DO-AHEAD
DINING

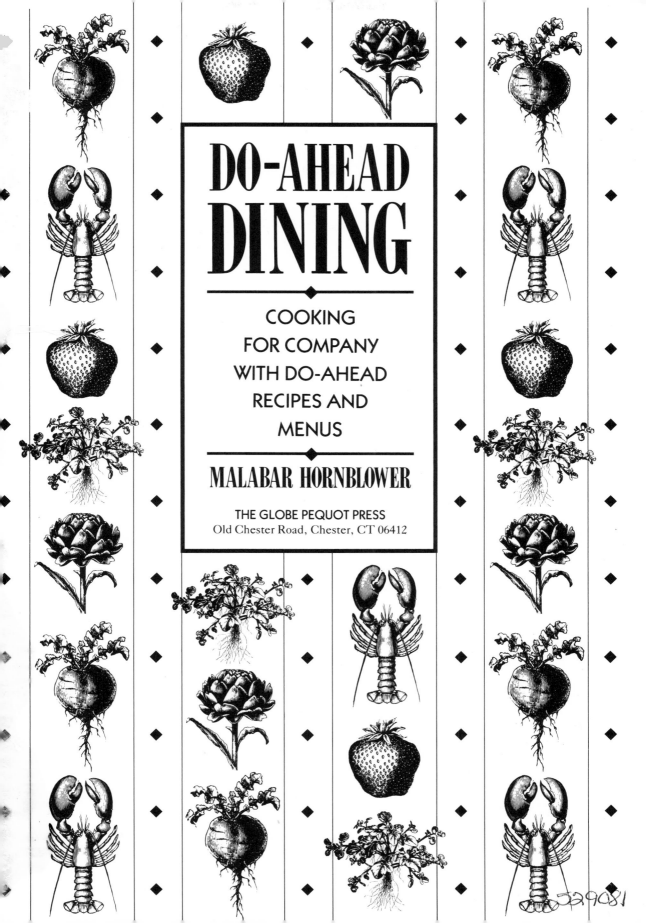

DO-AHEAD DINING

COOKING FOR COMPANY WITH DO-AHEAD RECIPES AND MENUS

MALABAR HORNBLOWER

THE GLOBE PEQUOT PRESS
Old Chester Road, Chester, CT 06412

Shown on front of jacket:

◆━━━━━━◆

STEAK BARBECUE FOR EIGHT

*Grilled Steak
Dijonnaise*

Vegetable Mélange

*Tomato and
Red Onion Salad
with
Vinaigrette Dressing*

*Hazelnut Cake
with
Lemon-Berry Filling*

◆━━━━━━◆

See page 114.

Manufactured in the United States of America.
First Edition/First Printing

COVER AND BOOK DESIGN BY BARBARA MARKS

Library of Congress Cataloging-in-Publication Data
Hornblower, Malabar. Do-ahead dining.
Includes index.
1. Entertaining. 2. Cookery. 3. Menus. I. Title.
TX731.H587 1986 641.5′55 86-22826
ISBN 0-87106-809-5

CONTENTS

THE SPIRIT OF DO-AHEAD DINING 1

ENTERTAINING IN THE SPRING 11

ENTERTAINING IN THE SUMMER 69

ENTERTAINING IN THE FALL 127

386913

ENTERTAINING IN THE WINTER 179

ENTERTAINING FOR A CROWD 237

RECIPE DIVIDENDS 285

INDEX TO MENUS ACCORDING TO NUMBER SERVED 303

INDEX 305

ACKNOWLEDGMENTS

No cookbook, I truly believe, has ever been conceived and executed by one person alone. Hidden behind the author's name there always exists a veritable army of family members and friends who form a vital part of the recipes' creation and evolution.

This was certainly true for me during the years when I wrote my "Do-Ahead Dining" column—the basis for this book—for *The Boston Globe*. My family and friends, whether they liked it or not, were the guinea pigs for my experimental endeavors, and I am indebted to each and every one of them.

Foremost on that list is my late and very dear husband, Harry, without whose continual encouragement, unfailing good humor, sensitive palate, and endless patience the recipes would never have been conceived, let alone tested. My children, Stephen and Rennie Brodeur, not only endured the seemingly endless routine of what they called "far-out food" (when all they wanted for supper were hamburgers) but even helped me with the mundane chores of preparation. So also did my stepchildren, Gusty, Hank, Hatzy, and Eleanor (listed in order of victimization, not favoritism).

The friends who submitted to the testing meals are far too numerous to thank individually, but without their interest, enthusiasm, and tolerance for dinners served appallingly late in the evening, the recipes would never have become what they are.

Lastly, there are my allies at the *Globe:* Patti Doten, who initiated the column; Jan Freeman, who caught the mistakes, typos, and inconsistencies; and Diane Nottle, who, with great energy and efficiency, helped me select and edit from more than three years of columns the menus gathered together in this book.

I owe the book to all of them.

TO HARRY

THE SPIRIT OF
DO-AHEAD
DINING

everal years ago I was invited to a dinner party by friends who lived in New York. Invitations to the Johnsons' (not their real name) were highly coveted, for Dorothy was a superb cook who was never satisfied with anything short of perfection. One time, I remember, she created three Tartes Tatins in succession simply because she was unhappy with the first two.

I arrived at the appointed hour. Heavenly odors were wafting through the apartment. Dorothy's husband greeted us and handed around tall frosted glasses. From the kitchen came the muffled sounds of feverish last-minute preparation. We guests sat chattering and gossiping and nibbling Dorothy's toasted pecans. But, despite the glorious anticipation we were all experiencing, there was something lacking in the evening.

What was missing was Dorothy. She did appear briefly, to be sure, and kissed each and every one with warm enthusiasm. But all too soon she excused herself and disappeared into the kitchen.

The party continued gaily. John circulated among the guests, keeping our glasses filled and the conversation flowing. But I remember thinking: "I wish Dorothy were out here, or we were in the kitchen." For we had come just as much to visit with her as to enjoy her food.

Later we were called to the table and Dorothy appeared, tidied up and radiant (cooking does that to her). But still her attention was drawn away from her guests because her mind, quite simply, was on the next course. It wasn't until the coffee at the end of the meal that we really were able to enjoy her company. Then, and only then, did the party peak.

I was a relatively young and inexperienced hostess at that point, but I realized I had learned something from Dorothy: I didn't want to be an absentee hostess at my own parties. I wanted to enjoy my guests. I wanted to be part of the party.

So I searched for solutions.

Caterers or extra hands in the kitchen could have helped, but I didn't have the money—or the inclination. Like Dorothy, I truly love to cook, and I had no desire to relinquish that pleasure to caterers or exotic take-out food emporiums.

Quick dishes made in minutes seemed a possibility, but closer scrutiny proved they were not the answer, at least not for me. Most require complex kitchen action at the last minute; or, to be more accurate, at the last sixty minutes—those very minutes I really want to spend, at least intermittently, with my guests. Moreover, a fair number of these "quick" recipes seem to demand that the cook possess the talents of a short-order chef. And how many of us really do?

Thus, by degrees, was born the concept of "do-ahead dining." Do-ahead dining means preparing—or partially preparing—in advance recipes that require only a little final attention, or serving dishes such as roasts and stews, which can rest on their own in an oven.

Do-aheads didn't happen overnight. It took me a long time to change my methods, my recipes, and my menus so that I could be the relaxed, serene hostess I envisaged. My goal was to produce meals that were as pleasing to the taste buds as they were well organized. That took quite a bit of experimentation and evolution.

But it worked. And it worked sufficiently well that friends, then friends of friends, began asking me to teach them how to do do-aheads. Cooking classes commenced with any number of eager would-be hostesses. As I worked up new recipes for these classes—and for my own repertoire—the recipes started to accumulate. From the positive reactions of my students, I realized there were many people I wanted to reach. Eventually it was *The Boston Globe*, in the person of an enthusiastic and encouraging editor, Patti Doten, who saw the potential in a food column devoted exclusively to do-ahead dining.

So, thanks to all those friends and friends of friends who first encouraged me, extensive preliminary preparation is a well-tested and successful method of home entertaining.

The menus are arranged by season, because I am a firm believer in the superiority of fresh foods. Each menu features at least three recipes, with additional suggestions given for the meal. Please remember that my menus are suggestions for foods that I consider to marry well with each other, but you are the person doing the entertaining. You know your guests' likes and dislikes. You must be happy with what you present in order to experience the host's ultimate reward: the knowledge that the guests enjoyed every part of the event, from the dishes served to the conversation and festivity their presence generated.

SECRETS OF SUCCESSFUL ENTERTAINING

When I was in high school in New York, I had a friend whose parents had a baronial-style but rather run-down mansion on the banks of the Connecticut River. They would retreat there every summer and as many spring and fall weekends as they could manage. The grounds had obviously at one time been magnificently planted, even to a once-splendid polo field. Instead of ribbon-bedecked ponies and riders, the field now sported merry crops of yellow dandelions. The immense building was covered with ivy; its slate roof was studded with turrets. Inside, mystery seemed to lurk in every corner. Every inch of wall space was packed with gloomy portraits of ancestors whose restless ghosts presumably still wandered about the place.

But! In spite of—or perhaps because of—the setting, my friend's parents threw simply wonderful parties there. At every gathering there were masses of people of all ages and from all walks of life. Perhaps that was one of the secrets of this family's success. Teenagers mingled with octogenarians, movie producers with neighborhood locals. Everybody had a memorable time.

But undoubtedly the real secret of their success was the apparent simplicity with which my friend's parents entertained. It all seemed *effortless.* Our hosts had no servants to ease the physical burden of entertaining. But the food was cooked beautifully, and presented artfully, and there was no hint of the amount of planning and preparing that undoubtedly had gone on in the background.

That's what a party, be it for four or forty, should be all about: It should *appear* effortless. But, in reality, it should be as well-organized as any military campaign.

A party begins with a guest list, and great thought should be given to the mix of people and their potential compatibility. This is not to say that seemingly strange combinations don't occasionally make magic, but a certain amount of preliminary character analysis and discreet selection reaps rewards. Of course, if a gathering is large, the compatibility issue is less intense. Somewhere in the crowd, everybody will find somebody of interest. It's simply a matter of their locating each other. One sure-fire rule, though, is to be certain that each person knows at least one or two other people attending the event. For a gathering of four or six, this is not crucial, but for a large dinner or a cocktail party, it works wonders. Allow the scale of acquaintances to rise in proportion to the size of the party: The larger the event, the more people who should know one another. Another role of the successful host or hostess follows the same theme: See that the guests circulate easily, making new friends, renewing old acquaintances.

After the guest list has been drawn up, the menu should be planned. If possible, the host or hostess should try to take into account not only the occasion, but his guests' idiosyncrasies. (Who's allergic to shellfish? Who's a vegetarian? Who dislikes both nouvelle cuisine and heavily sauced food? Who doesn't drink, and who shouldn't drink too much?) If it's a celebration, the menu should be festive—and hang the expense. If it's a more prosaic gathering, plan accordingly and less lavishly. Don't ever go overboard spending, though, if it's going to make you miserable and wipe out your food budget for the month. You should be as happy on the occasion as your guests. Don't be afraid to substitute peanuts for macadamia nuts. If your guests are having a good time, it won't make the slightest difference.

Also important to consider is the ease of last-minute preparation. If the occasion is informal, a cook's twenty-minute disappearance into the kitchen is of no great concern. On the other hand, if it's formal, host and hostess should be visible. One spring, some friends of mine were planning a formal dinner for twenty. They initially thought of preparing my grilled butterflied leg of lamb (see Chapter 4). But after some thought, they realized that the host would have to be tending the coals and the lamb during the cocktail hour, when he really should be mingling with his guests, making such introductions as were needed, and generally seeing to everyone's well-being. My friends opted for a beautiful roasted loin of veal instead.

After the menu has been settled—and by that I mean a *complete* menu, from cocktail nibbles to after-dinner peppermints—and the invitations issued, the moment comes for serious and intense organization. Time must be planned, and all contingencies prepared for. Nothing should be considered routine. Everything should be spelled out, and all needs anticipated.

One of the best places to start is with the table, or tables. Who will sit where? What arrangement will be the best in terms of happy companionship and good conversation? What accommodations should be made for ease of serving? This is also the time to plan the furnishings. Will there be enough chairs? Are there enough small tables to hold cocktail appetizers and ashtrays—or, in the case of buffet dining, each guest's plate and glass? At the other extreme, are the rooms packed with excess furniture? In that case, put unneeded furnishings in the basement, under the beds, or wherever, but get rid of them!

Then get down to the nitty-gritty. Are there enough plates? Enough glasses? Do some have to be rented or borrowed? Glasses are crucial. Remember that in large gatherings, guests often drift away from their glasses and accept new ones as proffered. No host should find himself in the role of collecting, washing, and returning glasses to the bar—or, for that matter, hunting desperately for wine glasses that should have been part of the place settings at the dinner table.

Also preselect the cooking utensils, serving pieces, and china that will be needed, and buy, rent, or borrow what is lacking. What could be worse for the cook than to discover at the last moment that there are no small soufflé dishes for the individual apricot-orange soufflés, or that that gorgeous teak salad bowl doesn't hold enough to serve sixteen? Actually, it doesn't hurt in the least to set the table or arrange the buffet the day before the party. The silver (if it is being used) can be taken out of its bags and polished, the special china retrieved from its storage shelves, the favorite crystal or glass rinsed and polished, the napkins counted and, if necessary, washed and ironed.

In short, do-ahead dining means not only do-ahead cooking but do-ahead planning; do-ahead shopping and stocking (don't forget the wine and liquor cabinet); do-ahead cleaning; do-ahead polishing; do-ahead table setting; and perhaps, depending on the occasion, do-ahead hiring.

Always give consideration to hiring help for special occasions. A waitress or a bartender, or an extra hand in the kitchen, can make the party a great deal happier for the host and hostess—and for the guests. Fortunately or unfortunately, guests have consciences, and few feel at ease watching their hosts laboring in the kitchen or clearing the table. Some even wash the dishes themselves—which is kind, generous, and *wrong*. Guests, quite simply, should be catered to. Sometimes hiring help makes all the difference.

Once these do-ahead planning chores are out of the way, then and only then should the host and hostess settle down to do-ahead food preparation. And that's why this book was designed: to help the hosts do as much ahead as is feasible, and to allow them to be with their guests, catalysts in the enjoyment of the moment.

USING THIS BOOK

◆

The core of this book is the do-ahead recipes that make up the next five chapters. On the assumption that you will be using the recipes for entertaining—whether for two or for twelve—they are presented in menu form. Do not feel that you have to follow my suggestions religiously; they are meant as guidelines only. If I offer a recipe for glazed ham steak, it is not necessary to present candied yams with it. I found that such a pairing worked well, but you may prefer to substitute something else. (Do take care, though, in multiplying or dividing other recipes to fit the number you need. Sometimes it works; sometimes it doesn't. It is best to experiment with your adaptation first.)

Immediately following each menu are the recipes for most of the dishes listed. Where a recipe for a certain dish is not given, the menu listing is often accompanied by an asterisk. Recipes for these items appear in Chapter 7, "Recipe Dividends."

The first four "core" chapters are divided by season; the fifth deals with entertaining large numbers of guests; and the sixth recipe chapter, "Recipe Dividends," consists of basic recipes for such things as mayonnaise or chicken stock, and, as mentioned, some dishes called for in the do-ahead menus but not actually given.

I am a zealot when it comes to taking advantage of seasonal products. Although so much is now available year round, nothing quite matches the quality of local produce, fresh from the garden, the trees, the sea, or the streams. Tomatoes are a perfect example. Only when they ripen locally are they fit for human consumption; then they're food for the gods. And I, frankly, am delighted that there are a few items out there—shad roe, for example—that science has not found a way to preserve or produce year round. If I could get shad roe every month of the year, it simply would not be the prize it is in spring. Furthermore, certain foods have greater appeal in certain weather. In the summer, light food is appropriate, and fresh native vegetables, fruits, and berries are then at their best. Conversely, in winter, hearty meals—soups, stews, root vegetables, rich desserts—help keep us warm. (Most of the time, our bodies burn up those extra calories.)

There are a few exceptions, of course. The chief one is salad greens, which, thanks to the miracle of modern transportation, are abundant year round. And, as you will note from my menus, I believe that salads should be served year round. Fresh and bright, full of texture, they complement every entree.

The do-ahead recipes tell you how far in advance they may be prepared or partially prepared and, if the latter, how much time must be allotted for the final preparation. Sometimes a dish may be partially prepared several days in advance, sometimes several hours. Some dishes are done very swiftly just before serving. Mostly, however, I have tried to create recipes that can be done sufficiently in advance to alleviate the last-minute crush. You will note—and this is very important for the timing of a recipe's final preparation—that I repeatedly urge you to remove refrigerated items from the icebox "at least one hour before final preparation." In these cases, the item must be at room temperature before you proceed if the timing I have given for the last steps is to be accurate. If you have an ice-cold piece of beef to roast, it's going to take a lot longer than if it has been brought to room temperature.

I learned this lesson the hard way, and my family has never let me forget it. I was experimenting with a large do-ahead dinner and wanted to feature an enormous roast of fresh ham. So big are fresh hams that they can take six or seven hours to roast. Pork must be cooked to an internal temperature of 170 degrees. I decided to preroast my fresh ham to 160 degrees the day before, then, on the day of the party, stick it in the oven for an hour or so to bring the temperature up from 160 to 170. Terrible reasoning!

I invited a few members of the family, and some friends, over to partake of the testing. I planned an 8:00 dinner. I think we finally sat down to the table, ravenous, at 11:30. I had (1) underestimated how long it would take to bring the meat to room temperature and (2) forgotten that the internal temperature of the meat had to rise from room temperature to 160—which took several hours—before it even began to progress toward 170. For months afterward, I had a hard time persuading any friends to partake of another testing dinner. "What time will we be eating?" they'd ask nervously.

TOOLS OF THE TRADE

None of these do-ahead recipes calls for esoteric or unusual kitchen equipment—unless you believe that a food processor falls into this category. I do suggest using a food processor for many dishes, and if you do not own one, I strongly urge you to consider buying one. You don't have to select the most elaborate food processor on the market. Some of the cheaper and simpler ones work just fine. So many chores can be done so much more rapidly and efficiently that a processor is well worth every cent.

Another kitchen gadget I consider indispensable is the salad spinner. To make a good salad, the greens must be dry. Wet greens mean limp salads when the dressing is applied. Of course, if you lack a salad spinner, there are other means of drying greens. I have even resorted to using the spin-dry cycle in a washing machine. (Place the washed greens in a pillow case, close the machine, set the control on "spin dry," and let 'er rip. The greens will not be bruised or shredded. They'll come out intact and very, very dry!) In the days before salad spinners, I used to throw my dripping lettuce leaves into a French wire basket especially designed for drying greens. To use these baskets, you had to go outdoors or into a room that you didn't mind soaking with water, and whirl the basket like a windmill until centrifugal force sent the droplets of water off at every angle. Even then, the leaves weren't half as dry as in a salad spinner. So for heaven's sake, indulge in one.

A hand-held electric mixer is nice, as is the heavy countertop variety, but if you don't have one, arm power will do.

A pepper mill is a must. My friends tease me because I always write "freshly ground black pepper," but "freshly ground" is important for the flavor of every recipe.

Stainless steel or enameled saucepans are musts, too, for they won't discolor vegetables or flavor sauces unpleasantly.

A *sautoir*, a large skillet with four-inch sides, is almost, but not quite, a necessity. It's nifty for browning meats over intense heat, and its high sides keep most of the spatters in the pan, not on the stove.

Nonstick frying pans have special uses, too, from making easy omelets to sautéing with little or no fat. I have them in a variety of sizes and wouldn't be without at least one.

A good, flexible, stainless steel whisk is a must. I emphasize "stainless steel" because aluminum imparts flavor to anything acid. In making such delectables as hollandaise and béarnaise sauces, which contain acid, aluminum utensils add a recognizable and distinctly metallic taste. This is true, too, of carbon steel knives, once highly coveted for the fine edge they could take. Now there are stainless steel knives on the market that are just as good. Test with your taste buds, if you don't believe me. Cut lemons for lemon curd, as for a lemon meringue pie, with a carbon steel knife. You will be able to taste the metallic flavor in the curd. It can ruin what would otherwise be a very special dessert.

Thermometers are important to a kitchen—both the instant-reading variety, which measures the degree of doneness of meat or the heat of boiling sugar or jelly, and an oven thermometer, which should always be in place to double-check the accuracy of your thermostat.

Finally, I have one little friend in my kitchen that I urge on everyone. It costs only about three dollars, can be found in most kitchen shops, and saves a lot of time. It's a sphere-shaped wire mesh ball, about three inches in diameter, designed to be filled with tea leaves and placed in your tea pot. I don't question its value for this purpose, but I have an even better use for it. Any time a recipe calls for a "bouquet garni" or herb bouquet, I fill the tea ball with herbs. That way I don't have to fuss with cheese-cloth and string. I simply compress my sprigs of parsley, bay leaf, thyme, and what-have-you into the ball, clamp it shut, and drop it into wherever it's needed. It works like a charm.

◆

For all the do-ahead planning and preparing that can make entertaining easier, I am afraid nothing can be done to eliminate the last few minutes of final preparation. Unless you are a sleight-of-hand magician or prefer to eat unheated food out of cans and boxes, you simply will have to leave your guests at some point and put the finishing touches on the meal. Only you know how you can best manage your time. But I implore you to scrutinize all the steps in the last-minute preparations and the "time allowances" at the end of the recipes, and a day or two before the party, make a little battle plan for those final minutes. Plan, for example, to whip the cream—or egg whites—while the fish is baking, the rice reheating, and the zucchini sautéing. Don't forget to include uncorking the wine. Or pouring the water, if you are serving it. Or lighting the candles. Or warming the plates.

When you have done everything that can possibly be done ahead of time, and when you are secure in the knowledge of how you will manage the last few steps, then you will have peace of mind. You will be a calm, relaxed host, and because of it your guests will enjoy your hospitality the more.

ENTERTAINING
IN THE
SPRING

When I was a young schoolgirl (in the third or fourth grade, I believe), my English class was assigned to write poems about spring. It was an agonizing assignment, for I was no budding poet, and I struggled mightily to give voice to my love for the season. Finally, in desperation, I resorted to plagiarism. Let me reprint what I wrote, with thanks to Carl Sandburg's "Fog":

> *The Spring comes*
> *on little cat feet.*
> *It sits looking*
> *over the hills and forests,*
> *the ponds and marshes,*
> *and, with silent footsteps,*
> *stealthily moves on,*
> *touching the earth with green.*

Perhaps it is a little late to start publishing my own (inept) poetry, but it seems to me that in my childish fashion, and with Sandburg's help, I managed fairly accurately to describe spring.

It is a season, certainly, that we all crave. Spring is particularly welcome after the rigors of a northern winter. After the mud and the slush, the piles of dirt-encrusted snow that never seem to melt, we have truly earned the joys of spring. I once lived in a winterless climate, where spring wasn't all that much different from winter, except for an almost imperceptible increase in temperature. When I became aware that I really hadn't noticed any difference, then—because I love spring so intensely—I realized I could, and did, appreciate winter.

Springs vary across the nation. I think perhaps my favorite ones have been spent in Virginia; the land slowly warms and the flowering trees and bushes seem to endure, suspended in time. The sun comes—and stays. There is rain, to be sure, but it is a caressing, gentle watering of the land.

Not so in New England. We have hot, sunny days in March, when I see rooftops and beaches alike packed with bikini-clad sun worshippers, followed the next day by a wild reversal of the elements and a return to winter. How the flowers and trees manage to survive, I'll never know. But eventually, in mid-May, spring weather finally takes hold.

When I entertain in the spring in New England, I like to take advantage of the spring's first crops: asparagus, shad roe, trout, soft-shell crab, wild morel mushrooms, the first shoots of sorrel, fiddlehead ferns, baby new potatoes, strawberries, and rhubarb.

Most of all, I like to fool myself into spring-thinking with spring flowers. I start things off in late winter by forcing forsythia. Although it often takes two or three weeks before the buds flower, there's something so inherently cheerful about the bright yellow branches; rays of sunlight seem to flood the room. Anemones, in their clashing mix of colors—white, red, and purple—are my next choice to fill as many vases as I can muster. If anemones are unavailable or very expensive, I'll just select masses of daffodils, jonquils, tulips, and iris, mixing and matching them indiscriminately, and position them on every table I can find. Branches of delicate fruit trees, like quince and cherry, are wonderful touches in a room, too; one or two to a vase, arranged asymmetrically. Sometimes, as the season progresses, when nurseries are full of flats of pansies, begonias, and impatiens I'll buy one or two, depending on the number of guests I anticipate, and transplant the flowers temporarily into demitasse cups, one for each place setting at the table.

Instead of white linens, I prefer to use gentle pastels when entertaining in the spring—pale peach, blue, yellow, or pink, subtle colors that enhance the flowers' tones. I like matching candles, too, to carry out the theme. Tinted glasses can be a pretty touch if you have them. I have some antique water goblets in a deep green. These, somehow, seem perfect in spring.

Above all, spring entertaining should be festive—even if the weather is not. Experience tells us that summer, wonderful summer, is just around the corner.

As for my spring poem: I am afraid I got an F. While the sentiment may have been appropriate, the teacher, it seemed, knew her Sandburg too well.

SPRING FEAST
FOR EIGHT

Chunky Mushroom Soup

Minted Rolled Leg of Lamb

Potatoes Gratinées

*Asparagus with Brown Butter**

*Rhubarb Upside-Down
Shortcake*

To celebrate spring, I lure guests to dinner with a feast devoted to some of the season's favorite produce: lamb, mint, asparagus, and rhubarb.

I start the meal with a hearty cream of mushroom soup. The difference in this version lies in its texture: coarsely chopped sautéed mushrooms in a cream of mushroom base.

For the entree, the rolled leg of lamb is very special; its stuffing makes a dark green spiral whose minty fragrance permeates the tender, sweet flesh of spring lamb. Satisfying potatoes, pungent with cheese, and tender new asparagus, bathed in nutty brown butter, enhance the meat. And when you bring on the steaming, ruby-crested rhubarb upside-down shortcake, your ears will ring from the accolades.

CHUNKY MUSHROOM SOUP

MAY BE PREPARED UP TO 48 HOURS IN ADVANCE.

¾ pound mushrooms, ends trimmed
6 tablespoons unsalted butter
1 large leek (about ½ pound), roots and green leaves trimmed, cleaned and
  sliced thin
1 large potato (about ½ pound), peeled and cut in ½-inch dice
4 cups chicken stock, preferably homemade (page 286)
2 tablespoons Madeira wine (or substitute 2 tablespoons dry sherry)
1 cup medium cream
Salt and freshly ground black pepper to taste
1 tablespoon minced fresh dill weed

Divide the mushrooms into two equal portions. With a sharp knife, cut one-half into coarse pieces. Finely chop the rest. Set aside.

Melt 4 tablespoons butter in a 3- to 4-quart saucepan. Add the leek slices and the coarsely chopped mushrooms. Sauté over low heat, stirring occasionally, until the vegetables are wilted, about 5 minutes. Add the diced potato and chicken stock, and increase the heat. When the liquid is boiling, lower the heat and simmer, partially covered, for 25 minutes. Allow to cool somewhat.

While the soup is cooling, melt the remaining 2 tablespoons butter in a small skillet over low heat. Add the finely chopped mushrooms and sauté them, stirring occasionally, for 3 to 4 minutes, or until they just start to wilt. Remove from the heat and reserve.

Ladle about one-third of the cooled soup (it does not have to be cold, just not so hot that it will scald you if some should spill) into a blender, cover, and whirl until smooth. Transfer to a medium bowl. Repeat until all the soup is smooth. Add the reserved mushrooms, the Madeira, and cream, and stir to blend. Add salt and pepper to taste. Cover with plastic wrap and refrigerate until final preparation.

TIME ALLOWANCE FOR FINAL PREPARATION: 15 MINUTES.

Pour the soup into a large saucepan. Set the pan over moderate heat and slowly bring to the boiling point, stirring every now and then.

Divide the soup among 8 heated soup bowls. Sprinkle with a generous pinch of dill weed, and serve immediately.

SERVES 8.

MINTED ROLLED LEG OF LAMB

MAY BE PARTIALLY PREPARED UP TO 24 HOURS IN ADVANCE.

¼ cup fresh parsley leaves, stems removed, packed down
½ cup fresh mint leaves, stems removed, packed down
5 tablespoons unsalted butter, softened
1 large clove garlic, peeled and cut in 3 pieces
2 tablespoons red wine vinegar
1 whole leg of lamb (8 to 9 pounds), boned and butterflied
¼ teaspoon salt
Freshly ground black pepper

Place the parsley, mint, and 3 tablespoons butter in the bowl of a food processor fitted with a steel blade. With the motor running, drop in the garlic pieces. Add the vinegar and blend until a paste is formed.

Lay the boned leg of lamb out flat, skin side down. Spread the paste over the inside, distributing it as evenly as possible. Roll up the lamb lengthwise, tucking in any loose ends, and tie with kitchen cord at 1-inch intervals. Refrigerate, well covered, until 2 hours before roasting.

TIME ALLOWANCE FOR FINAL PREPARATION: 1½ TO 2 HOURS.

Preheat oven to 450 degrees.

Sprinkle lamb with salt and pepper. Spread with remaining 2 tablespoons butter. Roast, uncovered, for 20 minutes. Reduce heat to 350 degrees. For rare lamb, roast 1 hour longer. For medium lamb, roast at this temperature 1¼ hours; for well-done, 1½ hours. Remove lamb from oven and transfer to heated platter. Cut off cording. Allow to rest at least 10 minutes before carving. Meanwhile, make the sauce.

SAUCE
Juices from roasting pan
¼ cup red wine vinegar
1 cup water
2 teaspoons sugar
¼ cup minced fresh mint leaves

Skim off all the fat remaining in the roasting pan, but retain the juices and particles clinging to the bottom. Place pan over medium heat; add vinegar, water, and sugar.

to the bottom of the baking dish, and replace them on the cake. Serve the cake still warm with a bowl of whipped cream.

SERVES 8.

SOLE AND SPINACH CASSEROLE FOR FOUR

Sole Florentine

Baked Barley

Mixed Green Salad with Russian Dressing*

Individual Apricot-Orange Soufflés

When we speak of sole, or fillets of sole, we can mean any number of species of flat fish found in salt water, from local flounder to the epicurean delights of Dover sole from the English Channel. (The word "sole" actually comes from the Old French and refers to the sole of the foot—or the shape of the fish.) Like chicken, sole is infinitely adaptable.

This popular sole Florentine is a subtle combination of fish, tomato, spinach, and sour cream. Since it incorporates so many vegetables, I like to serve with it a crunchy barley casserole, skipping other vegetables entirely except for a mixed green salad. Many people underestimate barley's potential, assuming it is simply meant for soups. I use it frequently in place of potatoes or rice, and it always brings forth exclamations of surprise and pleasure at the table.

For dessert, try the sumptuous but not too high-caloric individual apricot-orange soufflés. They're a host's dream dessert because the puree may be prepared as long as two days in advance. All that needs to be done at the last moment is to beat the whites, fold in the puree and fill the molds—steps that can be taken while the fish is baking and the barley reheating—because the soufflés hold their shape for up to forty-five minutes before baking. Just remember to tear yourself away from the table halfway through dinner to put them into the oven. At the moment when the guests are eagerly anticipating the pièces de résistance, the soufflés will be ready—puffed and gorgeous.

SOLE FLORENTINE

MAY BE PARTIALLY PREPARED UP TO 12 HOURS IN ADVANCE.

2 tablespoons unsalted butter
4 tablespoons oil
4 large tomatoes (about 1½ pounds), peeled and sliced ½ inch thick
1 teaspoon minced garlic
⅓ cup flour
1½ pounds fillet of sole, about 8 to 12 pieces, depending on size
1 tablespoon strained fresh lemon juice
½ teaspoon salt
Freshly ground black pepper
2 cups finely chopped fresh spinach (about ½ pound), tough stalks trimmed
2 cups sour cream
4 tablespoons grated Romano or Parmesan cheese

In a 12- to 14-inch skillet, melt the butter and 2 tablespoons of the oil over high heat. When it is foaming, add a layer of tomato slices and the minced garlic, and fry the tomatoes 1 minute on each side. (They will not brown; this step just precooks them slightly.) With a spatula, transfer the tomatoes and garlic to a buttered baking dish, about 9 by 12 inches or the equivalent. Repeat until all the tomatoes have been briefly fried. To the fat remaining in the skillet, add the remaining 2 tablespoons oil.

Spread the flour out on a piece of paper toweling. Dust the fish fillets in the flour, shaking off any excess, and fry them two or three at a time without crowding, 1 minute on each side or until they are just brown. As they are finished, transfer them to the baking dish, distributing them evenly on top of the tomatoes. (They may overlap a bit.) Sprinkle them with lemon juice, salt, and pepper.

In a small mixing bowl, combine the chopped spinach with the sour cream, mixing them thoroughly. Spread the spinach evenly over the fish. Sprinkle with the grated cheese. Cover with plastic wrap, and refrigerate until 1 hour before final preparation.

TIME ALLOWANCE FOR FINAL PREPARATION: 50 MINUTES.

Preheat oven to 300 degrees.

Remove plastic wrap from fish. Place baking dish in the oven and back 40 minutes, or until the juices in the pan are bubbling. (If the broiling unit is separate from the oven, preheat it the last 10 minutes of baking time.) Transfer baking dish to broiler, and broil 5 minutes, or until the surface becomes golden brown. Serve immediately.

SERVES 4.

BAKED BARLEY

MAY BE PARTIALLY PREPARED UP TO 48 HOURS IN ADVANCE.

2 tablespoons unsalted butter
2 tablespoons minced shallots
¼ pound mushrooms, coarsely chopped
¾ cup medium-grain barley
1½ cups chicken stock, preferably homemade (page 286)
¼ cup water
3 tablespoons thinly sliced scallions, including green leaves
Salt and freshly ground black pepper to taste
2 tablespoons minced fresh parsley

Preheat oven to 350 degrees.

In a 2-quart flameproof casserole with a tight-fitting lid, melt the butter over low heat. Add the shallots and mushrooms and sauté until soft, about 5 minutes. Add the barley, stir to mix, then pour in the chicken stock. Bring to a boil over high heat, cover, and transfer immediately to the oven. Bake 45 minutes.

Remove from the oven and cool. Refrigerate, well covered, until 1 hour before final preparation.

TIME ALLOWANCE FOR FINAL PREPARATION: 35 MINUTES.

Preheat oven to 300 degrees.

Uncover the casserole, add the water and scallions, and stir the mixture well. Cover and bake 30 minutes, or until the barley is steaming hot. Taste and adjust seasoning. Add parsley and toss thoroughly to mix. Serve immediately.

SERVES 4.

INDIVIDUAL APRICOT-ORANGE SOUFFLÉS

APRICOT-ORANGE PUREE MAY BE PREPARED UP TO 48 HOURS IN ADVANCE.

1 cup firmly packed dried apricots
¾ cup water
¾ cup plus 4 teaspoons sugar
½ cup strained orange juice
1 egg yolk
1 tablespoon strained fresh lemon juice
1 tablespoon finely grated orange rind
2 teaspoons unsalted butter, softened
3 egg whites at room temperature
Pinch of salt
½ cup heavy cream, whipped

Place the apricots in a small saucepan, cover with ¾ cup water, and soak 45 minutes. Add ½ cup sugar and the orange juice. Bring the mixture to a boil and cook, stirring occasionally, until the sugar is dissolved. Reduce heat, cover, and simmer 15 minutes, or until the apricots are very tender. Cool.

Transfer the fruit and its juices to a blender or a food processor fitted with a steel blade. Add the egg yolk, lemon juice, and orange rind, and whirl until very smooth. With a rubber spatula, scrape the puree into a bowl; cover tightly with plastic wrap and refrigerate until 1 hour before final preparation.

TIME ALLOWANCE FOR FINAL PREPARATION: 50 MINUTES.

Preheat the oven to 375 degrees. Place a large kettle of water on to boil.

Spread the insides of four individual 1-cup soufflé molds with ½ teaspoon each of softened butter. Sprinkle each with 1 teaspoon sugar, rotating the molds until all the sides are coated with sugar. Shake out any excess. (If you do not have individual soufflé molds, a 1-quart mold may be substituted. Butter a wax paper "collar" and tie it around the mold. Extend the cooking time to 35 minutes.)

In a large mixing bowl, beat the egg whites with the pinch of salt until soft peaks form. Slowly beat in the remaining ¼ cup sugar, and continue beating until the egg whites are stiff. Spoon one-third of the whites into the apricot-orange puree to lighten it; then gently fold the mixture back into the whites and continue folding until all traces of white have disappeared. Divide the soufflé mixture evenly among the molds, smoothing the surfaces with a spatula. (The filled molds may be held, uncooked, in a cool corner of the kitchen for up to 45 minutes before baking.)

Place the molds in a shallow baking pan, and add enough boiling water to reach halfway up the sides. Bake 30 minutes. Serve immediately, leaving the soufflés in their individual molds. (If you are using a 1-quart mold, remove the paper collar and serve at the table on dessert dishes.) Serve with whipped cream.

SERVES 4.

INTIMATE DUCKLING DINNER FOR TWO

Cream of Carrot Soup

Roast Duckling with Orange Glaze

Easy Wild Rice

Fruit Salad on Lettuce Beds with Poppy Seed Dressing*

Cheese and Crackers

Duckling is the perfect feast for two: Its five-odd pounds are more fat and bones than meat, which makes it too much for one and too little for three. It is, however, a smashing entree for entertaining someone special because it has the reputation of being both elaborate and troublesome to prepare. Not so this recipe. The secret lies in the four-hour slow-bake, which not only releases the bird's excessive fat but partially cooks it at the same time. A swift coating of something as simple as tart orange marmalade plus one last hour in the oven make the cook appear a veritable magician. This easy method for cooking wild rice is just as impressive. It's done with three washes of boiling water, and the resulting grain is full of body and flavor.

For a change, this menu presents the vegetable in the first course, as a soup. It can be prepared well in advance, reheated, and served with a fragrant garnish of tarragon leaves, preferably fresh ones. For a salad course, I suggest a pleasant fruit salad, with a poppy seed dressing, to counteract the richness of the duck. And for dessert? Why, there's nothing better than a special cheese, such as a goat cheese or a Saint André, to round off the meal.

All in all, a splendid evening to be enjoyed by two, with scarcely a moment apart.

CREAM OF CARROT SOUP

MAY BE PARTIALLY PREPARED UP TO 4 DAYS IN ADVANCE.

1 tablespoon unsalted butter
⅓ cup coarsely chopped onion
1 small potato (about ¼ pound), peeled and thickly sliced
½ pound carrots, peeled and thickly sliced
½ teaspoon dried tarragon
1 cup chicken stock, preferably homemade (page 286)
½ cup heavy cream
Salt and freshly ground black pepper
1 tablespoon whole fresh tarragon leaves (or substitute 1 tablespoon minced chives)

In a 1- to 2-quart saucepan, melt the butter over low heat. Add the onion and sauté until wilted, about 5 minutes. Add the sliced potato and carrots, dried tarragon, and chicken stock. Bring to a boil over high heat; then lower heat and simmer, partially covered, until the potatoes and carrots are very tender, about 15 minutes. Transfer contents of the pan to a blender or food processor fitted with a steel blade, and puree until smooth. Cool. Pour the puree into a container with a tight-fitting lid and refrigerate until time for final preparation.

TIME ALLOWANCE FOR FINAL PREPARATION: 10 MINUTES.

Pour the pureed potato and carrot mixture into a saucepan. Stir in the heavy cream. Taste and adjust seasoning and add salt and pepper if needed. Over medium heat, reheat just to the boiling point. Pour into individual heated soup bowls, sprinkle with fresh tarragon leaves or chives, and serve immediately.

SERVES 2.

ROAST DUCKLING WITH ORANGE GLAZE

MAY BE PARTIALLY PREPARED UP TO 24 HOURS IN ADVANCE;
MUST BE PARTIALLY PREPARED AT LEAST 5½ HOURS IN ADVANCE.

1 duck, 5 to 6 pounds
1 cup finely chopped celery
1 cup finely chopped onion
2 cups seedless grapes
½ teaspoon salt
2 tablespoons orange marmalade
1 tablespoon water
2 orange slices, cut in half
Watercress sprigs

Preheat the oven to 250 degrees.

Rinse out the duck's cavity with water; then pat dry with paper toweling. Pull out and discard any fat near the opening of the cavity. In a bowl, combine the celery, onion, and grapes, and toss to mix. Transfer to the cavity; then sew up the opening tightly. Prick the duck's skin all over with a fork. Rub with salt.

Place the bird on a rack in a roasting pan, and bake undisturbed for 4 hours. The duck will render most of its fat and become half cooked. Remove from the oven and pour off all the fat that has accumulated in the roasting pan. If you are not proceeding with the final preparation, cool the duck, cover it with plastic wrap, and refrigerate it until 1 hour before final preparation.

TIME ALLOWANCE FOR FINAL PREPARATION: 70 MINUTES.

Preheat the oven to 350 degrees.

Cut open the duck's cavity. Remove and discard the celery and grapes. Cut the duck in half lengthwise, and place it, skin side up, on a rack in a roasting pan.

Over low heat in a small saucepan, melt the marmalade with the water, stirring frequently, until it is liquid. Brush the glaze generously over the duck's skin. Bake 1 hour, or until the skin is dark brown and very shiny. Transfer to a heated platter, or plates, and garnish with orange slices and watercress.

SERVES 2.

EASY WILD RICE

MAY BE PARTIALLY PREPARED UP TO 24 HOURS IN ADVANCE.

½ cup wild rice, well rinsed
Boiling water
1 tablespoon unsalted butter
Salt and freshly ground black pepper

Select a strainer or colander that will fit compactly into a deep saucepan. Place the rice in the strainer and the strainer in the saucepan. Pour enough boiling water over the rice to cover it by 2 inches. (Do not have the saucepan over any heat.) When the water has cooled to lukewarm, drain and repeat with more boiling water. Again allow water to cool, then drain. If not proceeding to the final preparation, simply cover the rice and refrigerate it (if holding it over 4 hours) or hold it in a cool corner of the kitchen.

TIME ALLOWANCE FOR FINAL PREPARATION: 10 TO 15 MINUTES.

Bring a kettle of water to a rolling boil. Uncover the drained rice, and pour enough boiling water over it to cover by 1 inch. Allow the rice to soak in the water 5 minutes, not longer. (The point of this last "rinse" is to reheat the rice, not cook it.) Drain, return the rice to the saucepan, and, over low heat, toss with butter until the butter has melted and is well distributed. Taste and adjust the seasoning. Serve immediately.

SERVES 2.

POT ROAST FOR SIX

Sweet-and-Sour Pot Roast

Braised Carrots and Onions

Steamed Brown Rice*

Ginger Cake with Lemon Ginger Frosting

In New England, spring weather always plays games with us. Just when one thinks cool days are gone forever, a patch of cold, damp days arrive. On those unwelcome occasions, I am inspired to prepare hearty, robust stews and pot roasts that will take the chill out of our bones.

There are about as many versions of pot roasts as there are varieties of spring flowers. Sweet-and-sour pot roast is my adaptation of a special meal once served to me by a Swedish friend. The Swedes frequently use prunes in their cooking; I added a few apricots for a California flavor. It is pleasantly piquant and, with its use of dried fruit and lack of thickening agent, not as heavy as some of the more traditional versions. Rice makes a good accompaniment, although noodles would do nicely. Carrots and onions always seem to go hand and hand with pot roasts; a braised version, cooked separately from the meat, preserves the individual flavors.

To stick with the spicy spirit of the meal, we have for dessert a not-too-distant cousin of the familiar gingerbread. This ginger cake is lighter but, with its gingery frosting, every bit as heady.

SWEET-AND-SOUR POT ROAST

MAY BE PREPARED UP TO 48 HOURS IN ADVANCE.

¼ cup flour
1 teaspoon salt
½ teaspoon freshly ground black pepper
3 tablespoons oil
1 4-pound roast: chuck or top or bottom round
3 tablespoons unsalted butter
2 tablespoons minced garlic
2 cups coarsely chopped onions
2 teaspoons dried tarragon
1 cup tarragon vinegar
¼ cup sugar
1 cup pitted prunes, coarsely chopped
½ cup dried apricots, coarsely chopped

Preheat oven to 350 degrees.

On a piece of paper toweling, combine flour, salt, and pepper, mixing well with your fingers. Pour the oil into a heavy ovenproof casserole large enough to contain the roast comfortably, and place the casserole over moderately high heat. Coat the roast on all sides with the flour mixture, dusting off any excess. When the oil is hot, brown the meat on all sides, turning it with wooden spatulas or spoons. (Do not prick with a fork.) Transfer it to a plate and reseerve. Pour off the oil, clean the casserole, lower the heat, and melt the butter in the same casserole. Add the garlic, onions, and tarragon. Sauté them over low heat until the onions are transparent, about 10 minutes. Pour in the vinegar and sugar, and blend well. Return the roast to the casserole, bring the liquid to a boil, and cover the casserole with heavy-duty aluminum foil as well as with its own lid. Place in the oven and bake 2½ hours, turning the roast once or twice. Add the chopped prunes and apricots, and bake another ½ hour. If you are not planning to serve the meat immediately, allow it to cool and cut it into serving slices. (This facilitates reheating.) Transfer the meat to a clean casserole and pour the pan juices and fruit over it. Cover with its own lid, and refrigerate until 1 hour before final preparation.

If you are planning to serve immediately, set the pot roast on a warm platter and let it rest 15 minutes before slicing. Serve with pan juices and fruit.

TIME ALLOWANCE FOR FINAL PREPARATION: 30 MINUTES.

Preheat oven to 350 degrees.

Place the casserole, covered, in the oven. (The casserole and meat should have returned to room temperature.) Bake 20 to 30 minutes, until steaming hot.

SERVES 6.

BRAISED CARROTS AND ONIONS

MAY BE PARTIALLY PREPARED UP TO 48 HOURS IN ADVANCE.

1 pound small white onions, peeled
1 pound carrots, peeled and cut into ½-inch slices
4 tablespoons unsalted butter, in pieces
1 tablespoon sugar
½ teaspoon salt
Freshly ground black pepper
½ cup water
½ cup minced fresh parsley

In a flameproof, ovenproof casserole with a tight-fitting lid, place the onions, carrots, butter, sugar, salt, and pepper. Toss to mix. Add the water. Bring to a boil, lower the heat, cover, and simmer 15 minutes. If serving within 6 hours, reserve in a cool section of the kitchen. If preparing the dish well in advance, refrigerate, covered, until 1 hour before final preparation.

TIME ALLOWANCE FOR FINAL PREPARATION: 20 TO 40 MINUTES.

Preheat oven to 450 degrees.

Place the casserole over medium heat, uncovered, and bring the liquid to a boil. Immediately transfer the casserole to the oven, uncovered, and bake 15 to 30 minutes, until the onions and carrots are tender when pierced with the tip of a knife and most of the liquid has evaporated. (The timing depends largely on the size of the onions.) The vegetables should just be turning a delicate brown. Remove from the oven. Add the parsley, toss to coat the vegetables, and serve immediately.

SERVES 6.

GINGER CAKE WITH LEMON GINGER FROSTING

MAY BE PREPARED UP TO 24 HOURS IN ADVANCE.

CAKE
1 cup firmly packed dark brown sugar
¼ cup unsulphured molasses
½ cup unsalted butter, in pieces
½ cup milk
1 egg, well beaten
2 cups flour
1 tablespoon ground ginger
2 tablespoons baking powder
½ teaspoon baking soda
¼ teaspoon salt

To make the cake: Preheat oven to 350 degrees.

Generously grease an 8-inch square baking pan. Line it with wax paper to fit. Grease it again. Dust it with flour, shaking out any excess. Set aside.

In a small saucepan, combine the sugar, molasses, and butter. Set over low heat. Stirring frequently, cook until the butter is melted and the sugar dissolved. Remove from the heat and add the milk. Stir until well blended. Beat in the egg until all the ingredients are thoroughly mixed. Reserve.

Place a sieve over a large mixing bowl, and in it place the flour, ginger, baking powder and soda, and salt. Rub them through the sieve. With a beater, preferably electric, add the reserved sugar mixture slowly, beating constantly. Beat at least one minute, until the batter is smooth. Pour the batter into the prepared baking pan, place it in the oven and bake 45 to 50 minutes, or until a knife inserted in its center comes out clean. Let it rest 5 minutes; then turn it out on a cake rack to cool. Peel off the wax paper. When completely cool, spread with lemon ginger frosting.

FROSTING
4 tablespoons unsalted butter, softened
1½ cups confectioners' sugar, sifted
1 tablespoon grated lemon rind
2 tablespoons strained fresh lemon juice
2 tablespoons minced crystallized ginger

To make the frosting: Place the softened butter and the confectioners' sugar in a medium-size mixing bowl. Beat until smoothly combined. Add the lemon rind and lemon juice, and beat until the mixture is spreadable. (Add more lemon juice, perhaps 1 teaspoon, if you want a thinner frosting.) Finally mix in the crystallized ginger. Let the frosting sit 10 to 15 minutes to allow the flavor of the ginger to permeate it nicely. Spread on the sides and top of the cake.

YIELD: 1 EIGHT-INCH-SQUARE CAKE.

VEAL CHOPS FOR TWO

Veal Chops with Basil Cream

Brown Rice with Slivered Almonds

String-Bean Salad with Sweet-and-Sour Vinaigrette

Strawberries Spanish Style

Veal must be catching on with consumers, for more and more supermarket chains are devoting a sizable portion of their meat cases to it. Furthermore, better-quality veal is becoming readily available.

Probably one of the tastiest cuts of veal is the loin chop—the baby version of what we know as T-bone steaks in beef. The meat is delicately flavored and melt-in-the-mouth tender. Sadly, like most good things, it's expensive; so if you are going to splurge on this special dinner for two, make sure you get the best. It should have a pale pink hue.

Our veal recipe calls for simple pan-frying and an unobtrusive cream sauce infused with fresh basil. (Please do not substitute dried basil. It just doesn't taste the same, particularly in this sauce.) To enhance and absorb the sauce, try brown rice made extra crunchy with the addition of toasted slivered almonds. As a light foil to the richness of the sauced veal, I suggest a salad of string beans and mushrooms.

Spring is the season for strawberries, of course, and every week they seem brighter, sweeter, and juicier. Enjoy them while they're relatively native—either pure and simple without any embellishments; or with cream; or, my favorite, Spanish style with fresh orange juice.

VEAL CHOPS WITH BASIL CREAM

THIS DISH SHOULD BE EXECUTED JUST BEFORE SERVING.
TIME ALLOWANCE: 25 MINUTES.

1 tablespoon unsalted butter
2 veal loin chops, about 1 inch thick
1 tablespoon minced shallots
½ cup dry white wine
1 cup heavy cream
¼ cup firmly packed coarsely chopped fresh basil leaves
Salt and freshly ground black pepper

In a skillet large enough to hold the chops comfortably, melt the butter over moderate to high heat. When it is foaming, add the chops and fry 5 minutes on each side. They will feel resistant when prodded with a finger. They should be golden brown on each side, but do not allow them to become completely firm when prodded. You want them juicy, with perhaps just a tinge of pink to the interior flesh. When you consider them done, transfer them to a heated platter while you prepare the basil cream.

Add the minced shallots, lower the heat to moderate, and sauté them briefly until they are just beginning to become translucent. Add the wine, scraping up any particles clinging to the bottom of the skillet; increase the heat to moderately high, and boil the wine away until the skillet is nearly dry. Add the cream and the basil and, stirring frequently, reduce the cream by half. Taste and add seasoning as desired. Return the chops to the pan to reheat briefly with the sauce, turning once or twice. Spoon the sauce over the chops and serve.

SERVES 2.

BROWN RICE WITH SLIVERED ALMONDS

MAY BE PREPARED UP TO 24 HOURS IN ADVANCE.

⅓ cup brown rice, rinsed
½ teaspoon salt
1 tablespoon unsalted butter
¼ cup slivered almonds

Fill the top of a large double boiler with water to within one inch of its rim. Add the rice and salt and bring the water to a boil over high heat. When it has come to a boil, reduce the heat to low and simmer, partially covered, about 50 minutes, or until the rice is tender but not mushy. Drain thoroughly.

Meanwhile, in a small skillet, melt the butter. Add the almonds and, over moderate heat, fry them, stirring frequently, until golden. Be careful; they can burn easily. (If they become too dark, don't try to salvage them. Toss them out and start again.)

When the rice has drained (it does not have to be completely free of moisture), return it to the top of the double boiler. Add the almonds and any browned butter remaining in the skillet, and toss well. Taste and adjust seasonings. (Add butter if you like.)

If you are planning to serve the rice within 6 hours, simply reserve it, covered, in a cool spot in the kitchen. If you are preparing it well in advance, refrigerate, covered, until 1 hour before final preparation.

TIME ALLOWANCE FOR FINAL PREPARATION: 25 MINUTES.

Place the top of the double boiler containing the rice mixture over boiling water. Reduce the heat and steam for 15 to 20 minutes or until the rice is thoroughly heated. Transfer to a warmed serving dish or plates, and serve immediately.

SERVES 2.

STRING-BEAN SALAD
WITH SWEET-AND-SOUR VINAIGRETTE

MAY BE PARTIALLY PREPARED UP TO 6 HOURS IN ADVANCE.

DRESSING
½ teaspoon Dijon-style mustard
½ to 1 teaspoon honey
½ teaspoon dried basil leaves
¼ teaspoon salt
Freshly ground black pepper
2 tablespoons wine vinegar
⅓ cup vegetable oil

To make the dressing: In a small jar with a tight-fitting lid, combine the mustard, honey (the amount depends on your taste), basil, salt, pepper, and vinegar. Stir until the salt is dissolved and the other ingredients well combined. Add the oil, stir again, then put on the lid and shake vigorously. Store, covered, until ready to use.

SALAD

½ pound fresh string beans, ends trimmed
4 to 6 large green leaves of Boston lettuce, washed and dried
6 white mushrooms, ends trimmed, sliced very thin
8 slices peeled cucumber
2 tablespoons minced red pepper (about ¼ pepper)
1 tablespoon minced fresh chives

To make the salad: Drop the string beans in boiling water to cover, return to a boil, lower the heat, and simmer until the beans are just tender but still bright green, about 10 minutes. Drain the beans and refresh them under cold water. Drain again and transfer to a plate. When they are completely cool, cover them lightly with plastic wrap until final preparation.

TIME ALLOWANCE FOR FINAL PREPARATION: 10 MINUTES.

Arrange the lettuce leaves on 2 individual salad plates, using 2 or 3 leaves each, depending on size. Arrange the string beans, laying them parallel, on top of the lettuce. Scatter the mushrooms and cucumber slices on top of the beans, and the red pepper and chives on top of them. Shake the dressing vigorously once more; then dribble it over the salads.

SERVES 2.

STRAWBERRIES SPANISH STYLE

MAY BE PREPARED 4 HOURS IN ADVANCE;
MUST BE PREPARED AT LEAST 1 HOUR IN ADVANCE.

1 pint strawberries, washed and hulled
1 to 2 tablespoons sugar
¾ cup strained fresh orange juice
2 tablespoons Grand Marnier or Cointreau (optional)

Place the strawberries in a serving bowl, cutting them in half if they are very large. Sprinkle with sugar, the amount depending on the sweetness of the berries or your personal taste. Toss a few times. Pour the orange juice over them, and toss again. (Please use fresh orange juice when making this dessert. There is simply no comparison in the end result if frozen or bottled juice is substituted.)

Cover loosely with plastic wrap and refrigerate, tossing once or twice, until ready to serve.

Just before serving, dribble the Grand Marnier or Cointreau over the berries if you like.

SERVES 2.

GLAZED PORK ROAST FOR FOUR

Glazed Pork Tenderloin

Straw Potatoes

Young Green Beans in Butter

Individual Floating Islands*

A cut of meat we're seeing more frequently in supermarkets these days is whole boned tenderloin of pork. Tender, tasty, adaptable to many different seasonings, pork tenderloin can be fully cooked in less than 30 minutes—a real plus for the hassled host.

If you haven't enjoyed pork tenderloin before, try this apricot-gilded version. You'll quickly learn you're on to a good thing. Size varies considerably, so in preparing dinner for four, try to obtain either two one-pound or four half-pound tenderloins to keep roasting time short. Straw potatoes are a deliciously crisp accompaniment, as are tender green beans. As a finale, I offer one of my very favorite desserts, a special version of floating island—light as a feather and smooth as silk.

GLAZED PORK TENDERLOIN

MAY BE PARTIALLY PREPARED UP TO 48 HOURS IN ADVANCE;
MUST BE PARTIALLY PREPARED 24 HOURS IN ADVANCE.

¼ cup oil
2 tablespoons soy sauce
2 tablespoons apricot jam
1 teaspoon rosemary
1 teaspoon minced garlic
1 teaspoon grated orange rind
¼ cup strained fresh orange juice
1 teaspoon Dijon-style mustard
*2 to 4 whole pork tenderloins, depending on weight (allow ½ pound per
    person)*
2 tablespoons cider vinegar

Make the marinade by combining the oil, soy sauce, apricot jam, rosemary, garlic, orange rind, orange juice, and mustard in a blender or a food processor with a steel blade. Whirl until the ingredients have blended and thickened slightly. Transfer to a glass or enamel dish large enough to contain the tenderloins. Add the tenderloins and coat them in the marinade. Cover with plastic wrap; refrigerate at least 24 hours or as long as 48. (Turn the tenderloins every few hours to recoat them.) Bring to room temperature 1 hour before final preparation.

TIME ALLOWANCE FOR FINAL PREPARATION: 30 TO 45 MINUTES.

Preheat oven to 450 degrees.

Remove the tenderloins from marinade and place them in a roasting pan, reserving marinade. Roast 20 minutes for ½-pound loins or 25 minutes for 1-pound loins. Transfer to a heated platter.

Over medium heat, deglaze juices in roasting pan with vinegar, scraping up any particles clinging to the pan. Add reserved marinade and stir constantly until very hot. Cut tenderloins into ⅓-inch slices and serve with the sauce.

SERVES 4.

STRAW POTATOES

MAY BE PARTIALLY PREPARED UP TO 6 HOURS IN ADVANCE.

1 pound new potatoes, peeled and coarsely grated
4 tablespoons unsalted butter
2 tablespoons oil
Salt and freshly ground black pepper to taste

Place the grated potatoes in a colander or sieve, and rinse thoroughly under cold water. If not preparing immediately, immerse potatoes in cold water to cover to prevent discoloration.

TIME ALLOWANCE FOR FINAL PREPARATION: 40 MINUTES.

Discard water in which potatoes have been soaking, and rinse once or twice more. Place potatoes on several thicknesses of paper toweling and dab with more toweling to absorb as much water as possible.

Over high heat, combine 2 tablespoons butter and 1 tablespoon oil in a 12-inch nonstick skillet. When it foams, add the potatoes in an even layer. Place a heavy plate weighted down by an iron or can on top of the potatoes, and cook them over medium to high heat for 15 minutes. (If they seem to brown too quickly, reduce heat somewhat.) Remove the weights, and cover the skillet with an inverted cookie sheet. Turn both over so that the potatoes are then resting brown side up on the cookie sheet. Add the remaining butter and oil to the skillet. When they are foaming, slide the potatoes back into the skillet, brown side still up. Cook another 15 minutes, weighing the potatoes down as before.

To serve, invert a large round or oval serving platter over the skillet, turn both over and cut the straw potatoes into wedges.

SERVES 4.

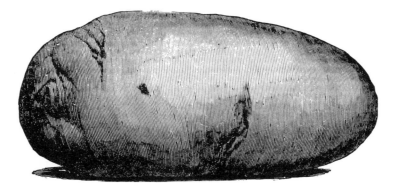

INDIVIDUAL FLOATING ISLANDS

MERINGUES MAY BE PREPARED UP TO 8 HOURS IN ADVANCE;
CRÈME ANGLAISE MAY BE PREPARED UP TO 24 HOURS IN ADVANCE.

MERINGUES

6 egg whites at room temperature
Pinch of salt
¼ teaspoon cream of tartar
¾ cup plus 2 teaspoons sugar
1 teaspoon vanilla
1 tablespoon unsalted butter
Boiling water

To make the meringues, preheat oven to 275 degrees.

Beat egg whites with the salt and cream of tartar until foamy. Gradually add ¾ cup sugar, a tablespoon at a time. Beat until stiff. Beat in the vanilla. Generously coat four 10-ounce custard cups or soufflé dishes with butter and dust them with the 2 teaspoons sugar. Divide the meringue among the cups and tap firmly to knock out any air pockets. Place the custard cups in a roasting pan, and fill it halfway up the sides of the cups with boiling water. Bake 1 hour or until a knife inserted in the center of one of the meringues comes out clean. Remove meringues from water bath and cool. Allow to rest in their cups at room temperature.

CRÈME ANGLAISE

6 egg yolks
½ cup sugar
1½ cups light cream, scalded
1 teaspoon vanilla

To make the Crème Anglaise: In a medium-size mixing bowl, beat the egg yolks. Gradually add the sugar, beating, until the yolks turn pale yellow. Slowly pour in the scalded cream while continuing to beat. Return mixture to the saucepan in which the cream was scalded, and cook over medium heat, stirring constantly, until the custard coats the back of the spoon. (Do not allow to come to a boil or mixture will curdle.) Remove from heat. Add vanilla and cool. Refrigerate covered until ready to assemble.

TIME ALLOWANCE FOR FINAL PREPARATION: 5 MINUTES.

4 tablespoons currant jelly, melted

To assemble: In shallow saucers or rimmed dessert plates, spoon generous amounts of the crème anglaise. Run a knife around the edges of the meringues, and invert one onto each plate of crème anglaise. (The meringue should appear to be "floating" in the crème.) Drizzle 1 tablespoon melted currant jelly over each meringue.

SERVES 4.

TWO
FOR THE ROE

Sautéed Shad Roe with Brown Butter

Boiled Baby Red Potatoes

Buttered Asparagus or Fiddlehead Ferns

Mushroom Salad

Strawberry Pudding "Parfaits"

Among the many delectables spring brings to our table are the delicately flavored and fragile roes, or eggs, extracted from fish that fight our swollen rivers to spawn upstream. Roes are particularly precious because their season is so brief, barely six weeks. They must be absolutely fresh to taste their best, and no one has yet devised a satisfactory way to preserve them.

Of our New England roes, there is no question that shad roe is queen, and, as such, deserves to be treated with great love and respect. While it is traditional to serve shad roe accompanied by bacon, I favor a purer approach, because I feel that bacon overwhelms the subtle flavor of the roe. After being lightly sautéed, with care taken not to overcook, the shad roe should be drizzled with brown butter, then perhaps, if you like, sprinkled with a few chives.

Tradition also calls for fresh asparagus, and with this I concur, although fiddlehead ferns are a nice alternative in this dinner for two. For a salad, I suggest a simple one of raw mushrooms decorated with endive leaves and watercress sprigs, and for dessert, an unusual offering: a pretty pink-red pudding "parfait" made from fresh strawberries and garnished with whipped cream and strawberry sauce.

SAUTÉED SHAD ROE WITH BROWN BUTTER

THIS DISH SHOULD BE EXECUTED JUST BEFORE SERVING.
TIME ALLOWANCE: 15 MINUTES. ROE MAY BE MILK-SOAKED
FOR UP TO 12 HOURS.

1 pair shad roe (about 1 pound)
½ cup milk
¼ cup flour
¼ teaspoon salt
Freshly ground black pepper
2 tablespoons unsalted butter
1 tablespoon oil
1 teaspoon minced fresh chives
2 lemon wedges

Immediately upon bringing the shad roe home from the fish market, unwrap them and carefully sever the pair by cutting through the membrane linking them. Lay the two pieces in a shallow bowl and cover with milk. Refrigerate until ready to use.

Place the flour, salt, and pepper on a piece of paper toweling and blend with your fingers until the salt and pepper are evenly distributed. Melt 1 tablespoon butter and the oil in a large skillet over medium to high heat. At the same time, melt the remaining tablespoon of butter in a small skillet or saucepan over low heat. When it browns, remove it instantly from the heat. Do not let it burn. Set aside.

Remove the roes from the milk, pat dry with paper toweling, and roll them one at a time in the flour mixture until well coated. Shake off any excess. When the oil and butter are foaming, place the roes in the skillet, lower the heat to moderate to low, and sauté 5 to 7 minutes. Turn the roes over and sauté for another 5 minutes. At this point, they should be nicely brown on both sides and cooked all the way through, but not overcooked. To make certain, prod the surface of the roe with your finger. It should feel firm to the touch but not hard; it should not feel mushy. If they feel too soft, cook a little longer, turning once or twice. Transfer to warm plates. Drizzle with brown butter and sprinkle with chives. Garnish with lemon wedges.

SERVES 2.

MUSHROOM SALAD

◆

DRESSING MAY BE MADE SEVERAL DAYS IN ADVANCE;
SALAD SHOULD BE PREPARED NO MORE THAN THREE HOURS IN ADVANCE.

LEMON OREGANO DRESSING
4 tablespoons strained fresh lemon juice
½ teaspoon Dijon-style mustard
¼ teaspoon salt
Freshly ground black pepper
½ teaspoon oregano
¾ cup good-quality olive oil
1 clove garlic, peeled and cut in half lengthwise

To make the dressing: In a 1½- or 2-cup bottle with tight-fitting lid, combine the lemon juice, mustard, salt, and pepper. Stir until the mustard has blended with the juice and the salt dissolved. Add the oregano and olive oil. Cover the bottle tightly and shake well. Drop in the garlic pieces. Cover again and store in a cool place. (For a mild garlic flavor, remove garlic pieces after 8 hours; for a stronger flavor, leave them in according to your taste.)

MUSHROOM SALAD
½ pound perfect white mushrooms, preferably at least 1 inch in diameter
10 endive leaves
4 sprigs watercress

To make the salad: Cut the stems off the mushrooms so that the caps lie flat. Slice caps thin. Place 5 endive leaves on each salad plate, fanning them out decoratively. Arrange the mushroom slices along each leaf. Tuck 2 sprigs of watercress on each plate. Cover the plates loosely with plastic wrap and refrigerate until ready to serve. Just before serving, give the dressing a few vigorous shakes and, if you haven't re-moved the garlic earlier, remove it before spooning the dressing over the salad. (Any excess dressing may be stored in a cool cupboard or refrigerated for 2 weeks.)

SERVES 2.

STRAWBERRY PUDDING "PARFAITS"

MAY BE PREPARED UP TO 24 HOURS IN ADVANCE.

1 pint strawberries, washed and hulled
¼ cup sugar
2 tablespoons strained fresh lemon juice
Pinch of salt
1 tablespoon arrowroot (or 1 tablespoon cornstarch)
2 tablespoons water
⅓ cup heavy cream, chilled

Place the strawberries and sugar in the bowl of a food processor fitted with a steel blade, and whirl until pureed, scraping down the sides as necessary. Remove ¼ cup of the puree and reserve it, covered tightly, in the refrigerator.

Transfer the remaining puree to a stainless steel or enamel-covered saucepan. Add the lemon juice and salt, and bring to a boil over medium heat, stirring constantly. Mix the arrowroot or cornstarch with the water in a small cup and blend until dissolved. Pour into the strawberry puree and, still stirring, heat to just below the boiling point, until the pudding has thickened. Be careful the pudding doesn't scorch.

Cool; then pour into two parfait or large wine glasses. Chill at least three hours, covered with plastic wrap.

TIME ALLOWANCE FOR FINAL PREPARATION: 5 MINUTES.

Just before serving, whip the cream until stiff. Place a generous dollop on top of each pudding. Then drizzle the reserved strawberry puree over the cream to create a "parfait" effect.

SERVES 2.

CHICKEN DINNER FOR TWELVE

Broiled Marinated Chicken Breasts

Peas and Onions, French Style

Midnight Salad

Chocolate Amaretto Cheesecake

When I am planning a large dinner in the spring, I like to think of a main dish that can be grilled outdoors, if the weather's warm enough, or under the broiler if it's still too cold. These chicken breasts are equally good either way. They smack of lush Hawaii with their marvelous Polynesian mix of ginger and soy sauce, sugar and fruit. Moreover, they are the do-ahead host's joy, for, after marinating a day or two, they cook in a matter of minutes. (If you're cooking outside for this many people, though, it does help to have someone else tending the grill.)

With the chicken breasts, I suggest an old favorite of mine, peas and onions French style, a dish which can also be prepared well in advance. Although generally I avoid canned produce (except tomatoes when fresh ones are out of season), the Le Sueur early peas, heightened with pearl onions and a generous pinch of thyme, take me right back to any number of Parisian bistros. I also love to serve "midnight" salad for a large crowd because, as its name implies, it can be assembled and dressed as long as twenty-four hours in advance without wilting one whit.

As for dessert, the chocolate Amaretto cheesecake is nothing short of spectacular. It's sinfully rich and chocolaty, with a follow-up whammy of almonds, and it could comfortably serve sixteen. But it's been my experience that when guests take one little forkful, their resolve falls by the wayside, and they come back for more . . . and more . . . and more.

BROILED MARINATED CHICKEN BREASTS

MAY BE PARTIALLY PREPARED UP TO 30 HOURS IN ADVANCE;
MUST BE PARTIALLY PREPARED 24 HOURS IN ADVANCE.

MARINADE

4 teaspoons minced garlic
2 tablespoons minced fresh ginger
6 ounces unsweetened pineapple juice
¼ cup orange juice, preferably strained fresh
¼ cup soy sauce
¼ cup cider vinegar
¼ cup honey
12 whole chicken breasts, split, skinned, and boned
¼ cup Chinese duck sauce (or more if needed)

In a blender or a food processor fitted with a steel blade, combine the garlic, ginger, pineapple juice, orange juice, soy sauce, vinegar, and honey. Whirl until well blended.

Place the chicken breasts in a large glass or enamel baking dish, and pour the marinade over them. Cover with plastic wrap. Refrigerate at least 24 hours, turning the breasts occasionally to redistribute the marinade. Remove from refrigerator 1 hour before final preparation.

TIME ALLOWANCE FOR FINAL PREPARATION: 20 MINUTES.

Preheat the broiler, positioning the rack 4 inches from the heat.

Transfer the chicken breasts from the marinade to jelly roll pans or cookie sheets. (The marinade may be refrigerated up to 1 month and used again.) Brush the surface of the breasts with the duck sauce. Broil 5 to 10 minutes without turning, until the breasts are firm to the touch. (Cooking time depends on thickness of breasts and heat of the broiler.) Serve immediately.

The breasts can also be grilled over charcoal, but allow additional time to prepare the coals, which should be red-hot but not flaming. Depending upon the fire's heat, turn the breasts after 5 minutes, brushing again with duck sauce—use ¼ cup more, if necessary—then grill an additional 5 minutes.

SERVES 12.

PEAS AND ONIONS, FRENCH STYLE

MAY BE PREPARED UP TO 24 HOURS IN ADVANCE.

3 (17-ounce) cans Le Sueur Early Peas
9 tablespoons unsalted butter, softened
1½ cups shredded lettuce leaves
1 pound frozen small white onions
½ teaspoon dried thyme
Salt to taste
Freshly ground black pepper
1 tablespoon sugar
3 tablespoons flour
¼ teaspoon freshly grated nutmeg
¼ cup minced fresh parsley

Drain the peas, reserving 1 cup liquid.

In a 2- to 3-quart heatproof casserole, melt 6 tablespoons butter, add the lettuce, and stir until the leaves are wilted. Add the reserved pea liquid, peas, onions, thyme, salt if desired, pepper, and sugar; toss to mix well. Bring to a boil, lower heat, and cover. Simmer 15 minutes or until the onions are tender.

In a small bowl, combine the remaining butter with the flour, blending well. Add to the peas along with the nutmeg and stir until the liquid has thickened. Remove from the heat and cool. Refrigerate, tightly covered with plastic wrap, if prepared more than 6 hours in advance. Remove from refrigerator 1 hour before final preparation.

TIME ALLOWANCE FOR FINAL PREPARATION: 10 MINUTES.

Reheat the peas and onions over low heat, stirring occasionally. Serve immediately garnished with minced parsley.

SERVES 12.

MIDNIGHT SALAD

MAY BE PREPARED UP TO 24 HOURS IN ADVANCE;
MUST BE PREPARED AT LEAST 12 HOURS IN ADVANCE.

1½ pounds fresh spinach, washed and dried
8 eggs
1 pound lean bacon
2 cups mayonnaise
2 cups sour cream
¼ cup strained fresh lemon juice
1 teaspoon salt
¼ teaspoon freshly ground black pepper
½ pound mushrooms, thinly sliced
1 head romaine lettuce (about 1 pound), shredded
¾ cup finely chopped red onion
1½ cups coarsely grated Swiss cheese
1 (10-ounce) package frozen peas, thawed in time for final preparation

Cut off tough stems from spinach, and coarsely chop the leaves. Immerse the eggs in water to cover in a large saucepan; bring to a boil and simmer for 12 minutes. Immediately drain and pour cold water over them to stop cooking. Peel and slice. Fry the bacon until crisp, drain on paper toweling and crumble.

To make the dressing, combine the mayonnaise and sour cream in a bowl; whisk lightly until well blended. Add lemon juice, salt, and pepper. Mix thoroughly.

In a large, deep salad bowl, arrange the ingredients in the following layers: first the chopped spinach, followed by the eggs, bacon, mushrooms, romaine, and red onion. Pour the dressing over the top, but do not mix. Sprinkle the cheese over all. Cover with plastic wrap and refrigerate 12 to 24 hours. Remove from the refrigerator 1 hour before serving.

TIME ALLOWANCE FOR FINAL PREPARATION: 5 MINUTES.

Sprinkle thawed peas on top of salad. Toss vigorously to coat ingredients thoroughly with dressing.

SERVES 12.

CHOCOLATE AMARETTO CHEESECAKE

MAY BE PREPARED UP TO 48 HOURS IN ADVANCE;
MUST BE PREPARED AT LEAST 12 HOURS IN ADVANCE.

CRUST

2 ounces slivered almonds
About 4 ounces chocolate wafers (about 22 wafers)
½ cup sugar
6 tablespoons unsalted butter, softened

To make the crust: Place the almonds in the bowl of a food processor fitted with a steel blade. Pulse them until finely chopped. (Do not grind them into a powder, however.) With your fingers, roughly crumble the chocolate wafers—there should be 1½ cups—and add them to almonds. Whirl the machine until the mixture is finely crumbed. Add the sugar and butter, and whirl until well combined. Generously grease a 9½-inch by 2-inch springform pan with butter. Pat the crumb mixture evenly over the bottom and up the sides of the pan. Chill in the refrigerator while proceeding with the filling.

FILLING

6 ounces semisweet chocolate bits
8 ounces Amaretti di Saronno cookies (available at specialty stores and some
*   supermarkets)*
4 ounces almond paste, cut into pieces
⅓ cup Amaretto liqueur
3 (8-ounce) packages cream cheese, softened
½ cup sugar
4 eggs
1 teaspoon vanilla
½ cup heavy cream
2 ounces semisweet chocolate, coarsely shaved

To make the filling: Preheat the oven to 350 degrees.
Melt the chocolate bits in the top of a small double boiler. Remove the double boiler from the heat when the chocolate is liquid, but hold the chocolate over the still-warm water.
With a rolling pin, crush the Amaretti di Saronno cookies. Transfer to a large mixing bowl and reserve.
Place the almond paste in the bowl of a food processor fitted with a steel blade.

Add the Amaretto and whirl until blended. (Or you may use an electric mixer for this and the following steps.) Scrape the mixture into the melted chocolate and stir to blend. Reserve over the warm water.

Without cleaning the processor, place the cream cheese in its bowl. Whirl until smooth. Pour in the sugar and whirl briefly. Add the eggs, one at a time, whirling only until each is assimilated. Scrape in the chocolate mixture, add the vanilla, and whirl to blend. (If you are doing this in a food processor, it is important not to over-blend.) Whirl in the cream, mixing only until smooth. Pour the batter over the crushed cookies and stir gently to mix. Pour the mixture into the prepared crust in the springform pan. Bake 45 minutes in the lower third of the oven. Do not bake any longer, even if the center is not firm, because it will solidify as it cools.

Place the pan on a rack to cool. Run a sharp knife around the edge of the cheesecake to loosen it, but do not remove the sides. Cover with plastic wrap and refrigerate for 10 hours.

TIME ALLOWANCE FOR FINAL PREPARATION: 5 MINUTES.

To present the cheesecake: Remove sides of the springform pan, running the knife around the edge once again if necessary. Set the cheesecake on a decorative platter and sprinkle the chocolate shavings on top. Serve while still chilled, in very small wedges. It is very rich.

SERVES 12 TO 16.

DILLED SHRIMP
FOR SIX

Shrimp in Dill Cream

Bulgur with Broccoli

*Grapefruit and Avocado Salad
with Oil and Lemon Dressing**

*Gatnaboor (Indian Rice
Pudding)*

Shrimp are decidedly a delicacy these days, a close second to lobster when it comes to expense. Fortunately, a few seem to go a long way, so you don't quite have to break the bank when planning a dinner for six. Two pounds of shrimp is more than adequate to serve six for this recipe, since the shrimp is supplemented by mushrooms and a rewardingly rich sauce. As a vegetable accompaniment, I suggest a combination of bulgur (otherwise known as cracked wheat) and broccoli flowerets. Small individual salads of grapefruit and avocado sections with a tart vinaigrette dressing might refresh your guests' palates before they are introduced to one of the easiest and best rice puddings imaginable: gatnaboor, an Indian version of a worldwide favorite. The dessert has the added plus of costing only pennies to prepare, thus helping you average out your total expenditure for the dinner.

SHRIMP IN DILL CREAM

MAY BE PREPARED UP TO 24 HOURS IN ADVANCE.

3 tablespoons unsalted butter
3 tablespoons minced shallots
½ pound mushrooms, thinly sliced
2 pounds large shrimp, shelled and deveined
¼ cup brandy
1 cup heavy cream
1 egg yolk
½ cup sour cream
1 tablespoon strained fresh lemon juice
½ teaspoon salt
Freshly ground black pepper
½ cup minced fresh dill weed (or 2 tablespoons dried)
¼ cup minced fresh chives

In a large skillet, melt the butter over low heat. Add the shallots and mushrooms, and sauté until soft. Increase the heat to medium-high and add the shrimp. Stir constantly until the shrimp turn pink-white on all sides. Dribble the brandy over the mixture, warm it, then ignite. When the flame has died down, transfer the shrimp and mushroom mixture with a slotted spoon to a bowl.

Add the heavy cream to the juices remaining in the pan. Reduce it by one-third over high heat, stirring constantly. Meanwhile, blend the egg yolk with the sour cream in a small bowl. Pour it into the hot sauce and blend well. Remove from the heat. Add the lemon juice, salt, pepper, dill, and chives, and allow to cool. Refrigerate sauce in its skillet, well covered. Refrigerate shrimp mixture tightly sealed with plastic wrap. Bring both to room temperature 1 hour before final preparation.

TIME ALLOWANCE FOR FINAL PREPARATION: 5 TO 10 MINUTES.

Place the sauce-filled skillet over medium to high heat and bring to just under the boiling point. Add the shrimp, tossing well to distribute them evenly in the sauce. Cook 2 to 4 minutes, or until the shrimp are hot. Do not overcook or shrimp will toughen. Serve immediately.

SERVES 6.

BULGUR WITH BROCCOLI

MAY BE PARTIALLY PREPARED 12 HOURS IN ADVANCE.

3 tablespoons oil
1 teaspoon minced garlic
2 cups coarse-grain bulgur (cracked wheat)
4 cups chicken stock, preferably homemade (page 286)
2 cups broccoli flowerets, stems removed
½ cup grated sharp cheddar cheese

In a flameproof casserole, heat the oil. Add the minced garlic and sauté 2 minutes. Add the bulgur, and stir until the bulgur is lightly toasted and all the grains are coated with oil. Cover and set aside off heat until ready to complete.

TIME ALLOWANCE FOR FINAL PREPARATION: 45 MINUTES.

Pour the chicken stock over the bulgur and stir well. Bring the liquid to a boil, lower heat, and cover. Simmer for 20 to 25 minutes, or until there is just about ¼ inch of liquid still to be absorbed. Scatter the broccoli flowerets on top of the bulgur; do not mix them in. Cover the casserole again, and simmer 10 minutes longer. The liquid should be completely absorbed and the broccoli cooked but still crisp. If not, simmer another 5 minutes. Sprinkle the grated cheese over the surface, turn off the heat, and cover so that the cheese will melt from the heat of the vegetables. Or, if you prefer, run the casserole briefly under a heated broiler to melt (and somewhat brown) the cheese. Serve immediately.

SERVES 6.

GATNABOOR (INDIAN RICE PUDDING)

MAY BE PREPARED UP TO 24 HOURS IN ADVANCE.

½ cup short- or medium-grain rice
2 cups milk
1 cup water
Peel from ½ lemon
½ cup seedless raisins
¼ to ½ cup sugar, according to taste
¼ teaspoon salt
1 teaspoon vanilla
¼ to ½ cup heavy cream
½ cup slivered almonds (optional)

Rinse the rice two or three times. Place it in a 2-quart saucepan and cover it with the milk and water. Add the lemon peel. Bring it to a boil over medium heat, stirring frequently; lower heat and simmer for 15 minutes. Add the raisins and simmer 5 minutes. Remove from the heat and, while it is still hot, mix in ¼ cup sugar, salt, and vanilla. Discard lemon peels. Taste for sweetness, adding more sugar if desired. When cool, refrigerate. (It will thicken as it cools.) Indian rice pudding may be served either cold or at room temperature. Remove it from the refrigerator accordingly.

TIME ALLOWANCE FOR FINAL PREPARATION: 3 MINUTES.

Blend in ¼ cup heavy cream, mixing well. The pudding should be creamy and soft, so add up to ¼ cup more cream if necessary. Transfer to a serving dish and sprinkle the almonds on top.

SERVES 6.

LUNCHEON FOR TEN SATISFIES EVERYONE

Bruce Ayer's Bloody Marys

Deviled Crab and Ham

Herbed Cherry Tomatoes

Baby Lettuce Vinaigrette

Pear Cream

Luncheon parties often pose a problem because appetites, habits, and capacities vary so widely at noon. Some people consume luncheons as hearty as most dinners; others are content to nibble on a lettuce leaf or a container of yogurt.

This luncheon was served to an assortment of friends on one of those typical gloomy, rainy spring Sundays. It was, frankly, an experiment to see if we could make everybody—men and women—happy. And the experiment worked. The Bloody Marys were smashing. The deviled crab and ham was enormously successful: It is a tasty but rich dish, so a little goes a long way. Those with "delicate" appetites were content with small portions, while hearty eaters could feel satisfied. The cherry tomatoes, bright and acidic, provided a nice foil to the creamy sauce binding the crab and ham, as did the simple salad. The dessert, a novel rendering of a familiar fruit, was very favorably received with its subtle essence of fresh pears.

BRUCE AYER'S BLOODY MARYS

MAY BE PREPARED UP TO 1 MONTH IN ADVANCE.

1 32-ounce bottle Beefamato
2 cups vodka
4 tablespoons horseradish
3 tablespoons Worcestershire sauce
10 lime wedges

In a large pitcher or shaker, combine the Beefamato, vodka, horseradish, and Worcestershire sauce and stir well. (Use a new bottle of horseradish, please. It loses its flavor so quickly once opened.)

Refrigerate the Bloody Mary mix, tightly covered, until ready to serve. It will hold in the refrigerator for up to 1 month.

TIME ALLOWANCE FOR FINAL PREPARATION: 5 MINUTES.

Fill 10 highball glasses with ice cubes. Give the Bloody Mary mix a final stir or shake and pour over the cubes. Garnish with a lime wedge in each glass.

SERVES 10.

DEVILED CRAB AND HAM

MAY BE PREPARED UP TO 6 HOURS IN ADVANCE.

5 tablespoons plus 10 teaspoons unsalted butter
1 cup finely chopped onion
3 tablespoons flour
1 tablespoon dry English mustard
3 cups light cream, scalded
1 teaspoon salt
¼ teaspoon freshly ground black pepper
1 tablespoon Worcestershire sauce
¼ to ½ teaspoon cayenne pepper (optional)
¼ cup dry sherry
2 tablespoons strained fresh lemon juice

2 hard-boiled eggs (page 46), coarsely chopped
¼ cup minced fresh parsley
2 pounds crabmeat, picked over for any stray pieces of cartilage and drained
½ pound baked ham, cut into julienne strips ¼ by 1 inch
¼ cup freshly grated Romano cheese
10 slices white bread, crusts trimmed

In a large 12- to 14-inch skillet, preferably with high sides, melt 4 tablespoons of butter over low heat. Add the onions and cook until wilted, about 5 minutes. Increase the heat slightly and sprinkle the flour over the onions. Stirring constantly, cook at least 1 minute so that the flour loses its raw taste. Mix in the mustard; then add the scalded cream and, continuing to stir, mix until thickened. Add the salt, pepper, Worcestershire sauce, cayenne pepper if desired, sherry, and lemon juice. Cook 2 or 3 minutes, until the flavors are nicely blended. Taste and adjust seasonings to your preference. Remove from heat and cool. Add the eggs, parsley, crabmeat, and ham, and mix well. Transfer mixture to 10 individual ramekins, lightly buttered, or one large, shallow ovenproof dish, lightly buttered. Sprinkle the surface with the grated cheese, and dot with the remaining tablespoon of butter. Cover with plastic wrap, and refrigerate until 1 hour before final preparation.

Spread the 10 slices of bread generously with ½ teaspoon butter on each side. Grill 2 or 3 slices at a time, preferably in a large, heavy cast-iron skillet, turning each piece as it becomes toasty and tan, then repeating with the other side. Transfer to a plate to cool. Cut each slice of toast with a serrated knife into 4 triangles, cover loosely with plastic wrap, and reserve for final garnish in a cool spot in the kitchen.

TIME ALLOWANCE FOR FINAL PREPARATION: 20 MINUTES.

Preheat oven to 375 degrees.

Remove plastic wrap from ramekins or casserole. Place in oven and bake 15 minutes, or until the edges begin to bubble and top is golden brown. (Run under the broiler if top is not brown enough.) Serve immediately, garnishing the ramekins or casserole with the toast points.

SERVES 10.

HERBED CHERRY TOMATOES

MAY BE PARTIALLY PREPARED UP TO 4 HOURS IN ADVANCE.

4 tablespoons unsalted butter
2 tablespoons minced shallots
2 tablespoons sliced scallions, including 1 inch of green leaves
¼ cup minced fresh parsley
2 tablespoons minced fresh dill weed
3 pints cherry tomatoes, washed and stems removed
Salt and freshly ground black pepper to taste

Melt the butter in a 12-inch skillet over moderate to low heat. Add the shallots and scallions and sauté until wilted, about 4 to 5 minutes, stirring occasionally. Toss in the parsley and dill. Turn off the heat and reserve the herbs in the skillet until final preparation.

TIME ALLOWANCE FOR FINAL PREPARATION: 10 MINUTES.

Place the skillet with the herbs over medium to high heat. Add the cherry tomatoes and sauté, stirring frequently, until they are heated through and are just about ready to burst. This will take no longer than 5 minutes. (If one bursts, they're done.) Sprinkle with salt and pepper to taste.

SERVES 10.

PEAR CREAM

◆

MAY BE PARTIALLY PREPARED UP TO 8 HOURS IN ADVANCE.

3 cups water
2 cups sugar
1 (1-inch) piece stick cinnamon
4 whole cloves
4 tablespoons strained fresh lemon juice
3 pounds Bosc or Anjou pears
1½ cups heavy cream, chilled
1 teaspoon vanilla

In a 3-quart saucepan, combine the water, 1 cup of sugar, cinnamon, cloves, and 2 tablespoons lemon juice. Place over moderate heat. Stir until the sugar is dissolved. Let come to a boil; then lower heat and simmer, covered tightly, for 15 minutes.

Meanwhile, half fill a large mixing bowl with cold water and add the remaining 2 tablespoons lemon juice. Peel, quarter, and core the pears, dropping them into the lemon-water to prevent discoloration.

When the syrup has simmered 15 minutes, add the quartered pears. Increase the heat to high, and bring the syrup to a boil. Lower the heat and simmer the pears, partly covered, for 15 to 30 minutes (depending on the ripeness of the fruit), until they are tender when pierced with the tip of a knife. As they cook, stir them occasionally to ensure even cooking.

With a slotted spoon, transfer the pears to a food processor fitted with a steel blade, add the remaining 1 cup sugar, and whirl until the pears are pureed. Transfer to a bowl. (Or press the pears through a ricer into a bowl, then beat in the sugar until pears are smooth.) After the pears have cooled somewhat, cover them with plastic wrap. Refrigerate until they are thoroughly chilled, up to 8 hours. Do not remove from refrigerator until ready for final preparation.

Remove the cinnamon and cloves from the syrup and discard. Over high heat, boil the syrup until it is reduced by one-third. Reserve at room temperature.

TIME ALLOWANCE FOR FINAL PREPARATION: 5 MINUTES.

In a large mixing bowl, beat the heavy cream until stiff, adding the vanilla as it stiffens. Gently fold the chilled pear puree into the cream, mixing only until it is well blended. Serve the reduced syrup in a small pitcher to drizzle over the pear cream if desired.

SERVES 10.

MIDEASTERN SPECIALTY FOR EIGHT

Egyptian Fathia

Sautéed Zucchini*

Parsnip and Carrot Salad with Creamy Curry Dressing

Lemon Meringue Cake

The Middle East offers many interesting dishes and taste combinations. Egyptian Fathia, while different, is not so novel that it will not appeal to almost every palate. Not too dissimilar to the familiar moussaka, with its ground meat, creamy cheese, and tomato sauce, it offers new gustatory sensations in its subtle use of fennel and fresh mint. It can be prepared well in advance—time enhances its flavors—and it is very easy on the pocketbook. Lamb is traditional in this dish, but if you cannot easily obtain good, lean ground lamb, substitute ground beef.

A bright green vegetable, such as sautéed zucchini or fresh beans, makes a pleasant visual accompaniment, as does a crisply textured salad of parsnips and carrots.

For dessert I offer a variation on theme: a lemon meringue *cake*. It makes a dramatic presentation, and it is one of those wonderful tart-sweet flavor combinations that round off a meal so satisfactorily.

EGYPTIAN FATHIA

MAY BE PREPARED UP TO 48 HOURS IN ADVANCE.

1 tablespoon plus one teaspoon salt
1 (8-ounce) package wide noodles
¼ cup unsalted butter
¾ pound mushrooms, stems trimmed, caps thinly sliced
1 cup small-curd cottage cheese at room temperature
1 (8-ounce) package cream cheese, softened
½ cup sour cream
1 green pepper, stem and seeds removed, finely chopped
2 pounds lean ground lamb (or lean ground beef)
1 (15-ounce) can tomato sauce
¾ teaspoon freshly ground black pepper
1 teaspoon fennel seeds
2 tablespoons finely chopped fresh mint

Fill a 5- to 6-quart saucepan with water to within 2 inches of the top. Add 1 tablespoon salt and bring to a boil. Drop in the noodles, stir to distribute, and boil rapidly for 5 minutes. They will not be done, but do not cook longer. Drain and rinse under cold water. Reserve.

Melt ¼ cup butter in a 12-inch skillet and, over low heat, sauté the mushrooms, stirring occasionally, until all the juices have evaporated, about 10 minutes. Meanwhile, combine the cottage cheese, cream cheese, and sour cream in a medium-size mixing bowl, and beat with a wooden spoon until they are well blended. Add the green pepper and the mushrooms and mix thoroughly. Reserve.

Using the same 12-inch skillet, break up the ground lamb into small pieces, and cook over medium-low heat, stirring frequently, until the meat turns gray and is relatively free of lumps. Add the tomato sauce, the remaining teaspoon of salt, and the pepper. Remove from heat and stir well.

With a mortar and pestle or a heavy rolling pin, crush the fennel seeds to a coarse powder. Add the mint leaves and continue to grind or crush until the two are well blended.

To assemble: Grease a 4-quart casserole (at least 4 inches deep) with butter. Layer the ingredients as follows: one-third of the noodles on the bottom, followed by one-third of the meat mixture (spooning it evenly over the noodles), followed by one-third of the cheese and mushroom mixture (spooning it evenly), and topped with one-third of the mint-fennel mixture. Repeat twice, ending with the mint-fennel. Cover tightly and refrigerate until 2 hours before final preparation.

TIME ALLOWANCE FOR FINAL PREPARATION: 50 MINUTES.

Preheat oven to 350 degrees.

Bake the casserole, covered, for 40 minutes or until steaming hot. Remove the lid and bake 5 minutes longer to brown the top. Serve immediately.

SERVES 8.

PARSNIP AND CARROT SALAD WITH CREAMY CURRY DRESSING

MAY BE PREPARED UP TO 4 HOURS IN ADVANCE.

SALAD
½ pound snow peas, ends trimmed, strings pulled off
1 pound carrots, trimmed and peeled
1 pound parsnips, trimmed and peeled
1 small red onion (about ¼ pound), peeled and sliced thin
½ cup minced fresh parsley

To make the salad: Plunge the snow peas into a saucepan of boiling water. When the water returns to a boil, immediately remove from the heat and drain the peas. Refresh under cold water. Drain and dry on paper toweling. Cut crosswise in ½-inch pieces. Reserve.

Coarsely grate or cut in thin julienne strips the carrots and parsnips. In a large salad bowl, combine the snow peas, carrots, parsnips, onion, and parsley, and toss with your hands to mix well. Cover loosely with plastic wrap and refrigerate while preparing the dressing.

DRESSING
1 egg yolk
½ teaspoon Dijon-style mustard
½ teaspoon salt
Freshly ground black pepper
1 teaspoon curry powder
1 teaspoon sugar

2 tablespoons cider vinegar
¾ cup salad oil

To make the dressing: In a small mixing bowl, combine the egg yolk, mustard, salt, pepper, curry powder, sugar, and vinegar. With a whisk, mix vigorously until well blended. Add the oil a few drops at a time, and whisk until each addition is completely absorbed. When half the oil has been added, each addition may be increased to about 1 teaspoonful, but the mixture must always be thoroughly incorporated before more oil is added. The dressing should have the consistency (but not the color) of a very light mayonnaise.

Pour the dressing over the salad, and toss until all the vegetables are coated. Re-cover with plastic wrap and refrigerate until ready to serve.

SERVES 8.

LEMON MERINGUE CAKE

CAKE AND FILLING MAY BE PREPARED UP TO 12 HOURS IN ADVANCE;
CAKE AND MERINGUE SHOULD NOT BE ASSEMBLED MORE THAN
1 HOUR BEFORE SERVING.

CAKE
5 eggs at room temperature
1 cup sugar
1 teaspoon vanilla
1 cup flour, sifted
6 tablespoons unsalted butter, melted and cooled

To make the cake: Preheat oven to 350 degrees.

Place the eggs in a large mixing bowl and, beating vigorously, slowly add the sugar. Continue beating until eggs are light yellow in color and tripled in volume. Beat in the vanilla. Using a rubber spatula, fold the flour gently into the egg mixture in three parts; then fold in the melted butter in three parts. Try not to break down the volume of the eggs.

Grease three 9-inch cake pans with butter. Line with circles of wax paper. Butter the wax paper. Dust with flour, knocking out any excess. Divide the batter evenly among the pans. Gently rap the pans to rid the batter of any air pockets. Place the pans in the middle of the oven and bake 12 to 15 minutes, or until the surface of the cake is firm and springy to the touch and is just barely colored. (The tops should not brown.) Transfer to a rack and cool. When the layers are no longer warm, remove from cake pans and peel off wax paper. Reserve. (Cover with plastic if holding longer than one hour.)

LEMON CURD FILLING

5 egg yolks
½ cup sugar
4 tablespoons unsalted butter
⅓ cup strained fresh lemon juice
2 tablespoons grated lemon rind

To make the filling: Combine the egg yolks, sugar, butter, and lemon juice and rind in a 1-quart saucepan. Stirring constantly with a wooden spoon, cook over medium heat until the curd thickens. Do not let it boil, or it will curdle. Remove from the heat and continue stirring until it has cooled somewhat. Cool completely before spreading on the cake. (Cover surface of curd with plastic wrap if executed well in advance, and refrigerate until 1 hour before assembling cake.)

TIME ALLOWANCE FOR FINAL PREPARATION: 20 MINUTES.

MERINGUE

3 egg whites at room temperature
Pinch of salt
1 cup sugar
1 teaspoon vanilla

To make the meringue: Place the egg whites in a mixing bowl with a pinch of salt. Beat until frothy, then add the sugar gradually, beating continuously, until the whites are stiff and glossy. Beat in the vanilla. Reserve.

To assemble: Preheat oven to 400 degrees.

Place a dab of meringue on an inverted 9-inch cake pan. This will serve to secure the cake as you assemble it. Set the first layer on top of the meringue on the cake pan. Spread its surface with half the lemon curd filling. Set a second layer on top of the first. Spread it with the remaining filling. Set the third layer on top. With a spatula, swirl the meringue over the top and sides of the cake as you would any frosting. Transfer the cake, still resting on the inverted cake pan, to the oven and bake for 8 minutes, or until the meringue is just barely beginning to brown. With two metal spatulas, carefully transfer the cake to a serving platter. Serve warm.

YIELD: 1 NINE-INCH THREE-LAYER CAKE.

GRADUATION BRUNCH FOR TWELVE

Orange Juice and Champagne Cocktails ("Mimosas")

Eggs in Baskets with Hollandaise Sauce

Squash Muffins

Summer Fruit in Raspberry Sauce

May and June bring a flurry of graduations. All those small children who used to play in the backyard are suddenly a lot taller, a lot bigger, and—surprise—a lot more educated.

It's time to celebrate. And there are parties galore—dinner parties, luncheon parties, pool parties, barbecues. For my graduating offspring, I dream up a brunch for twelve the morning of graduation.

The menu I've devised is as do-ahead as possible so that I will have time on my hands to oversee some of the young graduate's last-minute problems. We start with champagne and orange juice, known by some as "Mimosas." Eggs in baskets are a simpler rendition of eggs Benedict, which eliminates the chore of poaching eggs and toasting muffins just before serving. Although toasted ramekins themselves are a little tricky to make, you won't have any trouble if your bread is spanking fresh and you run a roller over the slices to make them more flexible. While the eggs are baking, you can whisk up the hollandaise—the only item on the menu that can't be done ahead of time and still be served warm.

The rest is a breeze. The squash muffins are moist, spicy creations that can be prepared the day before and warmed briefly before serving. Even the fruit in raspberry sauce can be assembled the night before, since the sauce acts as a protective coating and prevents the fruit from breaking down.

So give a brunch, then relax and join the fun.

ORANGE AND CHAMPAGNE COCKTAILS ("MIMOSAS")

MUST BE PREPARED JUST BEFORE SERVING.

2 (26-ounce) bottles champagne (or sparkling California blanc de blancs),
 well chilled
6 cups strained fresh orange juice, well chilled
Fresh mint sprigs

Pour equal amounts of champagne and orange juice into 4- or 6-ounce champagne glasses. Stir briefly to combine. Float a mint sprig on top as a garnish.

YIELD: SIXTEEN 6-OUNCE DRINKS OR TWENTY-FIVE 4-OUNCE DRINKS.

EGGS IN BASKETS

MAY BE PARTIALLY PREPARED UP TO 6 HOURS IN ADVANCE.

24 slices very fresh "very thin" white bread
½ cup unsalted butter, melted
24 slices imported ham 4 by 4 inches (about 1 pound)
2 (10-ounce) packages frozen chopped spinach, thawed
24 eggs at room temperature
Salt
Freshly ground black pepper

The "baskets" for the eggs in this recipe are simply toasted ramekins. To make them, roll a rolling pin back and forth a few times over each slice of bread to make it more flexible. Use a 3½-inch cookie cutter to cut one round from each slice of bread. (Save the scraps for homemade bread crumbs.) Brush the melted butter over the bottom and sides of 24 3-inch muffin tins (about 1¼ inches deep), and then apply it over the entire surface of one side of a bread round. Buttered side down, gently press the round into the bottom of the muffin cup, molding it to conform to the cup's shape. Repeat until all the muffin tins are filled. Next, center a square of ham in each cup. Cover the tins tightly with plastic wrap and hold until final preparation. At the same time, set the spinach in a sieve over the sink to drain, covering it loosely with wrap.

TIME ALLOWANCE FOR FINAL PREPARATION: 30 MINUTES.

Preheat oven to 425 degrees.

Remove plastic wrap from muffin tins. Making a fist, press down hard on the spinach in the sieve to remove any excess water. Place a scant tablespoon of spinach on top of the ham in each muffin cup. Break an egg into each cup on top of the spinach. Sprinkle with salt and pepper. Bake the eggs in the oven about 15 minutes, or until set. Run a knife around the edge of each cup before carefully transferring the "baskets" to a heated serving platter or individual plates. Serve immediately with warm hollandaise sauce (see following recipe).

SERVES 12.

HOLLANDAISE SAUCE

MAY BE PREPARED UP TO 30 MINUTES IN ADVANCE.

½ cup strained fresh lemon juice
3 tablespoons water
6 egg yolks
1½ cups unsalted butter, melted and cooled
½ teaspoon salt
Freshly ground white pepper

Combine the lemon juice and water in a stainless steel saucepan and, over moderate heat, stirring occasionally, reduce it until only 3 tablespoons liquid remains. Remove from heat and cool. Return the pan to very low heat and add the egg yolks. Whisk them until they have thickened, always watching the heat and lifting the pan off the heat if the bottom becomes too hot to touch with the bare hand. Add the melted butter, drop by drop, until it is completely incorporated, removing the saucepan from the heat briefly if necessary. Season to taste with the salt and pepper.

The sauce should thicken to the consistency of mayonnaise. If it separates from too much heat, immediately remove it from the heat and add 2 ice cubes. Beat vigorously. The sauce will be slightly thinner but will come together again.

Set the sauce aside in a warm corner of the kitchen, but not directly near or on heat. Do not attempt to reheat it. You may place the saucepan in a bowl of warm (not hot) water to help keep it warm, or in a Thermos.

YIELD: APPROXIMATELY 1½ CUPS SAUCE.

SQUASH MUFFINS

◆

MAY BE PREPARED UP TO 24 HOURS IN ADVANCE.

¾ cup unsalted butter, softened
1½ cups sugar
3 eggs
1½ cups squash puree
1½ cups seedless raisins
5 cups flour
5 teaspoons baking powder
1½ teaspoons cinnamon
½ teaspoon freshly grated nutmeg
1 teaspoon salt
*2 cups sour milk (or 2 cups fresh milk soured with 2 tablespoons lemon
    juice)*

Preheat the oven to 400 degrees.

In an electric mixer, or by hand, cream the butter with the sugar until well blended. Add the eggs, one at a time, beating well after each addition. Beat in the squash puree.

Dredge the raisins in a small bowl with ½ cup flour, then toss them in a sieve to shake off any excess.

In a large bowl, combine the remaining 4½ cups flour, baking powder, cinnamon, nutmeg, and salt; sift twice. Add the flour mixture to the squash mixture alternately with the milk. Do not overmix. Fold in the raisins.

Generously grease 2½-inch muffin tins to make about 36. Fill the cups two-thirds of the way with the batter. Rap the tins once or twice to eliminate any air bubbles. Bake 45 minutes. Remove and cool briefly on a rack. Serve hot or at room temperature.

Note: These muffins remain very moist in the center from the squash puree. Because of this, some people prefer to eat them without butter.

YIELD: ABOUT 36 MUFFINS.

SUMMER FRUIT IN RASPBERRY SAUCE

MAY BE PREPARED UP TO 6 HOURS IN ADVANCE.

(Spring can be an uncertain time for fruit. Feel free to make any substitutions that appear fresher than those suggested. If cherries are available, they are a happy addition. The amount of raspberry sauce in the recipe will generously coat at least 12 cups cut-up fruit or berries.)

> *2 (12-ounce) packages frozen, unsweetened raspberries, thawed*
> *2 to 3 cups superfine sugar*
> *5 large peaches (or substitute 1 large cantaloupe)*
> *2 bananas*
> *3 cups seedless grapes*
> *3 cups blueberries, washed and picked over, stems discarded*

Place the raspberries and 2 cups sugar in the bowl of a food processor with a steel blade. Whirl until pureed. Set a strainer over the bowl in which you plan to serve the fruit, and push the raspberry sauce through, discarding the seeds. Peel, stone, and slice the peaches (or cut cantaloupe in wedges, seed, peel, and slice it) and drop the slices into the sauce. Peel and slice the bananas, and add them, along with the grapes and blueberries. Toss to coat the fruit well with the raspberry sauce. Taste for sweetness, adding more sugar if needed. Cover with plastic wrap and refrigerate until serving time.

SERVES 12.

ENTERTAINING
IN THE
SUMMER

To me, summer is the best of all possible times to entertain. The only reason I could conceivably dislike it would be if I were stuck in a small, non–air-conditioned apartment in some hot and humid city in the middle of a heat wave. I've known such conditions in the summer in a number of cities—Boston, New York, and Chicago—and they can be a real test of friendship. Except under such circumstances, however, I adore summer.

Consider the options. Warm days and evenings present innumerable opportunities for all forms of entertaining. Have your friends over for a shade-dappled luncheon outdoors, the table covered in a gay floral print. Organize a picnic in some scenic spot. Call a group to a backyard buffet with the grill happily emanating the delicious scents of barbecuing food. Invite some fortunates for the weekend, and spoil them with sun-drenched breakfasts on a terrace or patio. Seduce some close friends with a quiet, late-evening meal on a screened porch, within earshot of crickets chirping and within sight of fireflies flickering in the distance. Or have a formal dinner indoors, with the cutlery shining on gleaming white cloths, the candles' flames protected by glass lamp-chimneys, and the soft summer breezes wafting through open windows.

Fruits and vegetables are at the height of their glory in the summer. Every menu you plan can be a meal to remember. The squash, the eggplants, the corn, the peas, the beans, the fruits, the berries will never again be so good—until next summer. Take the little extra trouble and do your buying at a nearby farm stand or a produce market. When the real thing is out there, don't compromise by buying fruits or vegetables that still need to be ripened. They will never taste as good as a vegetable that is only minutes away from its vine (with perhaps just a bit of soil left clinging to its skin) when it's scrubbed and plopped into its pot.

The menus and recipes I have selected for summer entertaining seek to take advantage of the season's munificence. I have also tried to include as many recipes for grilling as possible—without devoting the entire chapter to that particular method of cooking, satisfying as it is. In addition, I have included two menus for luncheon entertaining because I think folks have many more luncheon gatherings in the summer than they do in fall, winter, or spring. Undoubtedly the reason is that, for many, it's vacation time too—and vacations mean partying at any time of the week, not just the weekends. Bear in mind, too, that summer's heat often brings jaded appetites; these lunch recipes would be equally nice as light evening meals.

While I use summer flowers with great abandon for party decoration, platters of fresh fruits or vegetables also make dramatic centerpieces. I have a lovely copper *sautoir*—a high-sided skillet, to be precise—that I frequently fill with a mix of vegetables: shiny purple-skinned eggplants, a yellow squash or two, a handful of red and yellow cherry tomatoes, and a few green peppers. Anything that looks beautiful in the market will look just as good on the table. And the day after the party, the food won't go to waste. Sometimes I fill the *sautoir* with fat bunches of fresh herbs, perhaps a mix of lavender and rosemary, sage and basil, with trailing tendrils of tarragon. Not only are these bouquets beautiful to behold, their scent is subtle and intriguing.

The wonderful thing about summer entertaining is that it can be formal or informal, large or small, indoors or out. Unless it rains on your garden party or the air conditioning breaks down during a giant sit-down banquet, it can't help but be a great success.

LEISURELY LUNCHEON FOR SIX

Shrimp and Watercress Mousse with Tomato-Mushroom Sauce

Green and Yellow Beans with Vinaigrette Dressing

Hard Rolls with Sweet Butter

Baked Flamed Bananas

I enjoy giving luncheon parties when the air is full of the heady scents of flowers and warm earth. I always cross my fingers that the sun will not fail me and that it will be pleasant enough to eat outdoors.

Shrimp and watercress mousse is a marvelous medley of ingredients and colors. It tastes light as a mild summer's breeze but can be surprisingly filling. Before baking, the shrimp layers appear white and bland, but, with cooking, of course, the pink tones of the shellfish emerge. Thus the mousse is truly a visual delight when sliced, the green of the watercress layer sandwiched between the rosy hues of the shrimp.

Oddly enough, the robust tomato-mushroom sauce does not overwhelm the delicacy of the mousse. If anything, the mousse asserts itself grandly and the sauce acts as a satisfying foil to the richness of the mousse's cream base. (This is *not* a diet luncheon!) I suggest using canned tomatoes because, if fresh tomatoes are not at their peak of ripeness, they will not contribute much to the sauce. If you should happen upon some good ripe tomatoes, though, feel free to substitute them for the canned; the sauce will be the better for it. (You will need about six large ones, which must be peeled before chopping.)

Bananas make a dramatic dessert when baked and flamed. These can be slipped into the oven—at the same temperature used for the mousse—during the last minutes of the main course. Once the table is cleared, disappear discreetly, ignite the rum, and bring on the drama. You'll get all the oohs and aahs you deserve.

SHRIMP AND WATERCRESS MOUSSE

MAY BE PARTIALLY PREPARED UP TO 36 HOURS IN ADVANCE.

2 pounds large shrimp
2 egg yolks
⅓ cup fresh coriander leaves, packed down (or substitute ⅓ cup finely
  chopped fresh dill weed)
2 tablespoons strained fresh lemon juice
2 teaspoons salt
¼ teaspoon freshly ground black pepper
2 cups heavy cream
3 tablespoons unsalted butter
1 bunch watercress, tough stems removed, washed and dried
¼ cup minced scallions
4 small bunches parsley sprigs

Butter a 9-by-5-inch loaf pan. Cut a strip of wax paper the width of the pan and approximately 20 inches long. Press it into the pan and butter the paper. Set aside.

Shell and devein the shrimp. Reserve 4 for garnish. Place the rest in the bowl of a food processor with a steel blade. Add the egg yolks, coriander, lemon juice, salt, and pepper. Process until the shrimp are coarsely ground, about 10 seconds, scraping down the sides once or twice.

With the motor of the processor still running, slowly pour the cream down the feed tube and continue processing until the mixture is very smooth. Transfer two-thirds of the mixture to a bowl, and reserve it in the refrigerator.

Melt 2 tablespoons butter in a 1-quart saucepan over moderate heat. Add the watercress, cover the pan, and cook the cress, tossing it once or twice, until it is wilted. Add it, with the scallions, to the shrimp mixture remaining in the food processor. Process the mixture until the watercress is finely minced, about 10 to 15 seconds.

Spread half of the plain shrimp puree in the bottom of the loaf pan. On top of this, spread the watercress-shrimp puree and, finally, the remaining plain shrimp puree. Smooth the surface with a spatula, and rap the pan sharply to eliminate any air bubbles.

If you are not planning to finish the dish immediately, cover the top of the mousse with a sheet of buttered wax paper, cut to fit, laying it on the mousse so that a crust does not form. Next, cover the loaf pan with plastic wrap, sealing the mousse as tightly as possible. Refrigerate until 1 hour before final preparation.

Split the reserved 4 shrimp in half lengthwise. Melt the remaining tablespoon of butter in a small skillet. Over moderate heat, sauté the shrimp 2 minutes on each side, or until they just turn pink. Do not overcook, or they will toughen. Cool. Wrap in plastic and reserve until final preparation.

TIME ALLOWANCE FOR FINAL PREPARATION: 1¼ HOURS.

Preheat the oven to 375 degrees.

Bring a large kettle of water to a boil.

Remove the plastic wrap and top piece of waxed paper from the mousse. Cover the loaf pan with a double thickness of aluminum foil, and secure it with string. Set the loaf pan in a deep baking pan, and add enough boiling water to come halfway up the sides of the loaf pan. Bake the mousse 1 hour.

Remove the loaf pan immediately from the water, discard the foil, and pour any juices that have accumulated into the tomato-mushroom sauce (recipe follows). Loosen the mousse by running a knife around the edge of the pan. Invert it onto a heated serving platter, carefully peel off the wax paper, and arrange the reserved sautéed shrimp decoratively along the top of the mousse. Place sprigs of parsley at its four corners. Serve the mousse sliced, either hot or at room temperature, with the tomato-mushroom sauce.

SERVES 6.

TOMATO-MUSHROOM SAUCE

MAY BE PREPARED UP TO 36 HOURS IN ADVANCE.

4 tablespoons unsalted butter
3 tablespoons minced shallots
½ pound mushrooms, trimmed and thinly sliced
1 (28-ounce) can tomatoes (or 6 large ripe tomatoes, peeled)
1 tablespoon strained fresh lemon juice
½ cup dry white wine or dry vermouth
½ teaspoon salt
Freshly ground black pepper
1 teaspoon sugar
1 tablespoon water
1 tablespoon cornstarch

In a large skillet, melt the butter over moderate to low heat, and add the shallots and mushrooms. Sauté them, stirring occasionally, until the mushrooms have exuded their juices, about 10 minutes.

Drain the tomatoes, reserving ½ cup of their juice. Chop them coarsely. (If you are using the fresh, there won't be any juice, except what is exuded as you chop. Try to salvage whatever you can and add it to the pot.) Add the tomatoes, their juice, the lemon juice, wine, salt, pepper, and sugar to the mushrooms, and stir to mix. Cook 15 minutes over moderate heat, stirring frequently. (Cook the fresh tomatoes longer: about 25 minutes, or until they are nice and soft.) Meanwhile, in a cup, combine the water and cornstarch, and mix until the cornstarch is dissolved. Add to the sauce, blend well, and cook until the sauce has just thickened. If not using immediately, remove from heat, cool, and transfer to a refrigerator container with a tight-fitting lid. Refrigerate until 1 hour before final preparation.

TIME ALLOWANCE FOR FINAL PREPARATION: 15 MINUTES.

Transfer tomato-mushroom sauce to a medium saucepan. Add any juices that have accumulated from the shrimp and watercress mousse (see preceding recipe). Reheat over low heat, stirring frequently, until hot, about 10 minutes. Serve in a heated bowl with a ladle, as an accompaniment to the mousse.

YIELD: APPROXIMATELY 3 CUPS.

BAKED FLAMED BANANAS

MAY BE PARTIALLY PREPARED UP TO 4 HOURS IN ADVANCE.

6 tablespoons unsalted butter
6 bananas, peeled and sliced in half lengthwise
3 tablespoons strained fresh lemon juice
½ cup strained fresh orange juice
⅓ cup firmly packed light brown sugar
½ teaspoon cinnamon
2 tablespoons grated orange rind
⅓ cup medium-dark rum
1 cup heavy cream, whipped

In a 10- or 12-inch skillet, melt 4 tablespoons butter. Roll the bananas in the butter, making sure to coat all sides. Transfer them as you do so to an ovenproof baking dish, arranging them in one layer. (An oval au gratin dish is a natural for them as its contours fit the shape of the bananas.)

In a smaller bowl, combine the lemon and orange juices, brown sugar, and cinnamon. Mix until the sugar is dissolved. Pour the juices over the bananas. Sprinkle with the grated orange rind and dot with the remaining 2 tablespoons butter. Cover with plastic wrap, and set aside in a cool section of the kitchen until final preparation.

TIME ALLOWANCE FOR FINAL PREPARATION: 20 MINUTES.

Preheat oven to 375 degrees.

Remove the plastic covering from the bananas and bake 15 minutes. Heat the rum in a small pan until very hot. Remove the bananas from the oven, and pour the rum over the bananas and ignite. Spoon the sauce over the bananas until the flames die down. Serve with a bowl of unsweetened whipped cream.

SERVES 6.

BARBECUED LAMB CHOPS FOR FOUR

Grilled Marinated Lamb Chops

Green Peas with Prosciutto

Corn Fresh off the Cob

Fresh Pears

Spanish Almond Cake

Summer brings out my penchant for barbecuing. I simply love to serve and eat grilled foods. A subtle melding of the woody smoke—grapevine, mesquite, or plain old charcoal—with the flavors of the meat or vegetables adds a delightful new dimension to their character.

As a consequence, every summer I find myself experimenting with grilling something I haven't tried before. Some of my attempts have worked; some have been okay (i.e., the family barely accepted them); and some have been outright disasters. My grilled marinated lamb chops, I am happy to report, were received with great enthusiasm. I had never grilled lamb chops before and, loving lamb, I decided to see how they would work. Considering how costly loin chops are, though, I opted for caution in my "laboratory" and used shoulder chops instead, marinating them first for tenderness. The results were so pleasant, with the piquant flavor of lemon and the hint of oregano, that I decided a few weeks later to go for broke, using loin chops *and* the marinade. It's a real toss-up which is better, the shoulder or the loin. I'll let you and your purse decide.

I tend to abandon salads at the height of the season, reveling in the fresh produce available. The peas and prosciutto are a creation borrowed from Italy, a wonderful treatment of sweet garden peas complemented by the smoky Italian ham. (I must confess I have made the dish in winter with frozen peas, and it's not half bad—so don't relegate it just to summer.) My other vegetable on this menu, corn fresh off the cob, was invented for my husband, who loved summer corn but was less enthusiastic about the messy job of eating it. This recipe was the perfect solution.

The Spanish almond cake is an old family favorite that almost smells of Spain, with its essence of almonds and orange. There's no question that it serves more than four people, but I promise you that it will never go to waste.

GRILLED MARINATED LAMB CHOPS

MAY BE PARTIALLY PREPARED UP TO 6 HOURS IN ADVANCE;
MUST BE PARTIALLY PREPARED AT LEAST 3 HOURS IN ADVANCE.

1 teaspoon dry mustard
½ teaspoon salt
½ teaspoon Hungarian paprika
1 teaspoon minced garlic
3 tablespoons strained fresh lemon juice
2 teaspoons oregano
½ cup olive oil
8 shoulder or loin lamb chops, 1 inch thick, trimmed of all excess fat

In a glass or stainless steel baking dish large enough to contain all chops without crowding, combine the mustard, salt, paprika, garlic, and lemon juice. With a wooden spoon, stir until the mustard and salt are dissolved. Add the oregano and oil, and mix until well blended. Place the chops in the marinade, turning them several times to coat all sides. Cover them loosely with plastic wrap and marinate them, refrigerated, at least 3 hours but as long as 6. Remove them from the refrigerator 1 hour before final preparation. (Turn the chops several times during the marinating period.)

TIME ALLOWANCE FOR FINAL PREPARATION: 40 MINUTES.

Prepare the coals for grilling. They should be red-hot but not flaming.

Remove the chops from the marinade. Place them on a greased rack about 5 inches above the coals. If you have a grill with a cover, cover the chops. If not, watch the coals carefully. Try to prevent flaming by sprinkling them with water if flames rise up. For medium-rare lamb, grill the chops about 5 minutes on each side, or until they are somewhat resistant to the touch and the fat is brown and crisp. Transfer to a heated platter and serve immediately.

SERVES 4.

GREEN PEAS WITH PROSCIUTTO

MAY BE PARTIALLY PREPARED UP TO 4 HOURS IN ADVANCE.

2 tablespoons unsalted butter
½ cup finely chopped onion
2 cups green peas (about 2 pounds unshelled)
½ teaspoon sugar
¼ cup water
1 ounce prosciutto, cut in ¼-inch dice
Salt and freshly ground black pepper to taste

Melt the butter in a small saucepan. Add the onions and sauté them, stirring occasionally, until they are wilted, about 5 minutes. Add the peas, sugar, and water, and stir to mix. Cover and hold in a cool corner of the kitchen until final preparation.

TIME ALLOWANCE FOR FINAL PREPARATION: 20 MINUTES.

Place the saucepan over high heat. When the water is boiling, reduce the heat and cook the peas until tender, about 15 to 20 minutes. Add the prosciutto and continue to cook, uncovered, for 2 or 3 more minutes, until all the liquid has evaporated and the ham is warmed through. Take care not to burn. Taste for and adjust the seasoning.

(Frozen peas [10-ounce package] may be substituted for fresh peas when the latter are out of season. Thaw the peas before adding them to the onions; do not add any water; and steam them, covered, for about 5 minutes. Toss in the prosciutto, heat for a minute or two longer, and serve immediately.)

SERVES 4.

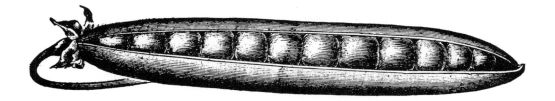

CORN FRESH OFF THE COB

MAY BE PARTIALLY PREPARED UP TO 2 HOURS IN ADVANCE.

6 very fresh ears of corn
3 tablespoons unsalted butter
¼ to ½ cup water
½ teaspoon salt
Freshly ground black pepper

Husk the corn, pulling off any silk threads left clinging to the cob. Hold the cob vertically over a shallow bowl or cutting block and, with a sharp knife, cut the kernels straight down, rotating the cob as each cut is completed. With the dull edge of a knife, scrape the cob on all sides to obtain any remaining liquid.

In a 10- to 12-inch nonstick skillet, melt the butter over low heat. Add enough water to cover the bottom of the skillet by ¼ inch. Add the corn, cover, and set aside in a cool corner of the kitchen until final preparation.

TIME ALLOWANCE FOR FINAL PREPARATION: 5 MINUTES.

Set the corn-filled skillet over moderately high heat. Keep the skillet covered. When you hear the water come to a boil, set the timer for 2 minutes. At the end of this time, remove the cover and cook 1 to 2 minutes longer, stirring frequently, until all the water has evaporated. Take care the corn does not burn. Season with salt and pepper. Serve immediately.

SERVES 4.

SPANISH ALMOND CAKE

MAY BE PREPARED UP TO 24 HOURS IN ADVANCE.

1 tablespoon plus ½ cup unsalted butter, softened
1¼ cups finely chopped almonds (two 2½-ounce packages)
1½ cups sugar
3 eggs, separated
2 cups flour
2 teaspoons baking powder
¼ teaspoon salt
1½ cups strained fresh orange juice
2 tablespoons grated orange rind
1 teaspoon almond extract

Preheat oven to 350 degrees.

Generously butter a 9-inch bundt pan with the tablespoon of butter, rubbing it well into all the surfaces. Drop ¼ cup of the chopped almonds into the pan, and roll and twist the pan to coat it with the nuts. Use a few more nuts from the total if necessary. Set pan aside.

In a large mixing bowl, beat the remaining ½ cup butter until soft. Add 1 cup of the sugar and continue beating. Add the egg yolks, one at a time, beating until they are all absorbed. Scrape down the sides of the bowl if necessary. In a sieve set over another bowl, combine the flour, baking powder, and salt. Rub the mixture through the sieve and add it in two batches, alternately with 1 cup of the orange juice, to the egg mixture. Beat in the orange rind and ½ teaspoon of the almond extract. Add the remaining almonds to the batter and blend well.

In a separate bowl, beat the egg whites until stiff. Fold them gently into the batter until all traces of white disappear. Pour the batter into the prepared bundt pan. Bake 1 hour or until a knife or straw inserted in the cake comes out clean.

Set the cake on a rack to cool for ½ hour. Run a knife around its edges to help loosen it, then turn it out, right side up, on a cake platter.

While the cake is cooling, make the orange glaze: In a small saucepan, bring the remaining ½ cup orange juice and ½ cup sugar to a boil, stirring until the sugar is dissolved. Lower the heat and boil 5 minutes. Stir in the remaining ½ teaspoon almond extract. Brush the glaze onto the cake while it is still warm.

YIELD: ONE 9-INCH BUNDT CAKE.

CHICKEN BREASTS
FOR SIX

Sesame Chicken Breasts

*Simple Baked Zucchini
with Cheese*

*Endive, Arugula, and
Mushroom Salad
with Vinaigrette Dressing**

*Pears with
Orange Currant Sauce*

A food-loving friend and I were passing the time of day recently playing a fantasy game we nicknamed "desert island." The object was not to decide with *whom* we'd like to be marooned on some deserted island, but with what . . . *food*. What if we were stranded for an indefinite period of time and had only *one* choice of meat, for example? What would that be? To our amazement, without any argument, we agreed that chicken would be our choice—plain, unromantic chicken. (We rationalized that we'd always be able to find fish, as it was an island.)

I'll go one step further: make it chicken *breasts*. Like chameleons, changing hue and texture with an addition here, a deletion there, they adapt to all embellishments. Sautéed, poached, breaded, herbed, or sauced, chicken breasts are one of the most versatile foods available and will withstand months of consecutive consumption.

I often prepare breaded and sautéed chicken breasts, varying them with different herbs or even a smattering of grated cheese. Sesame chicken breasts happened because one experimental evening I wondered how toasted sesame seeds would taste hidden among the breadcrumbs.

Because the sesame-breaded breasts are quite rich, I like to serve simple, non-starchy vegetables with them, such as baked zucchini. For a successful rendition of this easy dish, make sure you select young, fresh zucchini with smooth, glossy skins.

For dessert, I offer a serene melody of poached pears baked in an orange-currant sauce. It's a light but satisfying culmination to the evening meal. Perhaps, though, while you're dawdling over this dessert or coffee, you might like to indulge in a few rounds of "desert island."

SESAME CHICKEN BREASTS

MAY BE PARTIALLY PREPARED UP TO 8 HOURS IN ADVANCE.

½ cup sesame seeds (one 2⅜-ounce box)
1½ cups bread crumbs, preferably homemade
½ cup flour
½ teaspoon salt
Freshly ground black pepper
2 eggs
2 to 3 pounds boned, halved, and skinned chicken breasts (at least 8 to 12
    half-breasts)
3 tablespoons oil
2 tablespoons unsalted butter
6 lemon wedges (optional garnish)

The chicken breasts *must be executed at the very last moment* to be at their best. To facilitate the process, however, the ingredients can be set up ahead of time so that the final preparation is only a matter of minutes.

Toast the sesame seeds by placing them in a medium skillet, preferably nonstick, and setting the pan over moderate heat. They will begin to color rapidly. Shake the pan frequently, tossing the seeds, until they all have turned golden brown. Transfer to a shallow bowl or pie plate. When the seeds are cool, add the bread crumbs and mix thoroughly. Cover with plastic wrap and hold for final preparation.

In another shallow bowl or pie plate, combine the flour, salt, and pepper, stirring to blend well. Hold for final preparation.

Remove the eggs and chicken breasts from the refrigerator 1 hour before final preparation to bring to room temperature.

TIME ALLOWANCE FOR FINAL PREPARATION: 15 TO 20 MINUTES.

Preheat the oven to 250 degrees.

In a large skillet, preferably with 4-inch sides, bring the oil and butter to the foaming stage over moderate heat. (If your skillet is not large enough to hold all the chicken breasts without crowding, plan to cook them in two batches. Packing them too close together renders them soggy, which you do not want.) While the oil and butter are heating, break the eggs into a shallow bowl and beat them well with a fork. Working rapidly, one by one, dust the breasts on both sides in the flour mixture, then dip in the beaten eggs, and finally coat with the sesame bread crumbs, making sure they are well coated all over. Fry the breasts over moderately high heat for about 3 to

5 minutes on each side. (Timing depends on thickness of the breasts and the concentration of heat.) They should appear golden brown and feel firm when prodded with a finger. If you are frying them in more than one batch, transfer them to a platter lined with paper toweling, and hold them in the preheated oven until all are ready. Serve immediately, with or without lemon wedges as garnish.

SERVES 6.

SIMPLE BAKED ZUCCHINI WITH CHEESE

MAY BE PARTIALLY PREPARED UP TO 6 HOURS IN ADVANCE.

4 medium zucchini (about ½ pound each)
4 teaspoons unsalted butter, softened
1 teaspoon ground sage
1 teaspoon crushed rosemary
Salt and freshly ground black pepper
4 teaspoons freshly grated Parmesan cheese

Wash the zucchini and trim the ends. Cut them in half lengthwise. Place them, cut side up, in a baking dish or roasting pan small enough to contain them compactly. Spread about ½ teaspoon of the softened butter across the cut surface of each. In a small cup or bowl, combine the sage and rosemary. Sprinkle the mixed herbs on top of the butter; then sprinkle with salt and pepper to taste. Finally, spoon a generous dusting (about ½ teaspoon) grated cheese over each half. If not proceeding immediately, cover with plastic wrap and reserve in a cool section of the kitchen.

TIME ALLOWANCE FOR FINAL PREPARATION: 35 MINUTES.

Preheat the oven to 400 degrees.
Bake the zucchini for 20 to 30 minutes. The time will vary according to the freshness and size of the zucchini. Test by piercing with the tip of a sharp knife. Do not let them overcook. The cheese should be golden brown and the flesh still quite crunchy.

SERVES 6.

PEARS WITH ORANGE CURRANT SAUCE

MAY BE PREPARED UP TO 24 HOURS IN ADVANCE.

1 tablespoon grated orange rind
1 cup strained fresh orange juice
½ cup currant jelly
¼ cup water
½ cup sugar
6 pears (about 2 to 2½ pounds)
Whipped cream (optional)

In a small saucepan, combine the orange rind, juice, currant jelly, water, and sugar. Over moderately low heat, bring the syrup to a boil, stirring occasionally as the jelly melts.

Meanwhile, cut the pears in half and peel them. With a melon baller, scoop out their cores. Hold them in a bowl of cold water to prevent discoloration.

When the jelly has melted and the syrup is boiling, place the pears, cut side up, in a skillet large enough to contain them compactly. Pour the boiling syrup over them, return it to a boil, then lower the heat to a bare simmer. Cover the skillet and poach the pears for 20 to 40 minutes, turning them once. The cooking time will depend on the size and ripeness of the fruit. Test occasionally for doneness with the tip of a knife. The pears should offer no resistance.

With a slotted spoon, transfer the pears to a serving platter, cut side up. Increase the heat to high and, stirring constantly, reduce the syrup by half, about 10 minutes. Allow the syrup to cool somewhat before drizzling it over the pears. It should be quite thick. The pears should be served warm or at room temperature, with or without whipped cream. If preparing them well in advance, refrigerate them when they are cool, covered with plastic wrap. Allow at least 1 hour to bring them to room temperature.

SERVES 6.

A LUNCHEON SALAD FOR TEN

Chilled Cream of Watercress Soup*

Tex-Mex Salad

Cheddar Biscuits

Almond-Strawberry Tart

In summer my thoughts inevitably turn to leisurely weekend luncheons as one of the most pleasurable ways to entertain. I like to do cold luncheons on hot, balmy days. They're refreshing and very easy on the cook. Today's luncheon for ten is a fine example. It can be a hearty meal, but it requires no last-minute use of the stove or oven at all (unless perfectionism wins out and you want to serve the cheddar biscuits hot).

Aside from that traumatic decision, everything else can be readied ahead. The salad is a Tex-Mex combination of chicken, tomatoes, bacon, cheese, olives, and corn chips—the only thing missing, if you want to be a purist, are refried beans—all bound together with a rich avocado dressing with a peppery nip. Do try to beg or borrow a large bowl of clear glass or plastic in which to present this salad. It is as pretty as it is delectable, but only by looking through at its lovely layers will your guests be able to perceive the treat that lies ahead. Furthermore, restrain yourself from tossing the salad ahead of time. If you do, you'll ruin the stunning presentation.

As for dessert, the tart is beautiful to look at and just as beautiful to taste. It's not a breeze to make. It requires a good deal of patience and faith that it will actually work. (As it most certainly does.) If you become discouraged, keep your chin up and remember that, even if the crust and filling don't look quite the way they should, the gorgeously glazed strawberries will disguise everything, and in the end the tart will appear perfect.

TEX-MEX SALAD

MAY BE PARTIALLY PREPARED UP TO 12 HOURS IN ADVANCE.

SALAD

1 medium head iceberg lettuce
4 cups cooked white chicken meat, cut in ½-inch dice (about 2 pounds
  boneless chicken breasts)
2 large ripe tomatoes, cored and cut in ½-inch dice
1 cup sliced pitted ripe olives (about 13¼ ounce can)
½ cup sliced scallions, including 1 inch green leaves from each
10 pieces bacon, cooked, drained, and crumbled
1½ cups grated sharp cheddar cheese (about ½ pound)
2 cups crushed corn chips

To make the salad: In a large salad bowl, preferably clear glass or plastic, layer the lettuce, chicken, tomatoes, olives, scallions, bacon, and cheese in the same order as listed above. Cover with plastic wrap, and refrigerate until final preparation.

DRESSING

2 teaspoons minced garlic
2 ripe avocados, peeled, halved, and stoned
3 tablespoons strained fresh lemon juice
1 cup sour cream
½ cup vegetable oil
1 teaspoon chili powder
1 teaspoon salt
¼ teaspoon freshly ground black pepper
½ teaspoon ground cumin
¼ teaspoon Tabasco sauce

To make the dressing: In the bowl of a food processor fitted with a steel blade, place the garlic, avocados, lemon juice, and sour cream. Whirl until the avocados are pureed and the mixture is smooth. Add the vegetable oil, chili powder, salt, pepper, cumin, and Tabasco, and whirl until well mixed. Transfer to a bowl or jar, cover tightly with plastic wrap, and refrigerate until final preparation.

TIME ALLOWANCE FOR FINAL PREPARATION: 5 MINUTES.

Remove covering from salad. Spoon dressing over the top. Sprinkle with crushed corn chips. Refrain from tossing the salad until after its presentation, as it is very pretty to behold—particularly if served in a clear bowl.

SERVES 10.

CHEDDAR BISCUITS

MAY BE PREPARED UP TO 24 HOURS IN ADVANCE.

3½ cups flour
4 teaspoons baking powder
1½ teaspoons salt
6 tablespoons cold unsalted butter, cut in ¼-inch slices
1½ cups grated sharp cheddar cheese
1½ cups milk
1 egg
2 teaspoons cream
2 tablespoons sesame seeds (optional)

Preheat oven to 475 degrees.

In the bowl of a food processor fitted with a steel blade, combine 3 cups of the flour, the baking powder, and the salt. Whirl briefly to mix. Toss in the butter slices and pulse until the mixture resembles coarse meal. Repeat with the grated cheese. With the motor running continuously, pour the milk in through the feed tube, and whirl until a soft ball forms. Do not overprocess. Turn the dough out on a surface floured with the remaining ½ cup flour, and knead it briefly. With a rolling pin, roll it out to a thickness of ½ inch. Using a 2-inch round cutter, cut out as many biscuits as possible; transfer them to an ungreased cookie sheet. Knead the scraps, roll out again, and cut more biscuits. Repeat until all the dough is used up.

Beat the egg well in a small bowl. Beat in the cream. Brush the biscuits' surface with the egg wash. Sprinkle sesame seeds on top, if desired. Bake 15 minutes, or until the biscuits are a deep golden brown. Serve hot or at room temperature, with lots of butter. (Biscuits should be stored on a plate or platter, well sealed with plastic wrap. To reheat, place on baking sheet and warm in a preheated 300-degree oven for 10 minutes.)

YIELD: ABOUT TWENTY 2-INCH BISCUITS.

ALMOND-STRAWBERRY TART

MAY BE PARTIALLY PREPARED UP TO 12 HOURS IN ADVANCE.

PASTRY

⅓ cup finely ground skinless almonds
¾ cup flour
3 tablespoons confectioners' sugar
½ cup chilled unsalted butter, cut in slices

Preheat oven to 425 degrees.

To make the crust: Place the ground almonds in the bowl of a food processor fitted with a steel blade. Add the flour and sugar, and whirl briefly to mix. Add the sliced butter, and whirl just until a soft ball starts to form. Do not overblend. Press the pastry in small sections into an 11-inch French tart pan (the type with a removable bottom). The pastry will tend to be sticky and difficult to manage, but do not be discouraged. It is well worth the effort. To make things easier, cover your fingers with a piece of plastic wrap and simply work the pastry patiently across the bottom and up the sides of the pan. Prick the pastry liberally with the tines of a fork. Bake 10 minutes, or until golden brown. While it is still warm, run a knife gently around the edges of the tart pan to loosen the pastry. Set it aside on a rack to cool. Meanwhile, make the filling.

FILLING

1 (7-ounce) stick almond paste, cut into pieces
¼ cup confectioners' sugar
3 tablespoons unsalted butter, softened
1 egg yolk
1 quart ripe strawberries, washed and hulled
½ cup apricot preserves
1 tablespoon water
1 cup heavy cream

To make the filling: In the bowl of a food processor fitted with a steel blade, combine the almond paste, sugar, softened butter, and egg yolk, and whirl until very smooth and pale yellow, about 45 seconds. Scrape the sides down occasionally.

When the pastry has cooled, spread the almond filling across the base of the tart with a knife. The filling will be stiff. Wet the knife to aid in distributing it evenly. If too much moisture accumulates on the surface of the filling, "sponge" it up gently with a small piece of paper toweling. (The droplets of water will not affect the quality of the tart, but it will not look as pretty.) Next, arrange the strawberries, pointed ends up, attractively in concentric circles on top of the filling.

In a small saucepan, melt the apricot preserves with the water over moderately low heat. When it is sufficiently liquid, press it through a sieve so that you have a clear glaze. Brush the glaze generously over the strawberries and any almond filling that may be peeking through. Cover the tart loosely with plastic wrap, and refrigerate until ready to serve.

TIME ALLOWANCE FOR FINAL PREPARATION: 5 MINUTES.

Whip the cream until stiff peaks form. Scrape it into a pastry bag fitted with a decorative tip, and press out a circle of cream around the edge of the tart and a small round mound in the center. Then squeeze lengths of cream from the center to the edges, much like the spokes of a wheel. If you are not at ease with a pastry tube, simply serve the tart—removed from its rim but still resting on its base on a serving platter—accompanied by a bowl of whipped cream and let your guests help themselves.

SERVES 10.

SUNSET PICNIC FOR TWELVE

Mussels Rémoulade with Toast Points

Broiled Marinated Spareribs

Red, White, and "Blue" Salad

Roasted Marshmallows

Watermelon Slices

Sangria or Fruit Punch*

This evening picnic for twelve (although there's no reason it can't be held at midday) allows most of the meal to be prepared in advance, except for the grilling of the spareribs (what's an evening picnic without a fire?) and the roasting of the marshmallows. If the food seems a touch over-abundant, it should be: Eating in the open enhances appetites.

A successful picnic, of course, not only demands fair weather and toothsome food but thoughtful planning and packing. Don't forget any of those important incidentals, such as matches, barbecue tools, or can openers. And never forget about the dangers of spoilage in summer heat. Pack the food, well chilled, in insulated containers, with a bundle or two of ice as a precaution.

MUSSELS RÉMOULADE

MAY BE PREPARED UP TO 24 HOURS IN ADVANCE.

8 pounds mussels, scrubbed, "beards" pulled off
¼ cup sliced scallions, including 2 inches green leaves
½ cup capers, rinsed and drained
¾ cup minced fresh parsley
3 hard-boiled eggs, coarsely chopped (page 46)
¼ cup salad oil
1 cup unsweetened mayonnaise
2 tablespoons strained fresh lemon juice
2 tablespoons Dijon-style mustard
Salt and freshly ground black pepper
18 thin slices white bread, toasted, cut into "points"

Pour 2 inches of water into a 6- to 8-quart pot. Add the mussels. Cover and bring to a boil over high heat. Reduce heat to medium. Steam mussels, stirring once or twice to redistribute, until their shells have opened, about 10 minutes. (Discard all unopened ones.) Drain. When mussels are cool enough to handle, remove the body meat and discard shells. There should be about 4 cups of meat. If there is substantially (½ cup) more or less, increase or reduce the proportion of remaining ingredients accordingly.

With a pair of kitchen shears, cut each mussel in thirds, transferring them to a medium-size mixing bowl. Add the scallions, capers, parsley, and chopped eggs; toss well. In a separate bowl, beat the oil into the mayonnaise to lighten it. Beat in the lemon juice and mustard, and mix thoroughly. Pour the dressing over the mussel mixture, and toss until all the pieces are well coated. Taste for seasoning and adjust. Cover with plastic wrap and refrigerate until ready to serve.

Warning: No mayonnaise-based salad should be exposed to heat for a prolonged period. Mussels rémoulade must be stored in an insulated bag or cooler during picnic.

Serve spread on toast points.

SERVES 12.

BROILED MARINATED SPARERIBS

PRECOOKING MAY BE DONE UP TO 48 HOURS IN ADVANCE;
MARINATION MUST BE STARTED AT LEAST 24 HOURS IN ADVANCE.

10 pounds "country-style" spareribs, cut into ¾-inch- to 1-inch-thick ribs
(allow about 2 per person)
8 cloves
2 onions, peeled
4 bay leaves
1 tablespoon rosemary

MARINADE
3 cups soy sauce
1 cup medium-dry sherry
1 cup firmly packed dark brown sugar
4 tablespoons grated fresh gingerroot
½ cup thinly sliced scallions
1 tablespoon minced garlic

Place the spareribs into the 6- to 8-quart pot. Stick 4 cloves in each onion; add them, the bay leaves, and the rosemary, and fill the kettle with water. Cover, bring to a boil, reduce heat, and simmer the ribs for 45 minutes. Skim off any foam. Drain the ribs and cool them, discarding onions and bay leaves. (This thorough precooking will permit you to grill the ribs briefly over the coals and eliminates a lot of excess fat.)

To make the marinade: Combine the soy sauce, sherry, sugar, ginger, scallions, and garlic in a mixing bowl. Stir until the sugar has dissolved. Transfer the spareribs to a heavy-duty plastic bag to fit, and pour the marinade over them. Tie the bag securely. Shake and turn the bag several times so all the ribs are coated with the marinade. Refrigerate, turning the bag every 6 hours to recoat the ribs. Let them marinate 12 to 24 hours. Just before the picnic, untie the bag and drain the marinade. (It may be reserved and used again; it will keep for 1 month, covered and refrigerated.)

TIME ALLOWANCE FOR FINAL PREPARATION: ABOUT 1 HOUR.

In the case of outdoor grilling, the time allowance depends on wind, weather, and the talents of the grillmaker; hence no really firm time can be estimated. The charcoal should be red-hot but not flaming. The grill should be placed about 3 inches above the coals and should be pre-oiled with a product such as Pam to prevent sticking. If the coals seem ready but very hot, increase the distance of the grill from the coals to 4 inches. Broil the ribs in batches for about 5 to 8 minutes on each side (depending upon the heat of the fire) or until they are nicely brown and their remaining fat is crisp. Do not overcook, or they will dry out.

SERVES 12.

RED, WHITE, AND "BLUE" SALAD

SALAD AND DRESSING MAY BE PREPARED UP TO 24 HOURS IN ADVANCE.

DRESSING
½ cup white tarragon vinegar
½ teaspoon salt
Freshly ground black pepper
1 teaspoon Dijon-style mustard
1 teaspoon minced garlic
1 teaspoon oregano
1 cup salad oil

To make the dressing: In a 2- to 3-cup bottle with a tight-fitting lid, place the vinegar, salt, pepper, and mustard, and stir until the salt is dissolved and the mustard well blended. Add the garlic, oregano, and oil. Cover the bottle with the lid, and shake vigorously for 30 seconds. Open, taste for seasoning, and adjust if necessary. Cover and reserve in a cool spot until ready to use.

SALAD
1 teaspoon salt
2 cups rice
1 cup thinly sliced scallions, including 2 inches green leaves
2 (16-ounce) cans red kidney beans, rinsed and drained
1 green pepper, stem and seeds discarded, finely chopped
2 cups thinly sliced radishes
1 cup unpeeled cucumber cut in ¼-inch dice
1 cup minced fresh parsley
1 (10-ounce) package frozen peas, thawed
8 ounces ham, cut in ¼-inch dice
Freshly ground black pepper
8 ounces cherry tomatoes, sliced in half

To make the salad: Fill a 2- to 4-quart saucepan with water, add the salt, and bring to a boil. When it is rolling, add the rice slowly, stir to separate the grains, and bring to a boil again. Lower the heat to medium-low and cook, uncovered, 20 minutes. Drain. Rinse well under cold water; then drain for 10 minutes, tossing occasionally to help the rice dry out.

Transfer rice to a large salad bowl. Add the scallions, beans, pepper, radishes, cucumber, parsley, peas, and ham. Toss to mix thoroughly. Refrigerate, covered with plastic wrap, until ready to add dressing.

TIME ALLOWANCE FOR FINAL PREPARATION: 5 MINUTES.

Shake dressing vigorously again for a few seconds. Remove salad from refrigerator, uncover, and dribble dressing over the rice mixture. With a salad fork and spoon, toss well. Taste for seasoning and adjust. Arrange the cherry tomatoes decoratively around the edge of the bowl.

SERVES 12.

SANGRIA

◆

MUST BE PREPARED AT LEAST 6 HOURS IN ADVANCE.

1 cup sugar
2 cups water
2 limes, thinly sliced
2 oranges, thinly sliced, seeds removed
2 bottles dry red wine, chilled
1 cup brandy
1 10-ounce bottle club soda, chilled
Ice cubes

Combine the sugar and water in a 2-quart stainless steel saucepan and, over medium heat, stir until the sugar dissolves. When the mixture starts to boil, remove from the heat, and add the sliced limes and oranges. Allow the fruit to marinate in the syrup at least 6 hours, up to 24.

Fill a one-gallon thermal jug with the red wine, brandy, and club soda. Add the fruit-flavored syrup and stir well.

When ready to serve, pour into 8-ounce tumblers filled with ice.

YIELD: APPROXIMATELY EIGHTEEN 5-OUNCE DRINKS.

FOURTH OF JULY BRUNCH FOR TWELVE

Rum Punch

Roasted Almonds with Raisins

Cold Fruit Soup

Baked Eggs à la Flamenca

Buttered Toasted English Muffins

Citron Cheesecake

The Fourth of July is just about my favorite holiday. For me it heralds the official entrance of summer, with lovely, languorous days, balmy evenings, and the promise of burgeoning kitchen gardens.

I particularly like to entertain over the Fourth. Everyone seems to be in the same good spirits, full of laughter and conviviality. I often launch the weekend with a brunch for twelve favorite friends. We start things off around eleven o'clock with a fruity but not too potent punch, a blissful mix of orange and pineapple juices sparked with golden rum. We move on to a splendid cold fruit soup based on the superb fresh peaches and cherries in the market. While we're quaffing our frosty mugs of soup, a batch of eggs nesting on colorful sausage-vegetable mounds are baking in the oven. Served individually in ramekins, these eggs are hard to beat for ease of execution and serving convenience.

I finish the meal by offering my guests a frothy cheesecake imbued with orange and lemon. It's not the usual (and delicious) cheesecake, but a far lighter and less caloric version that was served me by an English friend. It's still guaranteed, however, to produce groans of appreciation. It is the perfect way to top off this Fourth of July celebration.

RUM PUNCH

MUST BE PREPARED JUST BEFORE SERVING.

For each serving:

4 to 6 ice cubes, according to size
1½ ounces gold Cruzan rum (or dark Mt. Gay rum)
3 ounces canned pineapple juice, well shaken
3 ounces strained fresh orange juice
Freshly grated nutmeg
½ orange slice

Drop the ice cubes into a 10-ounce highball glass. Pour the rum over the cubes; then add the pineapple and orange juices. Mix the drink well with a long iced-tea spoon. Grate nutmeg over the top. Garnish with the orange slice. Serve immediately.

MAKES 1 SERVING.

COLD FRUIT SOUP

MAY BE PREPARED UP TO 24 HOURS IN ADVANCE;
MUST BE PREPARED AT LEAST 4 HOURS IN ADVANCE.

4 large peaches (about 1½ pounds), peeled, pitted, cut in quarters
4 cups water
1 cup sugar
2 3-inch cinnamon sticks
4 cups cherries (about 1¾ pounds), stemmed and pitted
¼ teaspoon salt
1 tablespoon cornstarch
½ cup dry red wine
½ cup heavy cream
1 cup sour cream (garnish)

Combine the peaches, water, sugar, and cinnamon in a medium-size saucepan and bring to a boil. Lower the heat and simmer, partially covered, 10 minutes. Remove the cinnamon and reserve. With a slotted spoon, transfer the peaches to a blender or a food processor fitted with a steel blade and pour in about 1 cup of the fruit broth. Whirl until pureed. Return the puree and cinnamon to the saucepan, and add the cherries and salt. Stir to blend. Bring to a boil, lower the heat, partially cover, and simmer 30 minutes. Remove the cinnamon and discard.

Make a paste by combining the cornstarch with 3 tablespoons of the broth and stirring until smooth. Pour into the soup, stir well, and simmer, partially covered, 15 minutes. The soup should have thickened slightly. Remove from the heat and cool.

When the soup has come to room temperature, stir in the red wine and cream. Transfer to a large bowl or wide-mouth plastic jar, cover tightly, and refrigerate at least 3 hours or until thoroughly chilled.

TIME ALLOWANCE FOR FINAL PREPARATION: 5 MINUTES.

Spoon the soup into 12 individual bowls or oversized wine goblets. Garnish with a dollop of sour cream. Serve cold.

SERVES 12.

BAKED EGGS À LA FLAMENCA

◆

MAY BE PARTIALLY PREPARED UP TO 24 HOURS IN ADVANCE.

1 (12-ounce) package frozen pork sausage patties
4 tablespoons unsalted butter
⅔ cup finely chopped onion
2 red peppers (about ¾ pound), stemmed, seeded, and coarsely chopped
3 small yellow squash (about 1½ pounds), ends trimmed, cut in ½-inch dice
1½ teaspoons tarragon
3½ cups heavy cream
Salt and freshly ground black pepper to taste
12 eggs
2 tablespoons minced fresh parsley

In a large skillet, cook the unthawed sausage over medium heat for about 6 minutes on each side, or until golden brown. (If you do not have a skillet large enough to contain them in one layer, fry the patties in batches.) Drain on paper toweling. Cut into ¼-inch dice and reserve.

Rinse out the skillet, wipe dry, and return to moderately low heat. Melt the butter.

Add the onion, pepper, squash, and tarragon. Sauté the vegetables, stirring occasionally, for 10 minutes. Add 2 cups of the cream, increase the heat to moderately high, and cook, stirring constantly, until the cream has reduced by more than half and the vegetables are soft and very moist, about 5 minutes. Toss in the sausage and mix well. Taste and adjust seasoning. If not proceeding immediately, cool the mixture and transfer to a mixing bowl. Cover well with plastic wrap and refrigerate until 1 hour before final preparation.

TIME ALLOWANCE FOR FINAL PREPARATION: 20 MINUTES.

Preheat the oven to 375 degrees.

Generously butter 12 shallow ramekins about 4 inches in diameter. Cover the bottom of each with a layer of the vegetable-sausage mixture, making a well in the center. Break an egg into each one. Drizzle approximately 1 tablespoon cream over every egg. Bake 10 minutes, or until the eggs are set. Be careful not to overcook. Position each ramekin (they will be very hot) on a dinner plate. Garnish by sprinkling a tiny amount of parsley over each egg. Serve immediately.

SERVES 12.

CITRON CHEESECAKE

◆

MUST BE PREPARED AT LEAST 6 HOURS IN ADVANCE;
MAY BE PREPARED UP TO 24 HOURS IN ADVANCE.

1 tablespoon unsalted butter, softened
8 ounces ginger snaps, crushed
10 tablespoons unsalted butter, melted (1¼ sticks)
2½ to 3½ cups sugar
1 cup orange marmalade
1 cup water
½ cup strained fresh lemon juice
1 tablespoon plus 2 teaspoons unflavored gelatin
1 (8-ounce) package cream cheese, softened
1 cup evaporated milk, chilled
Sprigs of young fresh mint, washed and dried

Generously grease a 9-inch springform pan with the softened butter.
In a medium-size mixing bowl, combine the crushed ginger snaps with the melted

butter and 1 cup sugar. Toss until the butter has permeated all the crumbs. Press the mixture into the springform pan, building it 2½ to 3 inches up the sides. Hold in the refrigerator to chill while preparing the filling.

Place the orange marmalade, water, and lemon juice in a small saucepan. Sprinkle the gelatin over the water. When it has softened, heat the mixture slowly over low heat, stirring until the gelatin and marmalade have dissolved. Remove from the heat and bring to room temperature.

With an electric mixer or a wooden spoon, beat the cream cheese until fluffy, adding 1½ to 2½ cups sugar, according to taste. (The tartness of commercial marmalades varies greatly; start with 1½ cups sugar and increase if necessary. The cheesecake is being served here for brunch, and therefore a slightly tarter one is pleasant. If preparing the recipe for a general dessert, you may want to make it sweeter.) Beat the marmalade mixture into the cream cheese mixture. Refrigerate until thickened to the consistency of mayonnaise, about 2 hours.

In a separate bowl, whip the evaporated milk until stiff. Mix one-third of it into the gelatin mixture to lighten it; then gently fold in the rest. Pour the filling into the chilled crust and refrigerate until firm, about 5 hours. (Cover with plastic wrap if longer.) Serve cold.

TIME ALLOWANCE FOR FINAL PREPARATION: 5 MINUTES.

Run a knife between the edge of the cheesecake and the sides of the springform pan. Unlatch the springform and carefully remove. Transfer the cake (with the bottom of the springform) to a round serving platter. Garnish with sprigs of mint.

YIELD: ONE 9-INCH CHEESECAKE.

SWORDFISH DINNER FOR FOUR

*Swordfish Steak
with Gingered Hollandaise*

Sauteed Red Cabbage

Buttered Lima Beans

Double Blueberry Pie

One of the joys of summer in New England is the return to the fish market of the king of fishes, swordfish. Although we can find it in some markets off-season, it is never as good then as during the summer, and the reason is simple. There are two methods of catching swordfish: harpooning and deep-lining. Harpooning is done only in the summer, deep-lining year round. When harpooned, the fish is caught and brought in almost immediately. It dies quickly, by exposure to the air. When a swordfish is caught on deep lines, it dies by drowning. (The fishermen set their lines in the depths of the ocean and often do not return for several days to check their catch.) Deep-line swordfish, when cooked, is comparatively tasteless and can be downright mushy. Since swordfish is always expensive, no matter the season, be sure to check with your fishmonger to see how fresh it is and how it was caught. If he is a good fishmonger, he will be able to tell you.

I like to serve sautéed red cabbage with swordfish because visually they are such a nice combination. Take care not to overcook it, though—it is much better crisp. And a few native lima beans, nice and green this time of year, make the plate look really attractive.

For dessert, I offer one of my favorite pies: double blueberry. Invented many years ago by one of America's foremost cooks, Paula Peck, it combines cooked and uncooked berries. The cooked berries give the pie its juices, but not the usual flood tide of purple liquid; the uncooked contribute the crunchy, unmistakable texture of one of the most popular of our native bounties.

SWORDFISH STEAK WITH GINGERED HOLLANDAISE

MAY BE PARTIALLY PREPARED UP TO 4 HOURS IN ADVANCE.

GINGERED HOLLANDAISE

1 tablespoon strained fresh lime juice
3 tablespoons water
1 tablespoon minced shallots
3 tablespoons grated fresh gingerroot
1 egg yolk
½ cup unsalted butter, melted and cooled

To make the gingered hollandaise: In a small saucepan, place the lime juice, water, shallots, and grated ginger. Over low heat, allow the liquid to evaporate slowly until the shallots and ginger are barely moist. Still over low heat, add the egg yolk and whisk vigorously until the yolk thickens somewhat. Start adding the melted butter, drop by drop, over very low heat, always checking on the saucepan's temperature. The bottom of the pan should be warm, but not hot, to the touch. If necessary, remove it temporarily from the heat until it cools. Keep whisking in the butter steadily, drop by drop, until all is incorporated and the sauce has thickened to the consistency of mayonnaise. If the sauce should separate because of too much heat, remove the pan from the heat, add an ice cube, and beat vigorously. The sauce will be slightly thinner but will come together again. Cover the pan with its lid, and leave at room temperature until ready to serve. (Or transfer the hollandaise to a Thermos to keep warm.) Just before serving, whisk the sauce a few times. Never attempt to reheat it.

YIELD: APPROXIMATELY ½ CUP SAUCE.

SWORDFISH

2 tablespoons unsalted butter
2 tablespoons strained fresh lime juice
1 2-pound swordfish steak, about 1 inch thick
Salt and freshly ground black pepper

To cook the swordfish: Melt the butter and add the lime juice. Brush the bottom of a shallow baking dish large enough to hold the fish comfortably with some of the lime butter. Place the fish in the dish. Brush the surface of the fish with the remaining lime butter. Sprinkle with a small amount of salt and pepper. Cover with plastic wrap, and refrigerate until 1 hour before final preparation.

TIME ALLOWANCE FOR FINAL PREPARATION: 30 MINUTES.

Preheat the oven to 375 degrees. Preheat the broiler unit if separate from the oven.

Remove the plastic wrap from the fish. Bake 15 minutes. Turn on the broiler unit, or transfer the fish to the broiler, and broil 5 to 10 minutes, or until the top is nicely browned.

Serve immediately with gingered hollandaise.

SERVES 4.

SAUTÉED RED CABBAGE

MAY BE PARTIALLY PREPARED UP TO 6 HOURS IN ADVANCE.

3 tablespoons unsalted butter
½ cup thinly sliced red onion
4 cups coarsely sliced red cabbage (about 2 pounds)
Salt and freshly ground black pepper to taste

In a large skillet with a tight-fitting lid, melt the butter. Add the red onion, and sauté it over low heat until wilted. Remove from heat. Add the cabbage, toss briefly, and cover the skillet with the lid. Store in a cool corner of the kitchen until final preparation.

TIME ALLOWANCE FOR FINAL PREPARATION: 10 MINUTES.

Place the skillet over low heat, still covered. After 2 or 3 minutes, remove the cover and toss the cabbage well. Increase the heat to medium and continue to sauté, covered, 5 more minutes, stirring occasionally, until the cabbage has just begun to wilt but is still bright in color and crisp. Taste for seasoning and adjust.

SERVES 4.

DOUBLE BLUEBERRY PIE

MAY BE PARTIALLY PREPARED 12 HOURS IN ADVANCE.

4 cups blueberries, picked over, stems and soft berries discarded
½ cup currant jelly
½ to 1 cup sugar
1 teaspoon grated lemon rind
1 tablespoon strained fresh lemon juice
1 (9-inch) prebaked pastry pie shell
1 cup heavy cream, whipped

Combine 2 cups of blueberries, the currant jelly, ½ cup of sugar, and lemon rind and juice in a 2-quart stainless steel saucepan. Over medium to high heat, stir until the sugar and jelly have dissolved and the berries start to burst. Taste for sweetness and add up to ½ cup more sugar, bearing in mind that you will be mixing this "jam" with the remaining 2 cups of uncooked and unsweetened berries. Continue to cook, stirring occasionally, until the berry "jam" is reduced by almost half and the syrup coats the back of a spoon. Remove from heat and cool. Cover with plastic wrap and store in a cool spot in the kitchen. (Final preparation may be executed up to 2 hours before serving.)

TIME ALLOWANCE FOR FINAL PREPARATION: 5 MINUTES.

Place the 2 cups of uncooked blueberries in a mixing bowl. Spoon the blueberry "jam" over them, and gently mix until all the berries are coated. (If the jam has set somewhat, reheat it briefly, stirring, until it is liquid. Do not allow it to become too hot. It should be nearly at room temperature when mixed with the uncooked berries.)
Transfer the mixture to the baked pie shell.
Just before serving, top with whipped cream.

YIELD: ONE 9-INCH PIE.

MIDDAY BARBECUE FOR EIGHT

Grilled Italian Sausages with Tomato Sauce

Cauliflower and Broccoli Salad with Curried Mayonnaise

Peach and Blueberry Pie

One summer Sunday, I had the opportunity to observe the day's activities on a glorious stretch of Cape Cod's outer beach. There were all sizes and shapes of humanity, plus kites, coolers, beach umbrellas, wind shields, rubber rafts, beach towels, inner tubes, baseballs and bats, and Frisbees, as well as those most fundamental tools for American summer living: charcoal, lighter fluid, and the trusty portable grill.

At picnic time, I saw these lively groups kindle their fires. Out of the coolers came hamburgers, hot dogs, red-sauced chicken, steaks and kebabs, steamers and lobsters—you name it, someone had it, to be cooked in the open air. One family in particular caught my attention. The father was grilling a batch of Italian sausages, which he inserted in pieces of crusty Italian bread, then smothered in a pungent blend of onions, peppers, and tomatoes. From the way his family and friends devoured them, I knew his sausages must be special.

This recipe for grilled Italian sausages with tomato sauce is the result of that inspiration. With the sausage, I suggest a cauliflower and broccoli salad that really should be executed a few hours in advance to allow the flavors of the dressing to permeate the crunchy vegetables. For dessert, try the peach and blueberry pie. It is not so runny as to make transportation and picnic consumption a hazard; however, if you like it really oozing, forget the tapioca. Either way, the pie somehow imparts the essence of a sunny summer day.

GRILLED ITALIAN SAUSAGES WITH TOMATO SAUCE

MUST BE PREPARED JUST BEFORE SERVING.
TIME ALLOWANCE FOR FINAL PREPARATION: 30 MINUTES.

2 pounds sweet Italian sausages
1 medium onion, halved and thinly sliced
1 green pepper, halved, seeded, and cut in thin strips
1 (28-ounce) can Italian peeled tomatoes, drained
1 long loaf French or Italian bread, cut in 3-inch segments, each almost, but
  not quite, split in half lengthwise (at least 12 pieces)

This dish may be pan-fried or grilled over charcoal. However, the sausages are enhanced with a charcoal grilling.

For charcoal grilling: Prepare the coals. They should be red-hot but not flaming. Prick the sausages with a fork in several places so they will not burst.

Place the sausages on the grill, over the coals, and cook them, turning them frequently, until brown on all sides. Remove them from the grill and transfer them to a large frying pan, preferably cast iron. Place the frying pan on the grill over the coals, partially cover the pan, and cook the sausages about 5 minutes, or until they have exuded some of their fat and juices. Add the onion and green pepper, stir to mix, partially cover and cook another 5 minutes or until the onions have begun to wilt. Stir once more. Add the tomatoes, breaking them up as you scatter them among the pieces of sausage. Cook, uncovered, for 10 minutes or until the sauce has thickened considerably.

Meanwhile, spread the pieces of bread apart, and toast them over the coals to one side of the frying pan until they are golden brown.

Place one sausage in each piece of bread, smother in onion-and-tomato sauce, and serve immediately.

To pan fry: Follow the same directions, but fry the sausage—without any grease—in the skillet over moderately high heat, turning frequently, until brown on all sides. Reduce the heat to moderate, add the vegetables, and proceed as directed above. Toast the bread under a broiler or in a toaster oven.

SERVES 8.

CAULIFLOWER AND BROCCOLI SALAD
WITH CURRIED MAYONNAISE

MUST BE PREPARED AT LEAST 6 HOURS IN ADVANCE;
MAY BE PREPARED UP TO 12 HOURS IN ADVANCE.

CAULIFLOWER AND BROCCOLI SALAD

1 small head cauliflower, broken up into flowerets, stems removed
1 bunch broccoli, broken up into flowerets, stems removed
½ cup minced scallions, including 2 inches green leaves
1 cup cherry tomatoes, stems removed
1 tablespoon whole cumin seed, toasted

To make the salad: Combine the cauliflower and broccoli flowerets, scallions, cherry tomatoes, and cumin seed in a large salad bowl. Toss to mix. Pour curried mayonnaise over the vegetables, and toss thoroughly to coat all the vegetables. Refrigerate, covered, at least 6 hours or as long as 12. Remove from refrigerator 1 hour before serving.

SERVES 6.

CURRIED MAYONNAISE

3 egg yolks at room temperature
½ teaspoon salt
½ teaspoon dry mustard
1 tablespoon fresh lemon juice
1½ cups vegetable oil
1 tablespoon curry powder
2 tablespoons boiling water (optional)

To make the dressing: Drop the egg yolks into a food processor fitted with a steel blade. Add the salt, mustard, and lemon juice. Whirl about 30 seconds, or until the yolks have thickened. With the motor still running, pour the oil through the feed tube in a very slow, steady stream. Taste and adjust seasonings. Add the curry powder, and briefly whirl again. The mayonnaise should be thick. To make it creamier and lessen the danger of its separating, slowly add the boiling water with the motor still running. The mayonnaise may be refrigerated or used immediately on the salad.

YIELD: APPROXIMATELY 2 CUPS.

PEACH AND BLUEBERRY PIE

MAY BE PREPARED UP TO 8 HOURS IN ADVANCE.

2 eggs
3 tablespoons tapioca
¾ cup firmly packed dark brown sugar
Pinch of salt
¼ teaspoon freshly grated nutmeg
2 pounds ripe peaches, peeled and sliced (about 4 cups)
1 cup blueberries, picked over, stems and soft berries discarded
Pastry for 2-crust 9-inch pie
3 tablespoons heavy cream

Preheat oven to 450 degrees.

In a large mixing bowl, beat the eggs until frothy and well combined. Add the tapioca, and allow it to soften for a minute or two. Beat in the brown sugar, salt, and nutmeg. Add the peaches and blueberries, and toss well.

Spoon the fruit into a 9-inch pie plate lined with pastry. Roll out the top crust, cut 3 or 4 slits in it, and after moistening the edges of the bottom crust, lay the top crust over the fruit, pressing the edges firmly together. Trim off any excess dough, and crimp the edges decoratively. Brush the cream over the top crust for a glaze.

Place the pie on a cookie sheet on a rack in the top third of the oven. Bake it 15 minutes at 450 degrees. Lower the heat to 350 and bake 30 minutes longer, or until the pie is golden brown. Serve it hot or at room temperature.

SERVES 8.

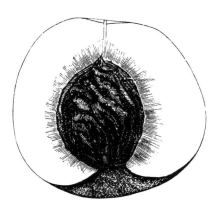

HOT-WEATHER LUNCHEON FOR EIGHT

Jellied Chicken Consommé*

Cold Poached Salmon with Cucumber Sauce

Snow Pea and Pasta Salad with Sherry Orange Mayonnaise Dressing

Cold Chocolate Soufflé

N o summer is truly a summer without one or more heat waves. This menu is what I feel to be the perfect meal for those days of outrageous temperatures when asphalt actually softens on city streets.

I suggest for the first course a chilled, translucent, jellied soup; for the entree, pink portions of sweet salmon, enhanced by a creamy, but not rich, cucumber sauce; a salad of crisp snow peas and pasta, with a tangy orange dressing; and for dessert, rich—but light and airy—cold chocolate soufflé moistened with a spoonful or two of heavy cream or silky crème anglaise. The portions recommended are moderate, nothing too big or overwhelming. To this lovely meal, any heat-jaded appetite would respond with pleasure.

COLD POACHED SALMON WITH CUCUMBER SAUCE

FISH STOCK MAY BE PREPARED UP TO 3 DAYS IN ADVANCE;
SALMON MAY BE POACHED UP TO 24 HOURS IN ADVANCE; SAUCE
MAY BE PREPARED UP TO 12 HOURS IN ADVANCE AND MUST
BE PREPARED AT LEAST 1 HOUR IN ADVANCE.

FISH STOCK
1 to 4 pounds salmon heads, bones, tail, etc.
½ to 3 quarts water
½ to 1 bottle dry white wine
1 to 2 large stalks celery, broken into sections
1 to 2 large carrots, broken into sections
1 medium onion, peeled
1 teaspoon salt
8 sprigs parsley, tied together

To make the stock: Select a poacher or roasting pan large enough to contain the salmon fillet (see below) in one piece, and measure its fluid capacity. For every quart of stock needed, allow one pound of fish heads or bones, 2 cups water, 1 cup dry white wine, 1 stalk celery, and 1 carrot. (For larger quantities, use 2 stalks celery and 2 carrots.) The other ingredients remain the same. You will probably need 2 to 3 quarts of stock, but pan sizes vary widely, as do salmon fillets, so precise measurements are difficult. As long as you use a good proportion of fish heads and bones, a little more or less of water or wine won't matter. (Add 1 extra cup of water for evaporation.)

Fill a large kettle with the appropriate amounts of fish heads and bones, water, wine, celery, carrot, onion, salt, and parsley. Bring to a boil. Lower the heat and skim off any scum that has risen to the surface. Partially cover the pan and simmer 30 minutes. Strain the stock and reserve, covered, in the refrigerator until ready to use. Discard the vegetables and fish particles.

1 salmon fillet, 2½ to 3½ pounds
1 bunch fresh dill weed
1 English cucumber
Lemon wedges

To poach the salmon: Center the fillet lengthwise in a long length of cheesecloth, bringing the sides up and over each other so that the fish is completely enveloped. Tie string around both ends of the fish so that it cannot slip out of its "bag." This will also permit the ends of the cheesecloth to be used as handles when you remove the fish from the hot stock.

Measure the fish at its thickest point. Allow 10 minutes of cooking time for every inch, and add 5 minutes for safety. A fish 2 inches thick should therefore cook 25 minutes; 3 inches, 35 minutes. Place the wrapped fish in its poaching vessel, and pour the stock over it until the fish is completely covered by at least ½ inch. Over moderate heat, bring the stock to a boil. Once it starts to boil, lower the heat to the barest simmer. Simmer the fillet for the appropriate time.

Remove the fish from the stock by lifting it gently by its cheesecloth handles, and transfer it to a serving platter. Carefully untie and fold back the cheesecloth and pierce the thickest section of the salmon with the tip of a knife just to check on its doneness. It should be completely opaque. If you think it needs a bit more cooking, rewrap it, return it to the stock, and simmer 5 or 10 minutes longer.

When the fish is poached to your satisfaction, allow it to cool somewhat. Using the cheesecloth for support, turn the fillet skin side up before discarding the cloth. Carefully peel off the skin with a sharp paring knife. (It is much easier to do this while the fish is still fairly warm.) To make the fish more palatable and attractive, scrape off the dark meat running down its center and discard. Refrigerate the fish, loosely covered with plastic wrap, until 1 hour before final preparation. Since salmon has such a delicate flavor, it should be brought to room temperature. While the fish is refrigerated, make the cucumber sauce.

CUCUMBER SAUCE
1 large cucumber
¾ teaspoon salt
8 ounces sour cream
8 ounces plain low-fat yogurt
2 tablespoons freshly grated onion
2 to 3 drops Tabasco
¼ cup minced fresh dill weed
Freshly ground black pepper

To make the sauce: Trim the ends off the cucumber and peel it. Cut it in half lengthwise. With the tip of a spoon, scrape out the seeds and discard. Cut the cucumber into thin slices, and place in a colander. Sprinkle with ½ teaspoon salt and toss to distribute. Allow to drain at least 1 hour. Transfer to paper toweling and pat dry.

Meanwhile, in a mixing bowl, combine the sour cream, yogurt, onion, Tabasco, dill, and pepper and, with a fork or whisk, blend thoroughly. Add the drained cucumber slices, mix again and taste for seasoning, adding another ¼ teaspoon salt if desired. Reserve, covered with plastic wrap, in the refrigerator until 1 hour before serving. Bring to room temperature and transfer to a serving bowl.

YIELD: APPROXIMATELY 3 CUPS SAUCE.

TIME ALLOWANCE FOR FINAL PREPARATION: 10 MINUTES.

Pour off any fish juices that may have accumulated on the serving platter. Mince 2 tablespoons dill, and sprinkle it over the salmon. Scrape the tines of a fork lengthwise down the unpeeled English cucumber on all its sides, and slice it very thin. Arrange the slices decoratively around the fish, interspersed with sprigs of dill and lemon wedges. Serve the fish whole, accompanied by cucumber sauce.

SERVES 8.

SNOW PEA AND PASTA SALAD WITH SHERRY ORANGE MAYONNAISE DRESSING

MAY BE PREPARED UP TO 12 HOURS IN ADVANCE.

SHERRY ORANGE MAYONNAISE DRESSING
½ cup dry sherry
3 tablespoons grated orange rind
½ cup strained fresh orange juice
2 tablespoons fresh lemon juice
1 small clove garlic, peeled and sliced
½ teaspoon salt
Freshly ground black pepper
1 egg yolk
½ cup olive oil
¼ cup half-and-half

To make the dressing: In a small saucepan, combine the sherry, orange rind, and orange and lemon juices and bring to a boil over high heat. Boil mixture until it has reduced to 3 tablespoons. Set aside and cool.

In a food processor fitted with a steel blade, whirl the sliced garlic until it is finely minced. Add the salt and pepper, the cooled reduced liquid, and the egg yolk; pulse until well combined. With the machine running, add the olive oil in a slow, steady stream, stopping every now and then to scrape down the sides of the bowl with a rubber spatula. Dressing will thicken to the consistency of mayonnaise. Add the half-and-half and pulse to mix. Reserve until ready to dress the salad.

SNOW PEA AND PASTA SALAD

1 (12-ounce) box rotini or rotelle
½ pound snow peas, ends trimmed, strings removed, cut in half crosswise
½ teaspoon salt
1 tablespoon vegetable oil
½ cup slivered almonds (1 2¼-ounce package)
1 red pepper, cored and seeded and cut into ½-inch dice
Freshly ground black pepper

To make the salad: Cook the pasta in boiling salted water according to package directions until *al dente,* or just tender. (Timing will vary according to manufacturer.) Drain in a colander and refresh under cold water. Cool.

Fill a 1- to 2-quart saucepan to within 2 inches of the top with water, add ½ teaspoon salt and bring to a boil. Drop the snow peas in and, when the water returns to a boil, immediately drain the peas in a sieve and refresh under cold water. Cool.

While the pasta and peas are cooling, heat the oil in a small skillet and add the slivered almonds. Toast them over moderately low heat until golden brown, stirring occasionally. This will take about 5 minutes. Do not allow to become too brown. With a slotted spoon, remove them to paper toweling to drain. Reserve for garnish.

In a large salad bowl, combine the pasta, snow peas, and red pepper, and toss well to mix. Pour the sherry orange mayonnaise over the salad, and toss vigorously to coat all the ingredients. Taste for seasoning and adjust. Cover with plastic wrap and refrigerate until 1 hour before final preparation.

TIME ALLOWANCE FOR FINAL PREPARATION: 5 MINUTES.

Remove the plastic wrap from the salad and toss thoroughly. Sprinkle the surface with the reserved toasted almonds.

SERVES 8.

COLD CHOCOLATE SOUFFLÉ

◆

SOUFFLÉ MAY BE PREPARED UP TO 24 HOURS IN ADVANCE
BUT MUST BE PREPARED AT LEAST 3 HOURS IN ADVANCE.

1 (12-ounce) package semisweet chocolate morsels
2 packages unflavored gelatin
1 cup water
6 eggs, separated
1 teaspoon vanilla
¼ teaspoon cinnamon
Pinch of salt
½ cup sugar
1 cup heavy cream, whipped
2 cups heavy cream or crème anglaise (see page 38)

Prepare a 1-quart soufflé dish by fashioning a collar of oiled aluminum foil or wax paper around the dish, extending at least 2 inches about its rim. Secure the collar with cord tied tightly around it, or fasten it with tape.

Melt the chocolate in the top of a double boiler set over moderate heat. Sprinkle the gelatin over the water to soften. When the chocolate has melted and the gelatin is soft, add the gelatin to the chocolate, and stir thoroughly. In a small bowl, beat the egg yolks well. Pour them into the chocolate mixture and continue beating for 3 to 4 minutes, or until the chocolate just starts to thicken. Remove the top of the double boiler from its lower section, add the vanilla and cinnamon, and cool to room temperature.

In a large bowl, beat the egg whites with a pinch of salt. Beat in the sugar very gradually, continuing until the whites are stiff and still glossy, but not dry. Fold the whites into the whipped cream. Blend one-fourth of the egg whites into the chocolate mixture to lighten it; then gently fold the chocolate mixture into the remaining whites, mixing only until all traces of white have disappeared. Gently transfer the soufflé into the prepared soufflé dish, and refrigerate it until firm all the way through, at least 2 to 2½ hours. If you are preparing the soufflé well in advance, make a lid of aluminum foil to set upon its collar and prevent the top from drying out.

TIME ALLOWANCE FOR FINAL PREPARATION: 5 MINUTES.

Cut off the cord or tape securing the collar to the soufflé dish. Carefully pull off the collar. The cold soufflé should look like a hot soufflé, nicely risen above the rim of its dish. Serve with heavy cream or crème anglaise.

SERVES 8.

STEAK BARBECUE
FOR EIGHT

Grilled Steak Dijonnaise

Vegetable Mélange

*Tomato and Red Onion Salad
with Vinaigrette Dressing**

*Hazelnut Cake
with Lemon-Berry Filling*

There's almost nothing I enjoy more than driving down country lanes around six or seven on a summer evening, when the heat of the day is just letting up and all manner of folk are congregated around their charcoal grills. My eyes catch glimpses of little plumes of smoke wafting upward; I hear the contagious laughter of children; my spirits soar just observing the variety of pleasures derived from the simple act of outdoor cooking. Even more tantalizing, though, are the aromas emanating from the fires. As I pass by, each fragrance seems more seductive than the last.

Not long after one of these drives, I started to plan the menu for a dinner for eight guests. Fired by my sensory trip, I decided that it must be a barbecued feast and that I would indulge our appetites in a great, big, lovely, thick steak. The next question was how to fashion a steak that would be novel. Why not a marinated steak, I thought, and boneless for easy carving? And why not, for the sake of the budget, select a cut that might benefit from the tenderizing effect of marination? The result was a two-inch-thick beauty from the top of the round that cost all of $13.50. That figure, of course, isn't peanuts—but it is when it feeds eight, and feeds them well.

To accompany the steak I prepared an easy, delicious mix of vegetables—carrots, leeks, and mushrooms—that required only a few final minutes of saucing and reheating.

Dessert required no effort at all because it had been done entirely ahead. The lofty hazelnut cake, layered with a lemon filling replete with fat raspberries and topped with still more berries, was a staggering delight to behold.

GRILLED STEAK DIJONNAISE

MUST BE PARTIALLY PREPARED 24 HOURS IN ADVANCE.

1 boneless top round steak, 4 to 5 pounds, about 2 to 2½ inches thick
2 teaspoons minced garlic
1 teaspoon rosemary, pulverized
1 teaspoon oregano
1 teaspoon marjoram
1 tablespoon Dijon-style mustard
¼ cup red wine vinegar
1 tablespoon chili sauce
½ teaspoon salt
¼ teaspoon freshly ground black pepper
1 tablespoon grated orange rind
½ cup olive oil

In a shallow glass or enamel pan large enough to contain the steak easily, combine the garlic, rosemary, oregano, marjoram, mustard, vinegar, chili sauce, salt, pepper, and orange rind. With a wooden spoon, mix until the mustard and salt are dissolved. Gradually add the oil, stirring constantly. Settle the steak in the marinade, turning it once or twice to coat both sides thoroughly. Cover with plastic wrap, and marinate in the refrigerator 24 hours. Turn the steak occasionally during this period, recoating it with the dressing. Remove it from the refrigerator about 1½ hours before final preparation to bring it to room temperature.

TIME ALLOWANCE FOR FINAL PREPARATION: ½ TO ¾ HOUR FOR PREPARING THE CHARCOAL; 20 TO 30 MINUTES FOR GRILLING THE STEAK.

For charcoal-grilling a piece of meat of this thickness, the coals should be red-hot but not flaming.

Remove the steak from the marinade, but do not scrape off any excess. (Discard what is left in the pan, however.) Place the steak on a greased rack about 3 inches above the coals. If you have a grill with a cover, keep the vents open but cover the meat while you cook it. If not, watch the coals carefully. Try to prevent flaming by sprinkling them with water if flames rise up. Allow about 10 minutes per side for rare but not raw meat. For medium meat, allow about 12 minutes per side; for well-done, 15 minutes per side. The heat of coals and grills' performances vary so greatly that you should not take the suggested time as law, but test the meat; either prod it with a fork or finger for resiliency (no resiliency indicates rare meat, great resiliency well-done) or make a small incision and look for yourself.

When the meat is grilled to your satisfaction, transfer it immediately to a heated platter. Carve it in thin slices, cutting across the grain and on a diagonal for extra tenderness.

SERVES 8.

VEGETABLE MÉLANGE

◆

MAY BE PARTIALLY PREPARED UP TO 6 HOURS IN ADVANCE.

¾ pound large white mushrooms
3 large leeks, roots and green stalks trimmed, thoroughly washed
1 pound carrots, peeled
3 tablespoons unsalted butter
½ cup water
1 teaspoon sugar
1 cup heavy cream
½ teaspoon salt
Freshly ground black pepper
3 tablespoons minced fresh dill weed

Trim the ends off the mushrooms and cut the caps in ⅓-inch slices. Cut the leeks into 3-inch-long strips. Julienne the carrots into ¼-inch by 3-inch strips.

Melt the butter over low heat in a large skillet with a tight-fitting lid. Sauté the mushrooms, turning frequently, until they just start to exude their juices. Add the leeks, carrots, water, and sugar. Stir to mix. Bring to a boil, cover, and steam over moderate heat for 5 minutes, or until the carrots are just tender. Remove the cover and continue cooking, tossing occasionally, for 1 to 2 minutes until all the liquid has evaporated. If, after 2 minutes, some liquid still remains, drain the vegetables thoroughly. Set the pan aside, covered, in a cool place until final preparation.

TIME ALLOWANCE FOR FINAL PREPARATION: 8 MINUTES.

Return the skillet to the range. Add the cream, salt, and pepper, and stir to blend. Cook uncovered over moderately high heat, stirring constantly, for 4 to 7 minutes or until the cream has reduced by half and thickened considerably. Add the dill, toss to distribute, and serve immediately.

SERVES 8.

HAZELNUT CAKE WITH LEMON-BERRY FILLING

CAKE MAY BE PREPARED UP TO 24 HOURS IN ADVANCE;
FILLING SHOULD BE PREPARED NOT LONGER THAN 4 HOURS IN ADVANCE.

CAKE
3 eggs
1½ cups sugar
1½ cups cake flour
2 teaspoons baking powder
¼ teaspoon salt
1½ cups heavy cream
2 teaspoons vanilla
*1 cup ground hazelnuts, available at specialty food stores (or substitute
ground pecans)*

To make the cake: Preheat the oven to 350 degrees.

Butter three 8-inch cake pans, line them with circles of wax paper cut to fit the bottoms of the pans, and butter again.

In a large bowl, beat the eggs until slightly thickened. Slowly beat in the sugar a few tablespoons at a time. Continue beating until the mixture is lemon-colored and fluffy. In another bowl, sift the flour, baking powder, and salt. Repeat and reserve. Whip the cream until soft peaks form. Beat in the vanilla.

In three parts, fold the cream into the egg mixture, alternating with the flour and hazelnuts. Fold gently but thoroughly. Divide the mixture evenly among the three cake pans, and bake for 30 minutes or until a knife or straw inserted in the center comes out clean. Cool 10 minutes on racks. Remove the cake from its pans and cool completely.

LEMON-BERRY FILLING
2 tablespoons grated lemon rind
½ cup strained fresh lemon juice
6 tablespoons unsalted butter
¼ teaspoon salt
1 cup sugar
3 eggs, beaten
1 pint cultivated raspberries or blueberries, cleaned and picked over

To make the filling: In a 1-quart stainless steel or enamel saucepan, combine the lemon rind, juice, butter, salt, and sugar. Over low heat, melt the butter, stirring occasionally. Add the eggs, increase the heat to moderate, and stir constantly until the mixture comes nearly to a boil and thickens sufficiently to coat the back of a spoon. Remove from the heat and cool, stirring once or twice to prevent a skin from forming. As it cools, the custard will become even thicker.

To assemble the cake: If the layers are not uniform, trim them with a serrated knife so that they will lie flat. Place one layer on a serving plate. Spread its surface with one-third of the lemon filling. Top with a single layer of berries, using about one-third of the pint. Repeat with the second and third layers. (Arrange the berries on the top layer as decoratively as possible, either spiraling them out from the center or arranging them in a spokelike fashion to the edge.) Do not attempt to coat the sides of the cake with the lemon filling; spread it to the edge of each layer, allowing it to dribble down the sides slightly if you want. It is not thick enough to adhere to the sides like traditional frostings.

Reserve the cake in a cool corner of the kitchen until ready to serve. It should not be exposed to heat. If in doubt, refrigerate it, protected lightly with plastic wrap. Bring it to room temperature before serving.

YIELD: ONE 3-LAYER CAKE.

FISH FEAST
FOR SIX

Bouillabaisse

*Cabbage Salad with Basil
Vinaigrette Dressing*

*Hot French Bread or
Crusty Rolls*

Hot Buttered Rum Peaches

Every summer I have an intense love affair with the plethora of fresh seafood around. That's when I offer my family and friends my favorite dish, a modified version of France's famous fish stew, bouillabaisse. The French dish—and there are as many varieties as America has chowders—often uses wine to generate a headier, more fluid, broth and a virtual aquariumful of nautical creatures, including their heads, tails, bones, and what-nots. I limit my list of ingredients, and I do not use whole fish. Bones do add flavor, but they make me nervous in a stew of this magnitude. Besides, bouillabaisse is wonderfully flavorful without them.

The base can be prepared several hours ahead of time, the ingredients thrown in on top, and the whole thing refrigerated until an hour before baking. All one needs is a very large casserole, a good fish market, and guests with healthy appetites.

Because bouillabaisse is so filling and delicious, one really doesn't need much else to accompany it. Bread is a must to absorb the abundant, self-generated broth; a light salad is nice but not strictly necessary.

For dessert, hot buttered rum peaches are spicy and wonderful, a good foil for the fish stew. In winter the same recipe can be done with canned peaches, but once you taste the dessert created with the fresh, you'll never be satisfied with substitutes.

BOUILLABAISSE

MAY BE PARTIALLY PREPARED UP TO 6 HOURS IN ADVANCE.

½ cup olive oil
1 cup coarsely chopped onion (1 large)
2 teaspoons minced garlic
2 teaspoons fennel seed
1 tablespoon grated orange rind
3 tablespoons minced fresh parsley
2 cloves
1 large ripe tomato, peeled and chopped (about ½ pound)
2 pounds fish fillets, skinned (striped bass, haddock, cod, scrod, or similar
  firm-fleshed white fish)
1 pound sea scallops
1 lobster, 2 or 3 pounds, uncooked, cut in 2-inch segments
18 littleneck or cherrystone clams
18 mussels, well scrubbed, "beards" removed
18 shrimp, unpeeled (about ½ pound)

Pour the olive oil into the bottom of a large (6- to 8-quart), deep ovenproof casserole equipped with a tight-fitting lid. Set it over moderately low heat. Add the onions and garlic, and sauté, stirring occasionally, until the onion is wilted. Add the fennel seed, orange rind, parsley, and cloves. Mix well. Toss in the tomato pieces and sauté until soft, about 5 minutes. Remove from the heat and cool.

When the bottom of the casserole feels cool to the touch, layer the fish, scallops, lobster pieces, clams, mussels, and shrimps (in that order) into the pot. Cover tightly and refrigerate until 1 hour before final preparation.

TIME ALLOWANCE FOR FINAL PREPARATION: 45 TO 60 MINUTES.

Preheat the oven to 375 degrees.

Place the casserole, covered, in the middle of the oven and bake 30 minutes. Remove the lid and check. If the clam and mussel shells have opened, the bouillabaisse is done. If not, bake 10 minutes longer and check again. Cook until the shells are wide open. It is not necessary to stir the ingredients in the pot. When the shells are open, everything will be cooked to perfection.

Serve the bouillabaisse in large, shallow soup bowls, making sure each bowl has a good proportion of the various ingredients and a generous ladling of the fish broth.

SERVES 6.

CABBAGE SALAD
WITH BASIL VINAIGRETTE DRESSING

SALAD MAY BE PARTIALLY PREPARED UP TO 4 HOURS IN ADVANCE;
VINAIGRETTE MAY BE PREPARED UP TO 1 WEEK IN ADVANCE.

CABBAGE SALAD

½ pound red cabbage, core removed, finely shredded
¾ pound green cabbage, core removed, finely shredded
1 tablespoon minced chives
½ cup minced fresh parsley

To make the salad: Line a large salad bowl with paper toweling. Place the red and green cabbages and chives in it. With your hands or with a salad fork and spoon, toss the salad until the ingredients are well mixed. Cover the bowl loosely with another sheet or two of paper toweling, and refrigerate it until time for final preparation.

BASIL VINAIGRETTE DRESSING

1 clove garlic, peeled and split
¼ teaspoon salt
Freshly ground black pepper
1 teaspoon Dijon-style mustard
½ teaspoon sugar
½ teaspoon dried basil
¼ teaspoon freshly grated nutmeg
2 tablespoons tarragon vinegar
6 tablespoons olive oil

To make the dressing: In a 1½ (or larger) jar with a tight-fitting lid, combine the garlic, salt, pepper, mustard, sugar, basil, nutmeg, and vinegar. Stir until the salt is dissolved and the mustard well combined with the vinegar. Add the oil, cover the jar securely with the lid, and shake the dressing vigorously. Set aside on a cool shelf until final preparation.

TIME ALLOWANCE FOR FINAL PREPARATION: 5 MINUTES.

Remove paper toweling from salad bowl. Give cabbage a final toss. Shake the dressing well. Remove garlic pieces and pour the dressing over the salad. With a salad spoon and fork, toss the cabbage until all the leaves are well coated with the dressing. Sprinkle the parsley on top, and toss a few more times.

SERVES 6.

HOT BUTTERED RUM PEACHES

MAY BE PARTIALLY PREPARED UP TO 4 HOURS IN ADVANCE.

1½ cups sugar
3 cups water
8 peaches, not too ripe (about 2 pounds), peeled, pitted, and halved
4 teaspoons unsalted butter, softened
Ground ginger
4 teaspoons dark brown sugar
½ cup golden rum
1 cup heavy cream, whipped

Combine the sugar and the water in a 3- to 4-quart saucepan, and bring the water to a boil. Stir until the sugar is dissolved. Lower the heat so that the syrup is barely moving, and gently transfer the peaches into it. Cook them, partially covered, for 5 minutes, or until they just start to become tender.

With a slotted spoon, transfer the peach halves to an ovenproof baking dish large enough to contain them in one layer. Place them cut side up and let them cool. Meanwhile, return the syrup to a high heat and boil it about 15 minutes, until it is reduced to about 1 cup. When the peaches are cool to the touch, place a scant ½ teaspoon of butter in each half, a bare sprinkling of powdered ginger over each one, and ½ teaspoon of brown sugar on top. Mix the reduced peach syrup with the rum, and carefully pour it into the baking dish without disturbing the peaches. Cover loosely with plastic wrap, and reserve in a cool section of the kitchen until final preparation.

TIME ALLOWANCE FOR FINAL PREPARATION: 20 MINUTES.

Preheat the oven to 350 degrees.

Place the peaches in the oven and bake them 15 minutes. Serve hot or warm, topped with whipped cream.

SERVES 6 TO 8.

PORK AND PEPPER DINNER FOR EIGHT

Chilled Avocado Soup

Pork with Red Peppers in Wine

Pan-Fried Potatoes with Parsley*

Mixed Green Salad with Creamy Basil Dressing*

Stewed Black Raspberries

Nothing is nicer in the summer than to beat the heat a little by starting dinner with a refreshing chilled soup. A popular tradition for years was to serve vichyssoise, that lovely French creation of chicken stock, pureed leeks and potatoes, and cream—or any of a number of variations on that basic theme. Potato-based cream soups, while still popular, are not so much in the limelight these days. Contemporary chefs are turning to lighter-tasting, more colorful fare, and today's avocado soup is just that: a gossamer-green blend of avocado, yogurt, and chicken stock, with a mince of cucumber thrown in for crunch.

After the soup, serve a special Spanish dish of pork and red pepper, an old favorite of mine. (Don't even consider it, though, if you aren't positively addicted to garlic. I once modified the amount of garlic for a garlic-hating friend, and, I am sad to report, the results just weren't what they should have been.) Not so long ago, red peppers were available only in August in the United States; so, back in those days, my family had to eat a lot of pork with red peppers every August. I can't say they complained, though.

For dessert I offer another personal favorite, this one from England: stewed black raspberries. (These imported berries are probably contributing to our balance-of-trade deficit. For the most part, the berries I have found in the market seem to have originated in Canada.) Stewed black raspberries are extraordinarily simple to prepare; the brief poaching softens the berries and releases a flood of intense, burgundy-colored juices. Topped with a cloudlike mound of softly whipped cream, the combination is heavenly.

CHILLED AVOCADO SOUP

MAY BE PREPARED AS LONG AS 24 HOURS IN ADVANCE;
MUST BE PREPARED AT LEAST 12 HOURS IN ADVANCE.

2 cups plain yogurt
2 ripe avocados, peeled, stoned, cut in chunks
3 tablespoons strained fresh lime juice
1½ cups canned chicken stock
5 to 10 drops Tabasco, according to taste
2 tablespoons grated onion
1 cup half-and-half
½ teaspoon salt
¼ teaspoon freshly ground black pepper
1½ cups English cucumber cut in ¼-inch dice (about ½ cucumber)
2 tablespoons minced chives

In the bowl of a food processor fitted with a steel blade, place the yogurt and avocado chunks. Whirl until the avocado is pureed and well blended with the yogurt. Add the lime juice, chicken stock, Tabasco, and grated onion, and whirl briefly. Transfer contents of processor to a large bowl and stir in the half-and-half, salt, and pepper. Mix well. Finally add the cucumbers, cover tightly with plastic wrap, and refrigerate until ready to serve.

TIME ALLOWANCE FOR FINAL PREPARATION: 5 MINUTES.

Divide the chilled soup among 8 soup bowls. Sprinkle a few chives on the top of each for garnish. Serve immediately.

SERVES 8.

PORK WITH RED PEPPERS IN WINE

MAY BE PARTIALLY PREPARED UP TO 12 HOURS IN ADVANCE;
MUST BE PARTIALLY PREPARED AT LEAST 3 HOURS IN ADVANCE.

5 teaspoons minced garlic (about 5 cloves)
1 teaspoon salt
½ teaspoon freshly ground black pepper
1 3- to 4-pound boneless pork loin, trimmed of fat, cut crosswise into
  ¼-inch-thick slices
3 tablespoons unsalted butter
3 tablespoons oil
5 red peppers, cored and seeded and cut lengthwise into ½-inch-wide strips
2 cups dry white wine

Combine the garlic, salt, and pepper in a mortar or small bowl and, with a pestle or the back of a spoon, mash them together into a paste. Spread a small portion of paste on one side of each pork slice. Arrange them in a bowl, toss briefly and cover well with plastic wrap. Marinate the slices, tossing them occasionally, at least 3 hours at room temperature or as long as 6 hours in the refrigerator. If you refrigerate them, bring them to room temperature at least 1 hour before sautéing.

In a 12- or 14-inch skillet, melt the butter with the oil over high heat. In batches, brown the pork slices well on both sides, transferring them to a platter as done. Lower the heat to moderate and, in the oil remaining in the skillet, sauté the red peppers, turning them frequently, until just slightly soft, about 5 minutes. Transfer the peppers to the platter with the meat.

Pour off any oil remaining in the skillet. Add the wine and bring to a boil over high heat, scraping up any particles left clinging to the bottom of the pan. Return the meat and peppers to the skillet. If you are not proceeding with the recipe immediately, remove the pan from the heat, cover it with its lid and store in a cool corner of the kitchen (for up to 3 hours) or in the refrigerator (for any longer period). Remove from the refrigerator 1 hour before final preparation.

TIME ALLOWANCE FOR FINAL PREPARATION: 30 MINUTES.

Return the skillet to the stove and bring the wine to a boil. Lower the heat, cover tightly, and simmer 25 minutes. With a slotted spoon, remove the meat and peppers to a heated platter. Increase the heat and boil the liquid remaining in the skillet until it is reduced by half, about 5 minutes. Pour the sauce over the meat and serve immediately.

SERVES 8.

STEWED BLACK RASPBERRIES

◆

MAY BE PREPARED UP TO 48 HOURS IN ADVANCE.

1½ pints black raspberries
¾ to 1 cup sugar
1 cup water
Pinch of salt
½ teaspoon vanilla
1½ cups heavy cream

Taste one of the black raspberries for sweetness. (Some are more tart than others.) Combine ¾ to 1 cup sugar (according to berries' sweetness) with the water and pinch of salt in a 2-quart stainless steel or enamel saucepan. Bring to a boil, and boil over moderate heat for 5 minutes. Add the vanilla and the berries, stir a couple of times, and return to a boil. The minute the berries have started to boil, remove the saucepan from the heat and allow to cool. Transfer the contents to a serving bowl, cover tightly with plastic wrap, and refrigerate until 1 hour before final preparation, or just before serving if you prefer your berries cold.

TIME ALLOWANCE FOR FINAL PREPARATION: 5 MINUTES.

Whip the heavy cream until soft peaks form. Serve the black raspberries in individual dessert dishes topped with generous dollops of whipped cream, or from the serving bowl itself, accompanied by another bowl containing the cream.

SERVES 8.

ENTERTAINING
IN THE
FALL

Fall is a lovely time of year. In New England, it is particularly special, for summer seems to linger—albeit erratically—well into October and sometimes, if we're lucky, even into November. Fall days, of course, are shorter and shadows longer, but the air can be seductively mild, inviting all manner of outdoor activities, from touch football games to leisurely walks through the vividly colored woods.

Fall is a splendid time for entertaining. During the summer, people have been away on vacation, and contact has been interrupted. Fall becomes a time to renew acquaintances and catch up on news. It's also the beginning of the "long" season—those months until next summer—so it's the perfect period for a flurry of imaginative entertaining. A football weekend? Why not a tailgate party? A spell of Indian summer forecast for Columbus Day weekend? Why not make the most of the weather before putting away the faithful grill? And never forget Election Night. That's a splendid evening for a party, with entertainment built in.

Thematically, I think of fall as reunion time, with all the qualities of celebration that that connotes: the pleasure of seeing old friends, of being together again, of good spirits and camaraderie. I think of much gaiety and laughter, enthusiasm and games. It is, after all, the lull before the storm of winter and a good chance to make hay while the sun shines.

Always, I like flowers in the fall. Chrysanthemums, which don't particularly appeal to me at other times of the year, seem a decorative must, especially the wispy, feathery kind. I like to take flowers in fall colors and mix them, long-stemmed and dramatic, in large vases. In other vases I intersperse dried red, orange, and yellow leaves with evergreen branches. I like to decorate the dining room table with mounds of fruits and nuts, displayed beguilingly so as to tempt guests to sample them, particularly at dessert time.

In fall, of course, we're still enjoying the fruits of the harvest—not as bountiful as in summer, but not half bad. Vibrant-hued squashes, from the deepest of greens to tangerine-orange. Pale green cabbages and Brussels sprouts. Root crops—carrots, turnips, and parsnips—whose flavors so intensify after a frost. And apples. Never are they so crunchy, juicy, and flavorful as when barely off the branches of their trees.

So see fall as a beginning—which it is, after all. It's the beginning of the school year, the beginning of a new social season, and probably the beginning of many new and valued friendships.

A DIFFERENT BARBECUE FOR EIGHT

Grilled Butterflied Leg of Lamb

Less-Calorie Ratatouille

Herbed French Bread*

Mixed Green Salad with Vinaigrette Dressing*

Peach Sorbet with Peach Sauce

As the leaves start to turn color and the evenings become chilly, we have limited time left to make the most of our outdoor grills. Operating on the theory that, by the end of summer, most of us are bored with barbecued steak, chicken, hamburger, and hot dogs, I offer something slightly different: a recipe for grilling a boned and butterflied leg of lamb. The meat is marinated to permeate the relatively lean flesh with oil, as well as to enhance its flavor. (It does not have to be grilled outdoors. It can be done very satisfactorily under a broiler in the kitchen. But the flavor of charcoal adds immeasurably to the dish.) Do not attempt to bone the leg yourself unless you have a degree in anatomy and previous experience. Let the butcher do the job for you.

Ratatouille—a Mediterranean mix of eggplant, zucchini, peppers, and tomatoes—seems the perfect blend of vegetables for lamb and requires no last-minute preparation at all. And fresh peach sorbet intensified by peach sauce makes the most of summer's many fruitful blessings.

GRILLED BUTTERFLIED LEG OF LAMB

MAY BE PARTIALLY PREPARED UP TO 8 HOURS IN ADVANCE.

½ cup vegetable oil
¼ cup strained fresh lemon juice
½ teaspoon salt
Freshly ground black pepper
2 teaspoons oregano
2 tablespoons minced fresh parsley
1 medium onion, thinly sliced
2 cloves garlic, thinly sliced
1 whole leg of lamb (8 to 9 pounds), boned and butterflied

Prepare a marinade by combining the oil, lemon juice, salt, pepper, oregano, parsley, onion, and garlic in the bottom of a glass or enamel roasting pan large enough to contain the butterflied leg of lamb. With a wooden spoon, mix until the ingredients are well blended. Lay the lamb in the marinade, turning it over once or twice to coat it well. Cover with plastic wrap, and refrigerate in the marinade 3 to 8 hours, turning it occasionally. Remove from refrigerator 1 hour before final preparation.

TIME ALLOWANCE FOR FINAL PREPARATION: 45 TO 90 MINUTES.

The lamb may be cooked either in a preheated, very hot broiler or over charcoal. In the latter case, the coals should be red-hot but not flaming. Because the thickness of the lamb varies, the final product will be done either rare in thick portions and medium in thin portions, for which you should allow 10 to 12 minutes per side, or medium in thick portions and well done in thin portions, for which you should allow 15 to 18 minutes per side.

To broil: Preheat broiler. Place lamb on rack about 3 inches beneath the broiler element. (Broil fat side up first.) Broil for the prescribed time according to doneness desired, turning once. Transfer to heated platter and serve immediately.

To grill: Prepare coals. Place lamb on greased rack about 5 inches above coals, fat side down. Sear meat for about 2 minutes. If you have a grill with a cover, cover the lamb. If not, watch the coals carefully. Try to prevent flaming by sprinkling the coals with water if flames rise up. Turn after prescribed time, keeping lamb covered, or else watching flames very carefully. Transfer to heated platter and serve immediately.

SERVES 8.

LESS-CALORIE RATATOUILLE

MAY BE PARTIALLY PREPARED UP TO 24 HOURS IN ADVANCE.

2 small eggplants or 1 large (about 1½ pounds), ends trimmed
1 medium zucchini (about ¾ pound), ends trimmed
2 teaspoons salt
¼ cup olive oil
1 teaspoon minced garlic
½ cup sliced onion
1 green pepper, seeded and julienned
½ pound mushrooms, cut in thick slices
3 large ripe tomatoes, peeled and cut in chunks (about 1½ pounds)
1 teaspoon oregano

Slice the eggplant, without peeling, into ½-inch slices. Quarter each slice. Slice the zucchini, without peeling, into ½-inch slices. Place one-quarter of the eggplant and zucchini pieces in a colander, and sprinkle with ½ teaspoon salt. Repeat three times until all the eggplant and zucchini pieces are salted and in the colander. Weigh them down with a teakettle filled with water or some other heavy object, and allow to drain for 30 minutes.

Meanwhile, pour olive oil into a large 12-inch skillet and turn heat to low. Add garlic, onions, peppers, and mushrooms, and sauté until soft, about 5 minutes. Remove from heat.

In a 2- to 3-quart ovenproof casserole, combine the eggplant and zucchini pieces with the onion-pepper mixture and the tomatoes. Sprinkle with oregano and toss to mix. Cover and refrigerate until 1 hour before final preparation.

TIME ALLOWANCE FOR FINAL PREPARATION: 1 HOUR.

Preheat oven to 325 degrees. Place casserole, still covered, in oven, and bake 45 to 50 minutes or until vegetables are soft. Serve immediately.

SERVES 8.

PEACH SORBET WITH PEACH SAUCE

MAY BE PREPARED UP TO 3 DAYS IN ADVANCE;
MUST BE PREPARED AT LEAST 2 HOURS IN ADVANCE.

1¼ cups sugar
¾ cup water
8 large ripe peaches (about 2½ pounds), peeled
¼ cup strained fresh orange juice
¼ cup plus 2 teaspoons strained fresh lemon juice

To make the sorbet: Combine ¾ cup sugar and the water in a small saucepan and bring to a boil, stirring only until the sugar is dissolved. Remove from heat and cool.

Cut 4 peaches into large chunks, discarding the pits. Place the peach pieces into the bowl of a food processor equipped with a steel blade. Add the orange juice and ¼ cup strained lemon juice and whirl until smooth. Pour in the sugar-water and whirl 10 seconds longer. Transfer to a mixing bowl, and chill in the refrigerator at least 1 hour. Pour the mixture into the container of a hand-cranked or electric ice cream freezer, and freeze according to the manufacturer's instructions. When frozen, remove from machine and pack into tightly covered freezer containers. Keep frozen until 15 minutes before serving.

To make the peach sauce: Cut the remaining peaches into thin slices, discarding the pits. Sprinkle with ½ cup sugar and the remaining 2 teaspoons lemon juice. Toss and refrigerate until ready to serve.

TIME ALLOWANCE FOR FINAL PREPARATION: 15 MINUTES.

Stir slightly softened sorbet with wooden spoon to break up any ice crystals. Spoon generous portions of sorbet into individual dessert plates or bowls. Serve with peach sauce.

SERVES 8.

GREEK-STYLE SHRIMP FOR TWO

Shrimp with Tomatoes and Feta Cheese

Spinach Salad with Avocado Dressing

French or Italian Bread

Blueberries Marinated in Cointreau

In Yarmouthport on Cape Cod, there used to be a restaurant, Myconos, that served splendid Greek food. One of my favorite dishes on Myconos's menu was shrimp with feta cheese. I ordered it many times, and it was consistently good, redolent of herbs, garden-fresh tomatoes, piquant cheese, and plump, juicy shrimp. I never asked the owner/chef for the recipe, always assuming I would do so on the next visit. Alas, the restaurant closed before I could acquire the recipe—a double tragedy.

Since then I have experimented with many versions of the dish. Although I can't say this one duplicates Myconos's, I hope it comes close. It is an unusual blend of flavors for shrimp lovers, and one that is especially nice for special company. Since it comes packed with tomatoes, a spinach salad with an avocado dressing makes a good, balanced accompaniment. Crusty French or Italian bread is a must to sop up the juices.

Dessert is simple but sophisticated: blueberries marinated in an orange liqueur. (You may substitute Grand Marnier for the Cointreau if you wish.) It's easy to make, yet presents a dessert with a little added zing.

SHRIMP WITH TOMATOES AND FETA CHEESE

MAY BE PARTIALLY PREPARED UP TO 12 HOURS IN ADVANCE.

1 tablespoon unsalted butter
1 teaspoon minced garlic
¼ cup finely chopped onion
2 cups chopped peeled tomatoes (about 2 pounds)
2 tablespoons finely chopped fresh basil leaves (or 2 teaspoons dried)
1 teaspoon Dijon-style mustard
1 teaspoon sugar
¼ cup dry white wine
¼ cup plus 2 tablespoons minced fresh parsley
1 tablespoon strained fresh lemon juice
½ teaspoon salt
Freshly ground black pepper
¾ pound large shrimp, peeled and deveined
2 tablespoons crumbled feta cheese

In a large skillet, melt the butter over low heat. Add the garlic and onions, and sauté until the onions are wilted, about 5 minutes. Add the tomatoes, basil, mustard, and sugar. Mix well to blend, and cook over low to moderate heat for 15 minutes or until the sauce is thick. Stir occasionally. Add the wine, ¼ cup parsley, lemon juice, salt, and pepper; mix well. Increase the heat to moderate, and add the shrimp. Cook them, stirring frequently, for 3 to 4 minutes, until they become opaque and are just done. Take care not to overcook them or they will toughen in the final cooking. Remove from heat and transfer the shrimp, in their sauce, to an open au gratin dish. When the sauce is cool, cover with plastic wrap and refrigerate until 1 hour before final preparation.

TIME ALLOWANCE FOR FINAL PREPARATION: 20 MINUTES.

Preheat the oven to 450 degrees.

Sprinkle the feta cheese over the surface of the shrimp. Bake the shrimp for 10 minutes, or until the sauce is bubbling and the cheese has melted. Briefly run the dish under the broiler to brown the top. Sprinkle the shrimp with the remaining 2 tablespoons of parsley, and serve immediately.

SERVES 2.

SPINACH SALAD WITH AVOCADO DRESSING

SALAD MAY BE PREPARED UP TO 4 HOURS IN ADVANCE;
DRESSING SHOULD NOT BE PREPARED MORE THAN 2 HOURS IN ADVANCE.

SPINACH SALAD

¼ pound fresh spinach, washed and dried, tough stems removed
4 large mushrooms, sliced
2 strips bacon, fried, drained, and crumbled

To make the salad: Line a salad bowl with paper toweling. Place the prepared spinach leaves in the bowl. Cover the bowl loosely with another sheet of toweling, and refrigerate until ready to dress the salad.

AVOCADO DRESSING

½ ripe avocado, peeled, pit discarded
¼ teaspoon garlic salt
3 tablespoons olive oil
¼ teaspoon Dijon-style mustard
½ teaspoon onion juice
1 tablespoon strained fresh lemon juice
Pinch of salt
Freshly ground black pepper

To make the dressing: Place the avocado in a shallow bowl, such as a soup bowl. With a fork, mash it well. Add the garlic salt and the olive oil, a tablespoon at a time, blending well after each addition. Stir in the mustard and onion juice. Finally, add the lemon juice, and mix until thoroughly blended. Taste and adjust seasonings. Cover with plastic wrap, and hold in a cool corner of the kitchen until final preparation.

TIME ALLOWANCE FOR FINAL PREPARATION: 5 MINUTES.

Remove paper toweling from salad. Add mushrooms and bacon. Give the salad dressing one final stir. Scrape the dressing over the salad (it will have a consistency similar to that of mayonnaise) and toss thoroughly to coat leaves.

SERVES 2.

BLUEBERRIES MARINATED IN COINTREAU

MAY BE PREPARED UP TO 12 HOURS IN ADVANCE;
SHOULD BE PREPARED AT LEAST 2 HOURS IN ADVANCE.

2 cups fresh blueberries, picked over, stems removed
2 tablespoons light brown sugar
½ teaspoon grated orange rind
3 tablespoons Cointreau or other orange-flavored liqueur
¼ cup heavy cream, whipped

Place the blueberries in a shallow mixing bowl. Sprinkle the brown sugar and orange rind over them. Toss well to coat all the berries. Pour the Cointreau over the berries, and toss again to mix thoroughly. Cover loosely with plastic wrap, and refrigerate until ready to serve, tossing once or twice to redistribute the flavorings.

TIME ALLOWANCE FOR FINAL PREPARATION: 5 MINUTES.

Remove plastic wrap, and toss blueberries briefly. Transfer the berries to a serving dish or individual bowls. Serve with whipped cream.

SERVES 2.

TAILGATE LUNCHEON FOR TWELVE

Hearty Pea Soup

Pita Surprises

Apples

Brown Sugar Pound Cake

A utumn is apple time and cider time and college football time, when we jaunt off to a nearby stadium to watch our team struggle against The Visitors.

And it's the perfect opportunity to do a little informal entertaining by gathering a few old friends, popping a cork or two, and, just a bit later as the afternoon sun fades, warding off the chill with a simple but satisfying soup-and-sandwich lunch.

This luncheon can be proffered at home before the game or toted to the stadium parking lot in the back of the car for a splendid tailgate picnic. All the latter demands is a couple of good-size Thermoses to keep the soup hot.

It's always easy to make soup a couple of days in advance, but sandwiches usually necessitate last-minute execution. Not so with pita surprises, which can be assembled a couple of hours before serving. The reason? These sandwiches are not made with mayonnaise, which is oily and runny, but rather coated with tasty spreads that solidify with cold. Furthermore, since pita (or Syrian) bread is unleavened, it does not absorb moisture and become soggy. As a result, the sandwiches remain remarkably fresh and unwilted.

The brown sugar pound cake, with its pecan glaze, is a rich, satisfying creation from the South, where the unstinting use of butter, sugar, and eggs seems to be a way of life. It has the additional picnic blessing of being fine finger food.

If your team doesn't win the game, at least your luncheon should gain you some very fast friends.

HEARTY PEA SOUP

MAY BE PREPARED UP TO 48 HOURS IN ADVANCE.

2 pounds dried split green peas, rinsed
6 pounds ham hocks (about 12)
3 cups coarsely chopped onion (about 2 large)
2 cups coarsely chopped celery (about 8 stalks)
4 quarts water
2 cups coarsely chopped carrots (about 1 pound)
1 pound ham steak, cut in ½ inch cubes, bone and fat discarded
Salt and freshly ground black pepper to taste
½ cup medium-dry sherry
½ cup minced fresh parsley

(For ham hocks and ham steak, you may substitute leftover ham, bone and remaining meat.)

Place the peas in an 8- to 10-quart kettle. Add the ham hocks or leftover ham, onions, celery, and water. Bring to a boil, stirring once or twice; then lower heat and simmer, tightly covered, for 1 hour. Transfer the ham hocks or the leftover ham to a chopping board, and remove and discard the skin and bones. Cut the meat into small cubes, and return it with the carrots (and the ham steak, if you are using the hocks) to the soup pot. You should have 2 to 3 cups cubed meat. (More is better than less.) Bring the soup to the boil again, lower the heat, and simmer uncovered for 30 minutes. Taste and adjust seasonings. Stir in the sherry.

If you are not planning to serve the soup immediately, allow it to cool; then transfer it to a large bowl and refrigerate it, well covered, until ½ hour before final preparation. (You may have to use two bowls.)

TIME ALLOWANCE FOR FINAL PREPARATION: 20 MINUTES.

Pour the soup back into the kettle, and warm it over moderate heat, stirring occasionally, until it is just below the boiling point. If it is too thick, add water, ½ cup at a time, until it reaches the right consistency. It is not supposed to be a very thick pea soup, but rather one with more ham and vegetables than is traditional.

Ladle the soup into bowls or mugs and sprinkle it with parsley. Serve immediately.

SERVES 12.

PITA SURPRISES

ALL MAY BE PARTIALLY PREPARED UP TO 6 HOURS IN ADVANCE.

Roast beef with tarragon mustard butter
Cucumber with Saga cheese
Smoked salmon with Boursin cheese

18 loaves of pita or Syrian bread, about 6 inches in diameter; white, whole-wheat, or a combination.
12 tablespoons unsalted butter, softened
6 tablespoons Dijon-style mustard
1½ teaspoons tarragon
6 to 8 ounces Saga blue cheese, softened, foil discarded
2 (5-ounce) packages Boursin cheese, softened
1 pound thinly sliced roast beef, trimmed of fat
1 medium red onion, peeled, halved lengthwise, and sliced into thin semicircles
1 bunch watercress, tough stems cut off, washed and dried
2 English cucumbers, unpeeled, ends trimmed, cut into ¼-inch slices
⅓ pound alfalfa sprouts
1 pound thinly sliced smoked Nova Scotia salmon (or lox)
4 tablespoons minced scallions, roots trimmed, white part only

Cut the pita bread in half crosswise. With the tip of a dull knife, gently pry each "pocket" open.

In a small bowl, mix the butter, mustard, and tarragon until well blended. Reserve.

Place the Saga cheese in a shallow bowl and mash it thoroughly with a fork. Put the Boursin cheese in another bowl and mash it.

Using about 1 tablespoon each, spread the insides of 12 pita halves with the butter mixture, another 12 halves with the Saga cheese, and the last 12 halves with the Boursin. (Extra quantities of cheese are allowed for, so don't worry if you are generous.)

Pack the pita halves in plastic bags according to their spreads. Tie firmly to seal and refrigerate until 1 hour before final preparation.

TIME ALLOWANCE FOR FINAL PREPARATION: 20 TO 30 MINUTES.

Arrange the pita fillings in front of you for easy access. Have the roast beef, sliced onion, and watercress in position together. Nearby, group the sliced cucumbers and alfalfa sprouts. Next to them, place the salmon and the scallions. To one side, position your serving platter; a large wooden salad bowl or shallow glass or pottery bowl is decorative as well as efficient.

To make the roast beef pita surprises: Remove the pita bread spread with the tarragon mustard butter. Holding one half in one hand, squeeze it gently to open it up. Drop in a slice or two of roast beef, a half-slice of onion (rings separated), and 3 or 4 sprigs of watercress. Transfer the filled pita half to the serving platter or bowl, cut side upright, and repeat with the remaining 11 halves.

To make the cucumber pita surprises: Take the pita halves with Saga cheese and drop into each half about 6 to 8 slices of cucumber and a generous clump of sprouts. Transfer the pita halves as they are completed to the serving platter or bowl, cut side up.

To make the salmon pita surprises: Take the Boursin-spread pita bread and drop into each half 1 to 2 slices of salmon. (The size of salmon slices varies enormously; judge the amount you have, and divide it equally.) Add about 1 teaspoon minced scallions. Transfer the pita halves to the serving platter or bowl. If you are making these sandwiches for a picnic, cover the whole bowl with plastic wrap until serving time.

This recipe allows three halves per person, which should be more than enough for the average appetite.

SERVES 12.

BROWN SUGAR POUND CAKE

MAY BE PREPARED UP TO 24 HOURS IN ADVANCE.

CAKE

1 cup unsalted butter, softened
½ cup solid vegetable shortening
3 cups firmly packed light brown sugar
5 eggs
3 cups cake flour
½ teaspoon baking powder
½ teaspoon salt
½ cup sour cream
½ cup heavy cream
1 teaspoon vanilla

To make the pound cake: Preheat oven to 325 degrees. Grease and flour a 10-inch tube pan.

Combine the butter, shortening, and sugar in a large mixing bowl; cream until light and fluffy. Add the eggs one at a time, beating well after each addition. In a sieve placed over another mixing bowl, combine the flour, baking powder, and salt. Sift them twice. Spoon the sour cream into a measuring cup until it reads ½ cup; add the heavy cream to the full cup level. With a spoon, gently combine them. Add the flour mixture alternately with the cream in three batches to the butter-and-egg mixture. Beat until smooth. Add the vanilla and mix until well blended. With a spatula, scrape the batter into the prepared tube pan. Rap it firmly on a hard surface to eliminate any air bubbles. Place it on a rack in the middle of the oven, and bake it 1½ hours or until a straw or knife inserted into the cake comes out clean. Cool it for 15 minutes on a cake rack; then remove it from its pan and let it completely cool, still on the cake rack.

GLAZE

4 tablespoons unsalted butter
½ cup coarsely chopped pecans
1 cup confectioners' sugar
1 teaspoon strained fresh lemon juice
Pinch of salt
½ teaspoon vanilla
¼ cup half-and-half

To make the glaze: In a small, heavy saucepan, melt the butter. Add the chopped pecans and, over moderate heat, bring the butter to a boil. Fry the nuts, stirring constantly, until they just start to brown. Be careful not to burn the butter. Remove the pan from the heat and set aside to cool.

When the butter and nuts are cool, add the confectioners' sugar. Mix well. The glaze will be very thick. Add the lemon juice, salt, vanilla, and half-and-half, and blend thoroughly. At this point the glaze should be the right consistency to spread; if not, add more half-and-half by the teaspoonful until it is.

Spread the glaze on the top of the cake with a spatula, allowing it to drip down the sides and center. Cover until ready to serve.

YIELD: ONE 10-INCH TUBE CAKE.

SOLE FOOD
FOR EIGHT

Baked Sole with Almonds

Beet Mix

Steamed Brown Rice*

Salad of Mushrooms and Artichoke Hearts

Hot Lemon Sponge

People are eating more and more fish these days. They're finding out that not only is fish good for the body but it tastes good too, if it's fresh.

Sole with almonds is delightfully easy to prepare and appears to the uninitiated to be more elaborate than it is. The recipe comes from the repertoire of my sister-in-law, Martha McCarthy, who lives in Florida. Martha makes it with that heavenly pompano, local to the Florida waters. Unfortunately, pompano has to be served straight out of the sea to be really good, so when the McCarthys were visiting us in Massachusetts, Martha and I decided to experiment, substituting some fresh fillet of sole. We were delighted with the results; but, I must say, if you have the opportunity to use fresh pompano, forgo the sole and grab it.

Beet mix came about when I became particularly exasperated with the perennial problem of which to use first, the beets or the beet greens. (Usually the beet greens won.) I decided to see if I could combine them into one vegetable dish. I think you will agree that it is indeed a nice treatment of the whole and eliminates the which-comes-first dilemma.

I always like to have a salad with my dinner, and one of my regular favorites for company is the combination of mushrooms and artichoke hearts in a French vinaigrette. Rather than using canned artichoke hearts, I cook the frozen, which I find very pleasing.

Hot lemon sponge, a piquant combination of cake with baked-in pudding, is a creation straight out of my childhood. I used to plead with my mother to make it for me, often as frequently as several times a week. (She never indulged me that much.) Whenever I smell its wonderful aroma wafting through the kitchen, I am transported back to my mother's kitchen and my seemingly endless joy in devouring lemon sponge, right from the oven. Perhaps when you try it, you will understand why I never have tired of it—at least in moderation.

BAKED SOLE WITH ALMONDS

MAY BE PARTIALLY PREPARED UP TO 4 HOURS IN ADVANCE.

12 fillets of sole (about 3 pounds), skinned
8 tablespoons unsalted butter
2 teaspoons strained fresh lemon juice
½ teaspoon salt
Freshly ground black pepper
5 tablespoons sliced almonds
8 lemon wedges

With 2 tablespoons butter, generously grease one large, shallow baking pan, or two smaller ones sufficient in area to contain the sole pieces in one layer. Lay the fillets in the pan. Dot with 2 tablespoons butter. Sprinkle with lemon juice, salt, and pepper. Cover tightly with plastic wrap and refrigerate until 1 hour before final preparation.

TIME ALLOWANCE FOR FINAL PREPARATION: 20 MINUTES.

Preheat the oven to 350 degrees. Preheat the broiler if it is a separate unit.

Meanwhile, melt the remaining 4 tablespoons of butter in a small skillet. Add the almonds and stir to mix. Hold over very low heat.

Remove and discard the plastic wrap. Place the fillets in the oven, and bake 10 minutes or until they are completely opaque. Remove the pan(s) from oven and switch the heating element to "broil" if it is the same unit. Spoon the almonds and melted butter evenly over all the fillets. Place the fillets in the broiler about 2 inches from the heat, and broil until the almonds just start to brown, about 2 minutes.

Serve immediately, garnished with lemon wedges.

SERVES 8.

BEET MIX

MAY BE PARTIALLY PREPARED UP TO 6 HOURS IN ADVANCE.

2 bunches medium-size beets with green leaves
2 bunches scallions with green leaves
3 tablespoons unsalted butter
¼ cup water
½ teaspoon salt
Freshly ground black pepper

Select two fresh bunches of beets with perky, not wilted, leaves. Cut the leaves with their red stems off the beet roots and reserve. Scrub the roots clean, place them in a saucepan filled with salted water, and bring to a boil. Lower the heat and cook 30 to 45 minutes, or until the beets show no resistance when pierced with a knife. (Timing depends on size of beets.) Drain and refresh under cold water. Trim the root and stem ends, slip the skins off, and cut the beets into ¼-inch julienne strips. Set them aside in a bowl covered with plastic wrap in a cool corner of the kitchen, and hold for final preparation.

Wash the reserved beet leaves and stems thoroughly. (They can pack a lot of dirt, and nothing is worse than a gritty vegetable.) Do not shake dry; the moisture retained on the leaves is necessary for the cooking process. Starting at the stem end, cut the stems and the leaves into strips 1 inch wide. Cut the green leaves off the scallions, reserving the white ends for another use. Wash the scallion leaves well, then cut into 1-inch lengths.

In a 14-inch skillet with high sides, melt the butter over low heat. Turn off the heat and cool. Add the water and the chopped beet and scallion leaves. Cover with the pan's lid, and set aside until final preparation.

TIME ALLOWANCE FOR FINAL PREPARATION: 15 MINUTES.

Set the heat under the pan containing the beet and scallion leaves to moderately high. Keep the pan covered tightly. Steam the leaves 5 minutes. Remove cover and turn leaves over so that the wilted ones are on top. Add the reserved julienned beets, scattering them across the surface of the leaves. Cover again and steam another 5 minutes. Remove lid and taste for doneness. The leaves should be wilted but slightly crisp; if not, toss and steam another 2 to 3 minutes. Add the salt and pepper, toss briefly, and serve immediately.

SERVES 8.

SALAD OF MUSHROOMS AND ARTICHOKE HEARTS

◆

SHOULD BE PREPARED 2 TO 4 HOURS IN ADVANCE.

2 (9-ounce) packages frozen artichoke hearts
¾ cup olive oil
6 tablespoons strained fresh lemon juice
½ teaspoon finely minced garlic
½ teaspoon salt
Freshly ground black pepper
1 teaspoon oregano
1 pound mushrooms, quartered
16 large green lettuce leaves, washed and dried
½ cup very thinly sliced boiled ham, cut in ½-inch dice

In a 2-quart saucepan half-filled with water, bring water to a boil. Drop in the artichoke hearts and return the water to a boil, separating the hearts as they thaw. Lowering the heat, continue to boil 4 minutes. (This is less time than the package directions call for.) Drain the hearts, and refresh them under cold water so that they stop cooking. Reserve.

In a medium-size bowl, combine the oil, lemon juice, garlic, salt, pepper, and oregano. With a wooden spoon, stir until they are well combined. Taste and adjust the seasonings. Immediately add the artichoke hearts and mushrooms, and toss to coat the vegetables thoroughly with the dressing. Cover with plastic wrap. Marinate at least 2 but as long as 4 hours. During this period, toss occasionally to redistribute the dressing. (It is not necessary to refrigerate them.)

TIME ALLOWANCE FOR FINAL PREPARATION: 5 MINUTES.

Remove plastic wrap. Toss vegetables one more time. Place two lettuce leaves each (or more, if you prefer) on 8 individual salad plates or bowls. With a slotted spoon, distribute the artichoke hearts and mushrooms evenly among the plates, reserving the marinade. Scatter the ham on top; then drizzle the remaining dressing over all.

SERVES 8.

HOT LEMON SPONGE

MAY BE PARTIALLY PREPARED 24 HOURS IN ADVANCE.

¼ cup unsalted butter, softened
1½ cups sugar
4 egg yolks
1 tablespoon grated lemon rind
½ cup strained fresh lemon juice
½ cup flour
Pinch of salt
2 cups sour milk (or 2 cups fresh milk soured with 2 tablespoons lemon juice)
4 egg whites at room temperature
1 cup heavy cream, whipped (optional)

With an electric mixer or wooden spoon, cream the butter with the sugar in a medium-size mixing bowl. Add the egg yolks, one at a time, beating well after each addition. Beat in the lemon rind and juice. Sift the flour with the salt over the mixing bowl, and blend well. Finally, stir in the sour milk and beat until all lumps have disappeared. Cover with plastic wrap and refrigerate until 2 hours before final preparation.

TIME ALLOWANCE FOR FINAL PREPARATION: 1 HOUR.

Preheat oven to 350 degrees. Bring a kettle of water to a boil. Remove plastic wrap from lemon base.

In a separate mixing bowl, beat egg whites until stiff. Add reserved lemon base, and fold until all trace of whites have disappeared. (The base and whites should blend completely.) Pour into a buttered 2- to 3-quart baking or soufflé dish, set in a *bain-marie* or small roasting pan, and fill the latter with boiling water halfway up the side of the baking dish. Bake 45 minutes or until the top is golden brown and somewhat crusty. Serve hot, with whipped cream if desired. The dessert can be served cold but is better steaming hot.

SERVES 8.

A DIFFERENT FALL DINNER FOR SIX

Kielbasa Stew

Baked Herbed Tomatoes

Chocolate Almond Pots de Crème

With frost comes hearty appetites. Here is a menu that suits that mellow time of year when the leaves and the weather turn, often overnight. The economical entree is an out-of-the-ordinary combination of spicy Polish sausage, broth-soaked potatoes, and delicately sweet leeks. I doubt that your family or guests will have tasted the like.

Since the stew is chock full of vegetables, I suggest serving baked herbed tomatoes with it. Baked tomatoes are a nice winter vegetable; in fact, baking is about the only way to use tomatoes out of season. Their color is handsome and their bland flavor is nicely disguised by a profusion of herbs and cheese.

To round things off, I suggest a heavenly-tasting, absurdly easy chocolate pudding so dense and rich it should be eaten in minute mouthfuls with dainty demitasse spoons.

KIELBASA STEW

MAY BE PARTIALLY PREPARED UP TO 4 HOURS IN ADVANCE.

3 tablespoons unsalted butter
3 bunches large leeks (about 9 or 10), green leaves and roots trimmed,
*   cleaned and cut in ½-inch slices*
4 teaspoons flour
6 large potatoes (about 2 to 2½ pounds), peeled and cut into ¾-inch chunks
1 cup chicken stock
1 to 1½ pounds beef kielbasa
3 tablespoons minced fresh parsley

Melt butter over low heat in a 4- to 6-quart flameproof casserole. Add leek slices. Tightly cover and steam, still over very low heat, until leeks are soft and have exuded a small amount of liquid, about 20 to 30 minutes. Remove from heat and cool. Sprinkle surface of leeks with flour, distributing it as evenly as possible. Add potato chunks, chicken stock, and kielbasa. Cover tightly and refrigerate until 1 hour before final preparation.

TIME ALLOWANCE FOR FINAL PREPARATION: 45 TO 50 MINUTES.

Place casserole over medium to low heat and, without disturbing, allow potatoes and sausage to cook until potatoes are tender when pierced with a tip of a knife, about 30 to 40 minutes. Remove kielbasa and carve it into ½-inch discs. Transfer potatoes and leeks to center of a preheated platter, ring them attractively with the kielbasa pieces, and sprinkle the surface with parsley. Serve immediately.

SERVES 6.

BAKED HERBED TOMATOES

MAY BE PREPARED UP TO 4 HOURS IN ADVANCE.

3 tablespoons soft homemade bread crumbs
1 tablespoon minced scallion
1½ teaspoons oregano
3 tablespoons freshly grated Parmesan cheese
¼ teaspoon freshly ground black pepper
3 large tomatoes (about ½ to ¾ pound each), rinsed

In a mixing bowl, combine the bread crumbs, scallion, oregano, cheese, and pepper, and mix well. Cut the tomatoes in half horizontally, and spread the crumb mixture evenly on each cut surface. Place the tomatoes on a baking dish, cover loosely with aluminum foil or plastic wrap, and reserve in a cool spot until ready to bake.

TIME ALLOWANCE FOR FINAL PREPARATION: 35 MINUTES.

Preheat oven to 375 degrees.
Bake tomatoes for 30 minutes. Serve immediately.

SERVES 6.

CHOCOLATE ALMOND POTS DE CRÈME

MAY BE PREPARED 24 HOURS IN ADVANCE.

½ cup blanched almonds (2¼ ounces)
6 ounces semisweet chocolate morsels (1 cup)
1 cup light cream, scalded
4 egg yolks
1 tablespoon unsalted butter, softened
½ teaspoon vanilla
Pinch of salt
Pinch of cinnamon

Place the blanched almonds in the jar of a blender, and whirl until the almonds are reduced to a fine powder. Lift the blender off its motor base and rap it firmly to dislodge and loosen the almonds (which will be packed around the blades), or free the almonds with a spoon. Add the chocolate bits and the scalded cream. Return the blender to its base, and whirl 10 to 15 seconds. Add the egg yolks and whirl again. Then drop in the butter, vanilla, salt, and cinnamon. Run the motor until the mixture is well blended, smooth, and shiny. Pour the mixture into 6 small pot de crème cups or demitasse cups, and cover with either pot de crème lids or plastic wrap. Refrigerate at least 2 hours.

SERVES 6.

CALVES' LIVER DINNER FOR FOUR

Calves' Liver with Apples

Swedish Roasted Potatoes

Steamed Spinach

Ginger Cream

This recipe for calves' liver with apples evolved from a friend's lyrical description of a similar dish he had eaten in New York. Because he and I were working together on a game cookbook, we decided to attempt to duplicate the dish, using some fresh venison liver he had in his larder. The results were beyond our fondest hopes. Even our spouses, our most severe critics, approved. The tartness of apples and apple cider perfectly complemented the richness of the liver. The recipe was duly written down and tucked away in our file.

Something bothered me, though: I hated to see such a good recipe used only by game fanciers. What about the rest of the world?

Without soliciting my friend's approval or even asking his permission to adapt the recipe, I must confess I went barreling ahead on my own, substituting calves' liver for the venison but otherwise sticking with our original recipe. It worked just as well as before.

With the liver, I recommend Swedish roasted potatoes. Partially presliced, they fan out decoratively during roasting and, with their crisp little edges, look unusually attractive on the plate.

For dessert, I offer an ambrosial ginger-flavored cream from the Far East. It is subtle, light, and sublime. Don't be put off by the high price of stem ginger. Even though only a small amount is used in this dessert, it lasts indefinitely in the refrigerator, tightly sealed, and can be used in all manner of ways. The Dutch, for example, place a slice of it on a cube of cheddar cheese, secure it with a toothpick, and serve it with cocktails—very different and very good.

CALVES' LIVER WITH APPLES

APPLES MAY BE PREPARED UP TO 4 HOURS IN ADVANCE;
LIVER MUST BE EXECUTED JUST BEFORE SERVING.

2 golden Delicious apples
3 tablespoons plus 1 teaspoon unsalted butter
½ cup flour
½ teaspoon salt
Freshly ground black pepper
½ teaspoon thyme
1½ to 2 pounds calves' liver, sliced thick (about ½ inch)
1½ cups apple cider

Leaving the apples whole, peel and core them. Cut them crosswise into ½-inch-thick slices. Melt 1 tablespoon butter in a 12-inch skillet, preferably a nonstick type. Add the apple slices and sauté them over moderately low heat, turning them once or twice, until they are slightly browned and have cooked through, about 5 to 6 minutes. Do not overcook. Remove the skillet to one side and reserve until final preparation.

TIME ALLOWANCE FOR FINAL PREPARATION: 15 MINUTES.

Place the apples, still in their skillet, over very low heat to warm, turning once or twice.

On a piece of paper toweling or in a large pie plate, combine the flour, salt, pepper, and thyme. Mix well. Melt 2 tablespoons butter over low heat in a skillet large enough to contain the liver pieces comfortably. (You may need to use 2 skillets; if so, allow 1½ tablespoons butter per pan.) As the butter is melting, dust the liver slices on both sides in the flour mixture, shaking off any excess. Increase the heat to moderately high and when the butter is foaming, add the liver. Cook it rapidly and turn after 2 minutes. For medium-rare liver, cook approximately 1 more minute. To judge liver for doneness, prod the surface with the tip of your forefinger. If the meat feels soft, it is rare. If it feels hard, it is well done. Medium-rare liver feels slightly resilient to the touch. Since intensity of heat and thickness of the meat vary considerably, prodding is a more reliable standard for judging doneness than time.

When the liver is cooked to your taste, transfer it to a heated platter and hold in a warm place. Pour off any excess butter remaining in the skillet. (If you have been using two skillets, use only one at this point.) Add the cider, and, with the heat at its highest, reduce the cider by half. Stir constantly, scraping up any particles left clinging to the bottom of the pan. When you have approximately ¾ cup sauce left in the skillet (and the cider has thickened somewhat), swirl in the remaining teaspoon of butter. When it is assimilated, turn off the heat and return the liver very briefly to the pan to reheat the slices. Transfer it to heated plates or a serving platter, spoon over the sauce, and garnish with apple slices. Serve immediately.

SERVES 4.

SWEDISH ROAST POTATOES

MAY BE PARTIALLY PREPARED UP TO 6 HOURS IN ADVANCE.

4 baking potatoes, about 4 by 2 inches, peeled
1 tablespoon unsalted butter, softened
2 tablespoons unsalted butter, melted
½ teaspoon salt
2 tablespoons fresh bread crumbs, preferably homemade

Using a deep-bowled slotted or wooden spoon, cradle one potato at a time in the bowl of the spoon and, starting about ½ inch from one end, cut slices about ⅛ inch apart, the length of the potato. (The bowl of the spoon will prevent the knife from slicing completely through the potato.) Hold the partially sliced potatoes in a bowl of cold water (to prevent discoloration) until time for final preparation.

TIME ALLOWANCE FOR FINAL PREPARATION: 1 HOUR.

Preheat the oven to 425 degrees.

Remove the potatoes from the water and pat them dry with paper toweling. Select a baking pan that will hold the potatoes snugly together and spread the softened butter over its bottom and sides. Arrange the potatoes in it, cut side up. Brush their surfaces with 1 tablespoon of the melted butter and sprinkle with the salt. Bake for 30 minutes. Brush with the remaining tablespoon of butter, then sprinkle with the bread crumbs. Return to the oven and roast until tender when pierced with the tip of a knife and golden brown, about 15 minutes longer. Serve immediately.

SERVES 4.

GINGER CREAM

MUST BE PREPARED AT LEAST 4 HOURS IN ADVANCE;
MAY BE PREPARED UP TO 24 HOURS IN ADVANCE.

3 egg yolks
⅓ cup superfine sugar
1 tablespoon grated ginger root
Pinch of salt
1 cup heavy cream
2 tablespoons syrup from stem ginger
1 tablespoon plus 1 teaspoon minced stem ginger (stem ginger, which is different from ginger root or crystallized ginger, is available in specialty food markets)

In a small mixing bowl, beat the egg yolks and sugar with an electric mixer until light yellow in color. Beat in the ginger root and salt. Set aside. In another mixing bowl, whip the cream until stiff. Beat in the ginger syrup. Take one-third of the cream and mix it into the egg yolks to lighten them. Fold the egg yolk mixture into the remaining cream, mixing only until the two are combined. Gently fold in the tablespoon minced stem ginger. Divide the ginger cream among 4 dessert bowls. Cover them tightly with plastic wrap and refrigerate until ready to serve.

Just before serving, garnish the ginger cream by sprinkling the remaining teaspoon of minced stem ginger over the tops of the dessert.

SERVES 4.

ROAST VEAL
FEAST
FOR EIGHT

Roast Veal with Red Onion

Pureed Celeriac

Creamed Peas and Onions*

Simple Salad Vinaigrette*

*French Cream
with Raspberry Sauce*

I have a passion for veal and a particular weakness for a roast loin. I first tasted it in Italy, where the quality of veal is truly superb. The Italians are entranced with the neutrality of its flavor, which lends itself to all sorts of harmonious marriages with other ingredients and sauces. Take *vitello tonnato*—veal with tuna fish sauce! Surely this must rate as one of the first *nouvelle cuisine* creations. Yet it's marvelous.

The best veal is raised in Europe, where it is generally slaughtered around two and one-half to three months of age and has spent its brief life living it up on milk and eggs, a diet that accounts for its beguilingly tender pink color. The quality of American veal is still erratic, but with more and more frequency we are able to find fairly respectable veal even in supermarkets. Veal is by no means cheap. A good loin, such as our recipe calls for, will make quite a dent in your pocketbook. Consequently, I urge you to save such a delicacy for only your most discriminating and favored friends. Since you will be paying a lot anyway, make sure you get the best available by buying it at a very reputable meat market. It will add to the price, but it will be worth it.

To accompany the veal, I suggest pureed celeriac. Celeriac, also known as celery knobs or celery root, is another European staple now starting to be found in our supermarkets. Whenever I am reaching for one of those rather strange-looking brown knobs in the market, it seldom fails that someone asks me what it is and what I do with it. The answer is that I frequently use it raw in salads, tossed with the greens and bathed in vinaigrette, or, also raw, coated with a mustard mayonnaise as in *celeri rémoulade,* a piquant starter found on many French menus. If you like the delicate taste of celery heart, from our stalk celery, you will love celeriac. Try it raw, and then try it cooked as in this recipe. Unfortunately, in America—like veal—it is quite expensive. Undoubtedly, as the demand grows, the price will drop.

The dessert offered in this menu is *not* expensive, and it tastes as good as it looks: a smooth, gelatin-based, slightly tart cream enhanced with a brilliant red raspberry sauce.

ROAST VEAL WITH RED ONION

MUST BE PARTIALLY PREPARED AT LEAST 4 HOURS IN ADVANCE;
MAY BE PARTIALLY PREPARED UP TO 8 HOURS IN ADVANCE.

1 3½- to 4-pound boned loin of veal
½ cup olive oil
¼ cup white wine vinegar
1 cup finely chopped red onion (1 large)
1 teaspoon minced garlic
3 tablespoons minced fresh parsley
¼ teaspoon crushed dried hot pepper
1 teaspoon salt
¼ teaspoon freshly ground black pepper

In a shallow glass, porcelain, or enamel baking dish large enough to contain the veal comfortably, combine the oil, vinegar, onion, garlic, parsley, hot pepper, salt, and pepper. Mix well. Roll the veal in the mixture, coating all sides, and allow it to marinate in the refrigerator, loosely covered with plastic wrap, at least 4 hours or as long as 8. Turn it 2 or 3 times during the marinating period. Remove from the refrigerator 1 hour before final preparation.

TIME ALLOWANCE FOR FINAL PREPARATION: 2 HOURS.

Preheat the oven to 450 degrees.

Remove the veal from the marinade, scraping it clean of any particles clinging to it. Transfer the marinade to a small saucepan and reserve. Place the veal in a roasting pan in the center of the oven, and roast it for 20 minutes. Reduce the heat to 350 and continue roasting for 1¼ hours. Set the veal on a carving board and let it rest for 10 minutes.

While it is resting, bring the reserved marinade to a boil. Reduce the heat to low and simmer 5 minutes.

To serve, carve the veal crosswise into ¼-inch slices and arrange them overlapping on a heated serving platter. Pour the simmering marinade over the meat and serve immediately.

SERVES 8.

PUREED CELERIAC

MAY BE PREPARED UP TO 48 HOURS IN ADVANCE.

2 to 3 large knobs celeriac or celery root (about 2 pounds total), peeled and
cut in ½-inch dice
1½ teaspoons salt
1 large potato (about 1 pound), peeled and cut in ½-inch dice
3 tablespoons unsalted butter, softened
½ cup light cream
Freshly ground black pepper
Paprika (optional)

Place the diced celeriac in a 3- to 4-quart saucepan. Sprinkle with 1 teaspoon salt and cover with water by one inch. Bring the water to a boil, lower the heat, and simmer, uncovered, for 15 minutes. Add the diced potato (and more water, if necessary), bring to a boil again, lower the heat, and simmer another 15 minutes. Drain the vegetables in a colander over the sink for several minutes until all the moisture has evaporated.

Transfer to a food processor fitted with a steel blade. Add the softened butter and the cream, and whirl until the vegetables are completely pureed and smooth. (Or, if you prefer, push the vegetables through a ricer, add the butter and cream, and beat until smooth.) Whirl in the remaining ½ teaspoon salt and the pepper.

Serve immediately or, if preparing well in advance, refrigerate the mixture, tightly covered, until 1 hour before final preparation. (If preparing 1 or 2 hours before serving, transfer to the top of a double boiler, cover, and hold in a cool corner of the kitchen until time for final preparation.)

TIME ALLOWANCE FOR FINAL PREPARATION: 20 MINUTES.

Place the pureed celeriac in the top of a double boiler over simmering water until steaming hot. Keep it covered, but stir occasionally. Reheating will take about 15 to 20 minutes. Spoon into a warmed serving dish and sprinkle with paprika, if desired.

SERVES 8.

FRENCH CREAM WITH RASPBERRY SAUCE

MAY BE PREPARED UP TO 24 HOURS IN ADVANCE;
MUST BE PREPARED AT LEAST 3 HOURS IN ADVANCE.

1 package unflavored gelatin
½ cup water
1 cup light cream
¾ to 1 cup sugar, according to taste
2 teaspoons grated orange rind
1 teaspoon vanilla
1 cup sour cream
1 (10-ounce) package frozen raspberries in light syrup, thawed

Sprinkle the gelatin over the water to soften it. Meanwhile, combine the light cream and ½ cup sugar in a small saucepan and, over low heat, stir the cream until the sugar dissolves. Add the softened gelatin and continue stirring until the gelatin dissolves. Remove from heat, add the orange rind and vanilla, and cool to room temperature. Spoon in the sour cream and whisk until thoroughly blended. Pour into a 3-cup melon mold or divide between 8 individual custard cups. Cover with the lid of the mold or plastic wrap and refrigerate until firm, about 3 hours, or until ready to serve.

Place the thawed raspberries in the container of a food processor fitted with a steel blade. Taste for sweetness, and sprinkle ¼ to ½ cup sugar over their surface, depending on taste. Let the berries sit until the sugar is nearly dissolved; then turn the motor on and whirl until the raspberries are pureed into a thin sauce. Strain the sauce into a sauceboat, cover with plastic wrap, and refrigerate until ready to serve.

TIME ALLOWANCE FOR FINAL PREPARATION: 5 MINUTES.

Unmold the French cream by placing the mold, or molds, in a bath of hot water, just to the rim to the mold(s). Hold for 5 seconds. Place a plate, upside down, on top of each mold, turn mold and plate over and give a brief shake. The cream should slide out. If not, repeat the procedure. Take care that you do not leave the mold in the hot water for too long, or the cream will soften. Serve accompanied by raspberry sauce, which should be drizzled over the cream.

SERVES 8.

PENNSYLVANIA DUTCH FLANK STEAK FOR EIGHT

Stuffed Flank Steak

Baked Cardamom Carrots

Baby Red Potatoes in Dill Butter*

Pseudo Crepes Suzette*

Flank steak was poorly named by whoever created the nomenclature for cuts of beef. The cut does indeed come from the flank, that section of flesh between the last rib and the hip; but, as for being a proper steak—forget it. It doesn't have the succulent flavor associated with beef steak. It's so tough and chewy it's advisable to cut it on the diagonal to break down the fibers. In fact, it was once considered such an inferior part of the beast that markets almost gave it away. (Not so today, sadly.)

However, it has one redeeming feature: chameleonlike, it lends itself to all kinds of doctoring. This recipe for stuffed flank steak is an excellent example of its versatility. In a manner inspired by an old Pennsylvania Dutch recipe, two steaks are sandwiched together with fragrant stuffing and then slowly braised on a bed of celery, carrots, and onions. Granted, the preparation takes a bit of time, as does the braising—but it's a period in which the host is free from cares. No basting, no raising or lowering of oven temperature. A nice, free time to spend with company.

With the stuffed steak, I suggest cardamom carrots. They echo the carrot base of the braising vegetables, but the cardamom gives them a definite identity of their own. Besides, they're extraordinarily simple to prepare.

For dessert, pseudo crepes Suzette are a gala dish and one I am sure you'll add to your repertoire. Without all the ballyhoo of chafing dishes and flaming liqueurs, they evoke the heady spirit of the original crepes Suzette, paper-thin pancakes served piping hot and bathed in a heavenly syrup of orange, orange rind, and orange liqueur. And, even better, there's no need to stand by with a fire extinguisher.

STUFFED FLANK STEAK

MAY BE PARTIALLY PREPARED UP TO 48 HOURS IN ADVANCE.

2 1½-pound flank steaks
16 tablespoons unsalted butter
6 or 7 slices thin white bread, cut into ½-inch cubes (3 cups)
1½ cups finely chopped onions
1 cup finely chopped celery
¾ pound lean ground beef or veal
¼ pound lean ground pork
1 egg plus 1 egg yolk
½ cup minced fresh parsley
¼ teaspoon crushed rosemary
1 teaspoon basil
½ teaspoon ground sage
1 teaspoon salt
½ teaspoon freshly ground black pepper
4 tablespoons vegetable oil
1 cup coarsely chopped celery
1½ cups coarsely chopped carrots
1 cup coarsely chopped onions
2 cups beef stock

Place the two flank steaks one on top of the other, arranging them to conform to each other's shape as closely as possible. With a long larding needle and a length of kitchen cord (or a regular needle and heavy thread), sew three of the four sides of the steaks together, leaving one lengthwise edge open.

Melt 8 tablespoons butter in a large skillet. Over medium to high heat, sauté the bread cubes, tossing frequently, until they are golden brown. Transfer them to a large mixing bowl. Add four more tablespoons of butter, lower the heat, and, when it is melted, add the finely chopped onions and celery. Sauté until wilted, about 5 minutes. Combine them with the bread cubes. Add the ground beef or veal, pork, egg, egg yolk, parsley, rosemary, basil, sage, salt, and pepper. Beat with a wooden spoon until all the ingredients are well blended. Pack the stuffing into the opening between the two flank steaks; then sew the opening securely closed.

Melt the remaining 4 tablespoons butter with the vegetable oil in a flameproof roasting pan. Over high heat, brown the steaks in the hot fat on both sides. Remove from the pan and reserve. Lower the heat and add the coarsely chopped celery, carrots, and onion and cook until tender, stirring occasionally, about 10 minutes. Pour in the beef stock. Place the stuffed flank steaks on top of the vegetables, cover securely with aluminum foil, and refrigerate until 2 hours before final preparation.

TIME ALLOWANCE FOR FINAL PREPARATION: 2 HOURS.

Preheat the oven to 350 degrees.

Without removing the foil, place the stuffed flank steaks in the oven and braise for 1¾ hours. Remove foil and pierce steaks all the way through with a sharp knife. If the meat offers no resistance, it is done; otherwise, rewrap the foil and cook 15 minutes longer. Transfer the meat to a heated platter. Cut off and discard all cords securing the meat.

Skim off any surface fat that has accumulated with the vegetables. Transfer the vegetables and the broth into a blender or a food processor with a steel blade and whirl until smooth. (This may have to be done in batches.) Pour the puree into a saucepan and bring to a boil. Taste the sauce for correct seasoning and adjust if necessary.

With a sharp carving knife, cut the stuffed flank steaks into ¾-inch-thick slices. Serve with the heated sauce.

SERVES 8.

BAKED CARDAMOM CARROTS

MAY BE PARTIALLY PREPARED UP TO 24 HOURS IN ADVANCE.

2 pounds carrots, peeled and cut into 1-inch lengths
2 teaspoons sugar
½ teaspoon salt
1 teaspoon ground cardamom
2 tablespoons water
3 tablespoons unsalted butter, cut into small pieces

Combine the carrots, sugar, salt, cardamom, and water in a 1-quart ovenproof casserole with a tight-fitting lid. Toss to mix well. Scatter the butter on top. Cover the casserole, and refrigerate until 1 hour before final preparation.

TIME ALLOWANCE FOR FINAL PREPARATION: 45 MINUTES.

Preheat the oven to 350 degrees.

Bake the carrots for 30 to 35 minutes, or until tender when pierced with the tip of a knife.

SERVES 8.

PSEUDO CREPES SUZETTE

CREPES MAY BE PREPARED AND FROZEN UP TO 1 MONTH IN ADVANCE;
COMPLETE DESSERT MAY BE PREPARED UP TO 24 HOURS IN ADVANCE.

CREPES
2½ cups milk
2 tablespoons unsalted butter, melted
4 eggs
2 tablespoons sugar
¼ teaspoon salt
2 cups flour
1 teaspoon oil

To make the crepes: Place milk, butter, eggs, sugar, and salt in the container of a blender and whirl for 4 seconds. Add flour and whirl until thoroughly blended. Let batter rest at least 1 hour before making crepes. (However, it may be refrigerated for up to 12 hours, if desired, and given another whirl before using, with 1 to 2 tablespoons more milk added to thin, if necessary.)

Put the oil in a medium-size skillet, preferably one with a nonstick surface. Swirl oil around pan over medium to high heat until bottom is lubricated. Pour out any excess. At same heat, ladle in about 2 tablespoons of batter, gently pushing batter with base of ladle to distribute it into an even 6-inch circle. As soon as the batter's surface seems dull and somewhat dry, turn crepe over. The first side should cook in about 1 minute, the second in half the time. Discard first crepe. Repeat process, transferring cooked crepes to a plate and topping each with a piece of wax paper (to facilitate separation), until all the batter is used. There is enough batter for 24 to 30 crepes, depending on their size. They may be stored 3 or 4 days, well wrapped, in the refrigerator, or for a month in the freezer.

FILLING
2 cups plus 1 teaspoon unsalted butter, softened
2 cups sugar
2 tablespoons grated orange rind
1½ cups strained fresh orange juice
¾ cup orange liqueur such as Cointreau or Grand Marnier
½ cup blanched slivered almonds, toasted

To make the filling: Melt 2 cups butter and sugar in a heavy 14-inch skillet over medium heat, stirring constantly until lightly caramelized (about 10 minutes). Add orange rind and juice, and continue to boil, stirring, until thick and somewhat syrupy, about 5 to 7 minutes longer. Add liqueur and cool.

Spoon about 1 tablespoon of syrup on one side of the crepe that was browned last (less attractive side). Spread over surface and fold crepe in quarters. Repeat with remaining crepes, allowing 3 or 4 per person. Grease with the remaining teaspoon of butter an ovenproof baking dish large enough to hold all the crepes. Arrange crepes in it. Cover tightly with plastic wrap. Keep refrigerated until 1 hour before final preparation. Transfer the remaining syrup to a container with a tight-fitting lid, and hold it refrigerated until 1 hour before final preparation.

TIME ALLOWANCE FOR FINAL PREPARATION: 20 MINUTES.

Preheat oven to 375 degrees.

Spoon remaining syrup over crepes. Slide baking dish into oven and heat for 10 to 15 minutes. Sprinkle the surface with toasted almond slivers. Serve hot.

SERVES 8.

NEW ENGLAND HARVEST DINNER FOR FOUR

Pan-Fried Oysters

Broiled Parsnips

Mixed Green Salad with Vinaigrette Dressing*

Apple Soufflé

In New England, fall is a magnificent harvest season. This menu incorporates three of its products: oysters, which always taste better in cool weather; parsnips, a universally underrated root crop; and, of course, New England's favorite fruit, apples.

Pan-fried oysters are an adaptation of a recipe I found one day many years ago while thumbing through a well-worn 1861 issue of *Godey's Ladies' Book.* The dish has since become a family favorite, sometimes as a main course, sometimes, in smaller quantities, as an appetizer. (Fried oysters are *very* filling.) Oysters vary so in size that it is hard to generalize on the time it should take to cook them. Just beware of overcooking, for like so many delectables, oysters toughen easily. Try the parsnips, too. They have a most delicate flavor and are worthy of inclusion on many menus. Finally, apple soufflé is light and frothy, a satisfying foil for the richness of the meal.

PAN-FRIED OYSTERS

MAY BE PARTIALLY PREPARED UP TO 3 HOURS IN ADVANCE.

1 pint shucked oysters (about 20 large)
1 egg
2 tablespoons light cream
1½ cups soft bread crumbs, preferably homemade
1 teaspoon lemon rind
1 tablespoon grated fresh ginger
1 teaspoon tarragon leaves, crushed
2 teaspoons minced scallions
4 tablespoons unsalted butter
4 tablespoons oil
4 lemon wedges

Keep the oysters covered and refrigerated until time for final preparation.

In a shallow bowl, beat the egg with the light cream. Cover with plastic wrap and set aside in a cool place.

On two sheets of paper toweling, combine the bread crumbs, lemon rind, ginger, tarragon, and scallions. With your fingers, toss and mix until well blended. Spread the mixture evenly over the towels.

TIME ALLOWANCE FOR FINAL PREPARATION: 15 MINUTES.

Preheat the oven to its lowest setting. While preparing the oysters, warm a platter in the oven.

Place the butter and oil in a heavy, large skillet, preferably one with high sides to keep spattering to a minimum. Over medium to high heat, bring to the foaming stage.

Meanwhile, drain the oysters and pat them dry with paper toweling. When the butter and oil are very hot, dip 10 oysters, one at a time, in the beaten egg, then coat each one with the herbed bread crumbs. Depending on the oysters' size, fry 1 to 3 minutes on each side, or until they are brown and crisp. Drain on paper toweling, remove to the hot platter, and keep warm in the oven. Repeat until all the oysters have been fried. Serve with lemon wedges.

SERVES 4.

BROILED PARSNIPS

MAY BE PARTIALLY PREPARED UP TO 8 HOURS IN ADVANCE.

1 pound parsnips, peeled, trimmed, and halved crosswise
1 clove garlic, peeled and halved lengthwise
4 tablespoons unsalted butter
1 tablespoon strained fresh lemon juice
¼ teaspoon freshly ground nutmeg
¼ teaspoon salt
Freshly ground black pepper
1 tablespoon minced fresh parsley

Drop the parsnips and the garlic into boiling salted water to cover. Boil over low heat until tender, about 15 to 20 minutes depending on size. Drain in a colander, and refresh under cold water. Cut the parsnips lengthwise into ¼-inch slices. Discard the garlic.

Generously butter a shallow baking dish large enough to hold the parsnips, slightly overlapping, in one layer. Dot with 2 tablespoons butter. Sprinkle with lemon juice, nutmeg, salt, and pepper. Cover with plastic wrap, and refrigerate until 1 hour before final preparation.

TIME ALLOWANCE FOR FINAL PREPARATION: 10 MINUTES.

Preheat the broiler and arrange the rack 8 inches below the heating element.

Place the parsnips in the broiler, and broil 5 minutes or until thoroughly heated. If in that time they have not browned delicately, move the rack closer to the heat and, watching carefully so they do not burn, broil them 1 to 2 minutes longer. Serve immediately, garnishing with minced parsley and the remaining 2 tablespoons butter.

SERVES 4.

APPLE SOUFFLÉ

MAY BE PARTIALLY PREPARED UP TO 6 HOURS IN ADVANCE.

4 cups peeled, cored, thinly sliced apples (about 7 medium)
½ to 1 cup sugar, depending on tartness of apples
1 tablespoon grated orange rind
⅓ cup strained fresh orange juice
4 eggs, separated
1 cup heavy cream, whipped (optional)

Combine the apples, ½ cup sugar, orange rind, and juice in a 1-quart saucepan. Over medium to low heat, cook them, covered, for 20 to 30 minutes, until the apples are very soft. If there is a lot of juice with the apples, uncover the pan for the last 5 minutes to permit the juices to evaporate somewhat. Remove from heat and cool. Transfer the apples to a food processor fitted with a steel blade, and whirl until finely pureed. Taste for sweetness, and add more sugar if desired. Drop in the four egg yolks, and whirl until completely incorporated. Cover the bowl of the processor and hold in the refrigerator until 1 hour before final preparation. Keep the egg whites, covered and unrefrigerated, in a mixing bowl until final preparation.

TIME ALLOWANCE FOR FINAL PREPARATION: 50 MINUTES.

Preheat the oven to 375 degrees. Bring a large kettle of water to a boil.

Generously butter a 1-quart soufflé dish and dust it with sugar. Take a piece of aluminum foil long enough to wrap around the soufflé dish, double it over lengthwise, and butter one side. Wrap it around the soufflé dish so that it extends at least 2 inches above the sides of the dish. Tie it securely with cord.

Beat the egg whites until stiff. Mix one-third of them into the apple puree to lighten it, then fold the puree gently into the remaining whites until all traces of white have disappeared. Spoon the mixture into the soufflé dish.

Place the soufflé dish in a *bain-marie* or baking pan and pour boiling water into it until the water reaches halfway up the sides of the soufflé dish. Bake 40 minutes, or until the soufflé is puffed and golden. Serve immediately, with whipped cream if desired.

SERVES 4.

AN INTIMATE THANKSGIVING DINNER FOR TWO

Sherried Consommé

Currant-Glazed Cornish Hens with Wild Rice Stuffing

Pureed Peas

Mashed Turnips* or Creamed Onions

Dried Fruit Tartlets

We tend to think of the holidays in terms of glorious scenes of large family reunions, full of laughter and camaraderie, where all generations come together and revel in one another's companionship. It's a valid image, of course; but there's another kind of Thanksgiving, or, for that matter, Christmas, gathering. It's the twosome, such as husband and wife, or mother and daughter, or two sisters, or two friends, who find themselves by themselves, and often feeling a little melancholy because of it.

One of the ways to beat those holiday doldrums is to plan a really good meal. Food is always comforting. Why should you and your companion settle for hamburgers or some such mundane creation for two when with a little time and effort (cooking is good therapy, too) you can enjoy a really smashing meal?

It may not be turkey, but what's wrong with Cornish hens, basted with currant jelly to crisp perfection? Or bright green pureed peas, not traditional, but so good. If you can manage another vegetable, go with the traditional mashed turnips or creamed onions . . . or both!

For dessert, forget pumpkin or mince pies. Try these individual dried fruit tartlets. The filling is reminiscent in texture of mince pie but has that unmistakable tang of dried apricots, apples, peaches, or pears. Let yourself go and slather the tartlets with whipped cream.

With good food, Thanksgiving can indeed be a joyous feast—even if only for two.

CURRANT-GLAZED CORNISH HENS

MAY BE PARTIALLY PREPARED UP TO 24 HOURS IN ADVANCE.

⅓ cup wild rice, rinsed
1¼ teaspoons salt
2 rock Cornish game hens, about 1½ pounds each
1½ cups water
1 carrot, broken into 3 pieces
1 stalk celery, broken into 3 pieces
1 bay leaf
4 tablespoons unsalted butter
2 tablespoons finely chopped pecans
2 tablespoons finely chopped onion
3 large mushrooms, coarsely chopped (about ¼ pound)
Freshly ground black pepper
½ cup currant jelly, melted
1 tablespoon flour

Drop the wild rice into a small saucepan full of boiling water to which ½ teaspoon of salt has been added. Bring it to a boil, lower the heat and simmer, uncovered, 50 to 60 minutes, or until the rice is just tender. Do not overcook it. Remove it from the heat immediately, drain it in a sieve, then refresh it under cold water. Set it aside to drain further.

Meanwhile, remove the giblets from the hens. Pull out and reserve any fat still clinging to their cavities. Wrap the fat well in plastic or foil, and refrigerate it until time for final preparation. Place the necks and all the giblets except the liver in another small saucepan, add ½ teaspoon salt, the 1½ cups water, and the carrot, celery, and bay leaf, and bring the water to a boil. Simmer uncovered for 45 minutes. With a slotted spoon, remove and discard all the vegetables. Add the liver to the broth, and simmer 5 minutes more. Transfer the liver and the giblets to a chopping board and chop fine. Wrap in plastic and reserve in the refrigerator if you are not planning to complete the dish immediately. Measure the broth; there should be ¾ cup. If not, add enough water to make the difference. Refrigerate, covered, if preparing ahead. If not, simply set aside and reserve.

In a 10-inch skillet, melt the butter over moderate heat. Add the pecans and toast, stirring frequently, for 2 to 3 minutes, or until the nuts begin to brown. Immediately lower the heat, add the onions and mushrooms, and sauté 5 to 7 minutes, or until the onions are soft and the juices the mushrooms exude have nearly evaporated.

Transfer the wild rice to a small bowl. Mix well with the mushroom-onion mixture. Add the remaining ¼ teaspoon of salt and a few grindings of pepper. Taste and adjust for seasoning. Cover the bowl with plastic wrap if preparing ahead, and refrigerate or set aside.

Wash the hens well. Pat them dry with paper toweling. Refrigerate them, well wrapped, until 1 hour before final preparation.

TIME ALLOWANCE FOR FINAL PREPARATION: 90 MINUTES.

Preheat oven to 450 degrees.

Place the reserved fat in a small skillet and, over very low heat, slowly render it.

Pack the hens loosely with the wild rice stuffing. There should just be enough. Sew the cavities closed, and truss the birds. Place them side by side in a roasting pan. Brush them well with the rendered fat; then sprinkle their surfaces with a few grindings of pepper. Transfer them to a rack in the upper third of the oven and roast them, undisturbed, for 15 minutes.

Lower the oven temperature to 350. Brush the birds again with the rendered fat. Roast another 15 minutes. This time, brush the skin with the melted currant jelly. Roast another 15 minutes, brush again with currant jelly, then roast them for a final 15 minutes. Make sure they are done by piercing a thigh with the tip of a sharp knife. The juices should run clear. If not, roast 5 minutes more, test again and repeat for 5 more minutes if necessary. Keep brushing with the glaze. When the juices run clear, set the birds aside on individual, warmed plates while you prepare the giblet gravy.

Pour off all but 1 tablespoon of the fat from the bottom of the roasting pan. Place the pan on top of the stove over moderately low heat. Add the flour, and blend it well with the fat, scraping up any particles left clinging to the bottom of the pan. Cook 1 or 2 minutes to remove any taste of flour. Slowly add the reserved broth, stirring well to prevent lumps from forming. Bring the gravy to a boil and, when it has thickened, pour it through a sieve into a saucepan. Add the reserved giblets; taste and adjust seasoning. Reheat and serve with the hens.

SERVES 2.

PUREED PEAS

MAY BE PARTIALLY PREPARED UP TO 6 HOURS IN ADVANCE.

1 (10-ounce) package frozen peas, thawed
½ teaspoon sugar
¾ teaspoon salt
½ cup water
1 tablespoon unsalted butter, softened
2 tablespoons heavy cream
Pinch of thyme

Place the peas in a small saucepan. Add the sugar, ½ teaspoon salt, and the water. Stir to mix. Bring the water to a boil; then lower the heat and simmer the peas, covered, for 4 minutes or until they are very tender.

Drain the peas well. Transfer them to a food processor fitted with a steel blade. Drop in the butter and cream, and whirl until the peas are smooth. (It may take as long as 60 to 90 seconds to puree the skins.) Add the thyme and the remaining ¼ teaspoon salt. Whirl briefly. Taste and adjust seasoning. Scrape the mixture into the top of a double boiler (or into its original saucepan) and set it aside, covered, in a cool section of the kitchen until final preparation.

TIME ALLOWANCE FOR FINAL PREPARATION: 15 MINUTES.

Half fill the bottom of the double boiler with water. Set the peas on top of it. (Or place the original saucepan in a shallow pan filled halfway with water.) Bring the water to a boil, lower the heat, and warm the peas for 10 to 15 minutes, stirring occasionally. Serve immediately.

SERVES 2.

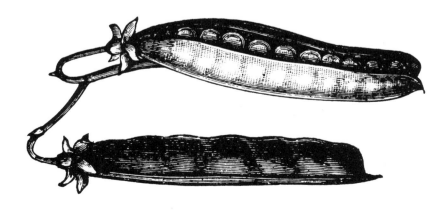

DRIED FRUIT TARTLETS

PASTRY MAY BE PREPARED UP TO 48 HOURS IN ADVANCE;
FILLING MAY BE PREPARED UP TO 1 WEEK IN ADVANCE;
TARTLETS MAY BE ASSEMBLED AND BAKED 24 HOURS IN ADVANCE.

PASTRY
1 cup flour
½ teaspoon salt
½ teaspoon sugar
¼ cup unsalted butter, cut in pieces and chilled
2 tablespoons vegetable shortening, chilled
1 to 2 tablespoons ice water

To prepare the pastry: In a medium-sized mixing bowl, combine the flour, salt, and sugar, and stir to blend. Drop in the pieces of butter and shortening. With your fingers, a pastry blender, or two knives, cut the fat in until the mixture looks like coarse meal. Add 1 to 2 tablespoons of the ice water (as little as possible) and toss with a fork until the mixture is just moist enough to form a ball. Shape the pastry into a round patty about 1 inch thick, wrap it in wax paper, and refrigerate it at least ½ hour or until ready to roll it out.

FILLING
½ pound mixed dried fruit, such as peaces, apples, pears, or apricots,
  coarsely chopped (about 2 cups)
½ cup golden seedless raisins
1 cup water
⅓ cup sugar
3 slices lemon
¼ teaspoon vanilla

To prepare the filling: Combine the mixed dried fruit, raisins, water, sugar, and lemon slices in a small saucepan. Over moderate heat, bring to a boil, stirring only until the sugar dissolves. Lower the heat and simmer uncovered for 20 minutes, or until the fruit is tender. Discard the lemon slices. Add the vanilla, stirring to mix, and allow to cool. If not preparing the tartlets immediately, transfer the mixture to a bowl, tightly cover with plastic wrap, and refrigerate until 1 hour before final preparation.

FINAL ASSEMBLY
1 egg yolk
1 tablespoon light cream
½ cup heavy cream, whipped

Preheat oven to 450 degrees.

On a lightly floured surface, roll out the pastry to ⅛ inch thick. Cut 2 circles of pastry 6½ inches in diameter. Transfer them to 5-inch pie plates (or substitute rame-kins) 1 inch deep, and press them gently in place. Divide the fruit mixture evenly between the two. Roll the remaining pastry again, and cut strips ½ inch wide. Make a lattice topping on both tartlets. Combine the egg yolk and light cream, mix well, and brush over the pastry.

Place the tartlets on a baking sheet, and bake 10 minutes in the center of the oven. Lower the heat to 350, and bake 30 minutes more. Serve hot or at room temperature, with whipped cream.

SERVES 2.

SUNDAY NIGHT SUPPER FOR FOUR

French-Style Fish Soup with Croutons

Spider Corn Bread

Cole Slaw with Light Mayonnaise*

Poached Apples

My family frequently enjoys what I call "Sunday night suppers." They're basically light meals, and they've always been a favorite, particularly with my children, who used joyously to devour French toast, cheese omelets, or some extra-special sandwich on those particular evenings.

While my children are grown now, they still ask for a "Sunday night supper" when they are at home. My son has not changed with the years—he still asks for French toast—but my daughter has become more sophisticated and prefers soups. When I first pondered a supper menu for *Do-Ahead Dining*, I considered a New England–style fish chowder, only to discard the idea as much too predictable. But then I had the idea of incorporating fish into a typical French potato-based soup, thus perhaps enjoying the best of two worlds. My family was enthusiastic, although it must be admitted that my son still sticks with the French toast.

With the filling soup, I suggest an old New England favorite, "spider" corn bread, which is very special, with a custardlike crust. (The name is derived from the three-legged frying pans—"spiders"—used in the old days in fireplace cookery.) Some may want to include a salad, so I have suggested cole slaw.

The poached apples are a real pleasure, delicate in flavor with just a hint of orange and caramel—a perfect foil for the meal. I think I prefer them to baked apples, but then, when I eat a really good baked apple, I reverse my opinion.

Oh, well. Isn't it a woman's privilege to change her mind?

FRENCH-STYLE FISH SOUP WITH CROUTONS

MAY BE PARTIALLY PREPARED UP TO 24 HOURS IN ADVANCE.

2 cups bread cubes, made from homemade-style bread, cut in ½-inch cubes
5 tablespoons unsalted butter
1 fish head and bones (for stock)
1 cup thinly sliced, well-cleaned leeks (about 3), white parts only, roots
*   trimmed*
1 pound potatoes (about 2 medium), peeled and cut in ½-inch cubes
1 skinless fillet (1½ to 2 pounds) of haddock, scrod, cod, or any other firm,
*   white-fleshed fish*
2 teaspoons salt
Freshly ground black pepper
4 drops Tabasco
3 tablespoons minced fresh dill weed
1 cup heavy cream

Preheat oven to 300 degrees.

To make the croutons, spread the bread cubes out on a cookie sheet and toast them in the oven, stirring occasionally, until they are uniformly tan, about 20 minutes. Transfer them to a small bowl. Melt 2 tablespoons butter and pour it over them. Toss well to coat all the cubes. Cover the bowl tightly with plastic wrap and reserve in a cool, dry spot until final preparation.

Meanwhile, place the fish head and bones in a large kettle, and just cover with water. Bring to a boil, lower the heat, and simmer, partly covered, for 20 minutes. Strain the broth into a mixing bowl and reserve. Discard the fish head and bones.

Melt the remaining 3 tablespoons butter in a large saucepan or in the same kettle. Add the leeks and sauté over low heat until just wilted, about 5 minutes. Add the potato cubes and layer the fish on top. (You may want to cut it into 3- or 4-inch pieces to make an easier fit.) Pour 3 cups of the reserved fish stock into the pot, cover it and bring the stock to a boil. Immediately reduce the heat and simmer, still covered, for 15 minutes. (Reserve remaining fish stock, if any, for another use, or discard.)

With a slotted spoon, remove the fish to a plate or bowl and reserve. In two or three batches, puree the broth, potatoes, and leeks in a food processor or blender until smooth. Transfer the mixture as it is completed to a large bowl. Break the reserved fish into bite-sized pieces and add to the soup. Season to taste with salt, pepper, and Tabasco. Add the dill weed. Cover tightly with plastic wrap, and reserve in the refrigerator until final preparation.

TIME ALLOWANCE FOR FINAL PREPARATION: 15 MINUTES.

Transfer the soup from the bowl to a large saucepan. Place it over moderate heat, and bring it to a low boil. Add the cream; stir briefly to mix and remove from heat. Spoon into individual heated soup bowls, scattering a generous portion of the reserved toasted bread cubes on top.

SERVES 4.

SPIDER CORN BREAD

BEST PREPARED JUST BEFORE SERVING;
DRY INGREDIENTS MAY BE MEASURED AND SIFTED WELL IN ADVANCE.

½ cup flour
2 teaspoons baking powder
1 teaspoon salt
2 tablespoons sugar
1½ cups white cornmeal, preferably stone-ground
4 tablespoons unsalted butter
2 eggs
3 cups milk, sour milk, or buttermilk

In a sieve, combine the flour, baking powder, salt, sugar, and cornmeal. Sift twice. Store in a plastic bag or similar airtight container until ready to use.

TIME ALLOWANCE FOR FINAL PREPARATION: 40 TO 45 MINUTES.

Place the butter in a 12-inch cast-iron skillet (with an ovenproof handle) in the oven to melt as you preheat the oven to 400 degrees. (If you do not own such a skillet, substitute a 9-by-13-inch baking dish.)

While the oven is warming, beat the eggs well. Add 2 cups of the milk, sour milk, or buttermilk. Mix thoroughly. Add to the cornmeal mixture, stirring only until the ingredients are completely moistened. Do not worry about lumps. Remove the skillet from the oven. Swirl the melted butter around to coat the bottom and sides of the pan. With a rubber spatula, scrape in the batter. Immediately drizzle the remaining cup of milk, sour milk, or buttermilk over its surface. Return the skillet to the preheated oven and bake 30 minutes, or until the top of the bread is just beginning to turn golden. Serve very hot, with butter.

Please note: As the recipe implies, this spider bread can be made with milk, sour milk, or buttermilk. Plain milk produces a blander bread than either the sour milk or buttermilk, both of which impart a tangy flavor to the cornmeal. No matter which milk is used, the trick of pouring the final cup over the batter results in a somewhat custardy crust—a pleasant variation on an old theme.

SERVES 4.

POACHED APPLES

MAY BE PREPARED UP TO 24 HOURS IN ADVANCE.

1 cup sugar
1 cup water
2 tablespoons strained fresh lemon juice
Peel of 1 orange
4 golden delicious apples, peeled and cored
Freshly grated nutmeg
½ cup golden seedless raisins
1 cup medium cream

Combine the sugar and water in a shallow pan with a cover, large enough to hold four apples. Place over moderate heat, and stir until the sugar is dissolved. Add the lemon juice and orange peel, and boil the syrup for 3 minutes. Add the apples, reduce the heat to low, and simmer, partially covered, for 15 minutes. Turn the apples two or three times while they are poaching. Do not overcook; the apples should be tender and soft but hold their shape. Transfer the apples to a serving dish and sprinkle them with grated nutmeg.

Discard the orange peel. Add the raisins to the syrup and, over high heat, boil vigorously for 2 minutes, or until it is slightly reduced and thickened. Cool; then spoon the syrup and raisins over the apples to give them a nice glaze. If not being served immediately, the apples may be stored in a cool section of the kitchen, covered with plastic wrap. Serve at room temperature, accompanied by a pitcher of cream.

SERVES 4.

CROWN ROAST OF PORK FOR EIGHT

Crown Roast of Pork with Apple Stuffing

Bourbon Sweet Potatoes

Stir-Fried Snow Peas with Yellow Peppers *

Bananas Cascais

A crown roast, whether it be lamb or pork, is what I call "feast food": dramatic and delicious. There is a popular misconception, though, that these roasts are difficult to prepare. Nothing could be farther from the truth. The only threat to success is your butcher. Many butchers stuff the ground-up trimmings of the chops into the crown's cavity. This completely confuses the cooking time. If your butcher unwittingly does this for you, smile bravely—but remove the ground trimmings. Don't throw them away, though. Freeze them for another use.

The bourbon-infused sweet potatoes go well with roast pork and are a superb version of a too-little-appreciated vegetable. Taste them, and I'm certain you'll make them a regular addition to your menus. The only chore in preparing the potatoes is eliminating the lumps, but with patience and a strong arm or sturdy beater, you will succeed.

The dessert is one of my family's favorites, borrowed from a dish my husband and I enjoyed—no, went mad over—in the Portuguese resort town of Cascais. It was made with fresh raspberries. It was truly sublime—so memorable, in fact, that I was home barely a day or two before I attempted to duplicate it. Since the availability of fresh berries is sometimes limited, I took the liberty of substituting frozen, which in no way detracts from the pleasure of the dessert. It is one of those rare treats that is unbelievably simple to execute yet tastes as if it has taken hours. I always keep a supply of Italian Amaretti di Saronno cookies and frozen raspberries on hand just in case I want to produce it for unexpected company. With a dessert like bananas Cascais, your meal will always be remembered.

CROWN ROAST OF PORK WITH APPLE STUFFING

MAY BE PARTIALLY PREPARED UP TO 6 HOURS IN ADVANCE.

3 cups bread cubes, made from extra-thin white bread cut in ¼-inch cubes
3 tablespoons unsalted butter
¼ cup coarsely chopped onion
2 tablespoons minced fresh rosemary (or 2 teaspoons dried, crushed)
2 teaspoons grated orange rind
¼ cup seedless raisins
¼ cup strained fresh orange juice
6-pound crown roast of pork
Freshly ground black pepper
1 red Delicious apple (about ½ pound)

Preheat oven to 300 degrees. Spread the bread cubes out on a cookie sheet and toast them in the oven, tossing occasionally, until uniformly tan, about 20 minutes. Transfer them to a mixing bowl.

Melt the butter in a medium-size skillet over low heat, and add the onions. Cook the onions until wilted, about 5 minutes, stirring occasionally. Pour the onions and the butter over the bread cubes and toss well. Add half the rosemary and the orange rind, and toss again.

While the onions are cooking, combine the raisins and the orange juice in a small saucepan and, over medium heat, bring the juice to a boil. Turn off the heat, and let the raisins plump for 10 minutes. When they are nice and fat, pour both the raisins and the juice over the bread cubes, and toss again. Cover with plastic wrap, and set aside in a cool section of the kitchen until final preparation.

TIME ALLOWANCE FOR FINAL PREPARATION: 2¼ HOURS.

Preheat oven to 450 degrees.

Remove the little white frills with which the butcher has probably decorated your crown roast, and reserve them until serving time. Cover each exposed rib bone with a small piece of aluminum foil to prevent burning. If your butcher has packed a wad of ground pork into the center of your roast, remove it and reserve it for another use. (Wrap it well and freeze; combine it with ground beef for a meat loaf.) Sprinkle the roast with pepper and the remaining rosemary. Place it in a roasting pan and roast, uncovered, for 1 hour.

Just before the hour is up, core the apple (do not peel it) and cut it into ½-inch dice. Mix the apple well with the stuffing. Remove the roast from the oven, and pack the central cavity of the crown with the stuffing, spreading the meat apart to get all of it in if necessary. Mound it slightly. Lower the oven temperature to 350, and continue to roast the pork another hour, or until the internal temperature registers 170 on a meat thermometer.

Transfer the roast to a heated serving platter. Remove the aluminum pieces from the bones, and replace with the reserved paper frills.

SERVES 8.

BOURBON SWEET POTATOES

MAY BE PARTIALLY PREPARED UP TO 24 HOURS IN ADVANCE.

4 pounds sweet potatoes
2 teaspoons salt
½ cup unsalted butter, softened
½ cup bourbon
2 teaspoons grated orange rind
¾ cup strained fresh orange juice
¼ cup firmly packed dark brown sugar
½ teaspoon cinnamon
¼ teaspoon freshly grated nutmeg
½ cup finely chopped pecans

Place the sweet potatoes in a large saucepan. Cover them with water to which 1 teaspoon of salt has been added. Bring them to a boil over high heat, covered. Reduce heat and simmer 30 to 45 minutes, depending on their size, until they feel very tender when pierced with a knife. Drain the potatoes and allow them to cool.

When they are cool enough to handle, peel them and push them through a ricer, or mash them well in a large mixing bowl. With a wooden spoon or hand-held electric beater, mix in the butter, bourbon, orange rind and juice, sugar, the remaining teaspoon of salt, cinnamon, and nutmeg. Beat them until the ingredients are thoroughly blended and the potatoes are very smooth. (This may take some time and muscle if you are using a wooden spoon, but the effort is worth it.) Transfer the potatoes to a well-buttered 9-by-12-inch baking dish or its equivalent, smoothing the surface with a spatula. Cover with plastic wrap and refrigerate if you are preparing the potatoes more than 4 hours in advance. (If 4 hours or less, they do not have to be refrigerated. Hold them in a cool section of the kitchen.) Remove them from the refrigerator 1 hour before final preparation.

TIME ALLOWANCE FOR FINAL PREPARATION: 50 MINUTES.

Preheat oven to 350 degrees.

Distribute the pecans evenly over the top of the potatoes. Bake 45 minutes. Serve immediately.

SERVES 8.

BANANAS CASCAIS

MAY BE PREPARED UP TO 4 HOURS IN ADVANCE;
MUST BE PREPARED AT LEAST 1 HOUR IN ADVANCE.

6 ripe bananas, peeled
2 (10-ounce) packages frozen raspberries, packed in syrup (not light syrup), thawed
1 cup heavy cream
4 tablespoons sugar
½ cup crushed Amaretti di Saronno cookies (available at specialty stores and some supermarkets), or crushed almond macaroons

In the bottom of a deep glass bowl, layer the bananas sliced very thin. Drain the raspberries through a strainer, reserving ½ cup of the syrup. Scatter the berries over the bananas and drizzle the reserved syrup over the top.

In a chilled bowl, whip the cream until thick, beating in the sugar 1 tablespoon at a time. Spread the cream over the fruit. Distribute the crushed cookie crumbs evenly over the surface of the cream. Cover with plastic wrap and refrigerate until serving time, allowing at least 1 hour for the flavors to develop and meld.

SERVES 8.

ENTERTAINING
IN THE
WINTER

My general reaction to winter, I must confess, is negative. Despite the hazards of the New England climate, however, I do enjoy entertaining in winter. There is a conviviality to winter get-togethers rarely found in the other seasons. Friends seem happier to see each other than usual, perhaps because, with fewer outdoor activities, everyone suffers a bit of cabin fever. Of course, there are those chancy evenings when a storm arrives instead of the invited guests. (At those moments, I always say a silent prayer of gratitude for the freezer.) And then there are those marvelous occasions when the elements generate impromptu meals for travelers seeking shelter. (Again I give thanks for the freezer, and the cupboard, too.) Whether planned or spontaneous, those occasions when cherished friends have foiled the whims of nature make for especially warm and hospitable meals.

Warmth and hospitality, then, are my goals for winter entertaining. The house, apartment, or room must seem particularly inviting, delightfully cozy. If there is a fireplace, then there must be a blaze burning brightly. Heady odors should come wafting from the kitchen. Flowers mean more in winter than in any other season, and I like to set massive bouquets in as many corners as I can manage—not careful arrangements, but an eclectic assortment of stems and blossoms plunked into vases to give an effect of abandon. I seldom place flowers on the dining table, however, because I prefer the warmth of candlelight on dark nights, and I often use an assortment of unmatched candlesticks of different heights to add another dimension of warmth. I will often put a floral arrangement on a side table, instead.

No one should be afraid to serve hearty foods in winter. A roast or a stew never tastes better than when the temperature is low and the wind is whistling. Give me a royal roast of beef, or a spectacularly aromatic lentil-sausage stew, or perhaps a loin of pork, redolent with garlic, its fat darkly crisp. If they're appropriate to the entree, add big baked potatoes topped with sour cream, or maybe even hot, freshly baked home-made bread. And never forget a treat for the sweet tooth. Much as I love fruit as a dessert in one form or another, chocolate—hot or cold, but in any case, lots of it—is meant for winter. The richer, the creamier, the better the dessert—at least, in winter.

So, all things edible considered, why don't I like winter? For the life of me, I can't remember.

BORROWED FROM BRITAIN: A CHRISTMAS FEAST FOR TEN

Tomato Bouillon

Rib Roast of Beef

Pecan Yorkshire Pudding

Broccoli Flowerets with Brown Butter*

Plum Pudding with Hard Sauce or Yule Log

Christmas is probably one of the most hectic days in any family's life—particularly one with small children. With this in mind, I offer a Christmas dinner that is perhaps as simple as any festive dinner for ten can be. It borrows inspiration from the British in a masterfully elegant rib roast of beef. While a goodly number of English families serve roast goose—a most splendid bird—for Christmas, it does require a great deal of time and effort in the kitchen, as the rendered fat must be drained off constantly. Thus, I favor the easier feast of roast beef, England's most cherished national dish. One Swedish visitor to England in the eighteenth century remarked: "Englishmen understand almost better than any the art of properly roasting a large cut of meat."

This very untraditional recipe for the roast, given a few years back by one of my favorite butchers, Bill Harris of Ellis's Market in Orleans, Massachusetts, is absolutely foolproof and demands no attention whatsoever during the busy day. The results are sublime: The roast turns brown and crisp on top and beautifully rare inside, flowing with juices.

Before the beef, I suggest a clear and beautiful tomato bouillon to whet the appetite without suppressing it. With the roast, serve the traditional accompaniment, Yorkshire pudding, with pecans added for flavor and crunch.

For dessert, I offer a choice (or you could serve both): English plum pudding or a French yule log. Many people rely on their local bakeries to avoid the headaches of elegant holiday desserts, but if you start early you can make your own. Plum puddings and yule logs keep well, so they can be made weeks ahead of time. Your family and guests will be entranced as the flaming plum pudding comes to the table or the yule log arrives. Either dessert makes a good gift, and the plum pudding recipe makes enough for three puddings. Just think—in one baking session, you can produce one family dessert and two gifts.

TOMATO BOUILLON

MAY BE PREPARED UP TO 4 DAYS IN ADVANCE.

10 cups beef stock (or six 13¾-ounce cans beef broth)
Two 28-ounce cans tomatoes with their juices
10 whole peppercorns
10 cloves
8 sprigs parsley
¼ cup chopped onion
1 teaspoon oregano
6 egg whites
6 eggshells
10 lemon slices, cut thin

Skim any fat from the surface of the beef stock. In a large enamel or stainless steel pot, combine the stock, tomatoes and their juices, peppercorns, cloves, parsley, onions, and oregano, and bring to a boil. Reduce heat and simmer, uncovered, 15 minutes. Set aside and let cool completely.

Lightly beat the egg whites in a medium-size bowl until they are frothy. Crush the eggshells with your hands or a rolling pin. Add both to the beef stock and tomato mixture. Bring to a boil, stirring constantly. Lower the heat, and allow to simmer undisturbed for 20 minutes.

Gently ladle the bouillon into a glass or porcelain bowl through a sieve lined with a double thickness of rinsed cheesecloth. Do not press down on the vegetables, or the broth will become cloudy. Taste for seasoning and adjust if necessary. Cover with plastic wrap and refrigerate until ready to use. Discard vegetables and eggshells.

TIME ALLOWANCE FOR FINAL PREPARATION: 15 MINUTES.

Transfer bouillon from bowl to stainless steel or enamel saucepan. Bring just to the boiling point over medium heat. Serve in preheated soup bowls. Garnish with lemon slices.

SERVES 10.

RIB ROAST OF BEEF

◆

MUST BE PREPARED JUST BEFORE SERVING.

1 5-rib oven-ready roast of beef from the first cut, well marbled, short ribs
*   cut off, weighing 12 to 15 pounds*
Salt
Freshly ground black pepper

Have your butcher carefully weigh the oven-ready roast. Based on its weight, allow 5 minutes per pound for the initial hot-roasting. This method produces an evenly rare piece of meat; the interior will not be raw. (For medium, allow 6½ minutes per pound.) Be sure to take into account the total trimmed weight of the meat in order to calculate cooking time accurately. Do *not* round off the pounds. In other words, if the meat weighs 13¾ pounds, allow 68¾ minutes, or 69 minutes, for a rare roast.

Bring the roast to room temperature for at least 2 hours before placing it in the oven. Sprinkle with salt and freshly ground black pepper to taste. Place it in a pan large enough to contain it comfortably, with room to spare.

Preheat oven to 500 degrees.

Set a timer for the correct hot-roasting time you have calculated for your particular roast. Place the roast in the oven, and leave it undisturbed. When the timer sounds, turn the oven off. Do not open the door at any time. Leave the roast in the oven at least 2 hours (up to 2½) as the heat slowly dies down. It is then ready to be served.

If you prefer, or if you have only one oven, the roast may sit at room temperature while you bake the pecan Yorkshire pudding. However, this extra sitting period, advised in cooking most roasts to ensure tenderness and ease in carving, is not necessary with this recipe.

SERVES 10.

PECAN YORKSHIRE PUDDING

MAY BE PREPARED UP TO 6 HOURS IN ADVANCE.

3 eggs
1½ cups milk
¾ cup flour
¾ cup ground pecans
½ teaspoon salt
6 tablespoons beef fat drippings (see instructions below)

Drop the eggs into a blender. Whirl 5 or 6 seconds, or until well beaten. Add the milk and whirl again. Add the flour, ground pecans, salt, and 4 tablespoons of the beef drippings.

(The beef drippings may be taken from the pan of the finished roast beef; however, *do not take them until the cooking has been completed.* Then let the beef rest on a preheated platter in a warm spot while the Yorkshire pudding is baking. If you have two ovens and prefer to bake the pudding during the final 30 minutes the roast is in its oven, render your own drippings before making the batter from a ¾- to 1-pound chunk of beef suet, placed in a baking dish in a 350-degree oven for about 45 minutes. Discard any excess suet or drippings.)

Blend the batter until all ingredients are well assimilated. Cover blender, and refrigerate until 1 hour before final preparation.

TIME ALLOWANCE FOR FINAL PREPARATION: 40 MINUTES.

Preheat oven to 450 degrees.

Place the remaining beef drippings in a baking dish about 10 by 14 inches, and swirl around until the bottom and sides are coated. Blend the batter for 2 or 3 seconds; then pour into the baking dish. Bake 15 minutes; then reduce heat to 375 and bake another 15 minutes. The pudding should be puffed and golden brown. Cut into squares, and serve immediately with the roast beef.

SERVES 10.

PLUM PUDDING WITH HARD SAUCE

MAY BE PREPARED UP TO 1 YEAR IN ADVANCE;
SHOULD BE MADE AT LEAST 2 WEEKS BEFORE SERVING.
THIS RECIPE MAKES THREE 1-QUART PUDDINGS.

2 cups currants
2 cups seedless raisins
2 cups golden seedless raisins
½ cup finely chopped candied fruit peel
½ cup finely chopped candied cherries
1 cup blanched sliced almonds
2 cups coarsely chopped peeled apple (about 2 apples)
2 tablespoons grated orange rind
2 teaspoons grated lemon rind
½ pound ground beef suet
2 cups flour
4 cups soft bread crumbs, preferably homemade
1 cup brown sugar
2 teaspoons allspice
1 teaspoon salt
9 eggs
⅔ cup molasses
⅓ cup strained fresh orange juice (about 1 orange)
¼ cup strained fresh lemon juice (about 1 lemon)
1 cup brandy or dark rum, plus ½ cup per pudding for flaming

In a large bowl, combine the currants, raisins, fruit peel, cherries, almonds, apple, orange rind, lemon rind, and beef suet. Toss until well mixed. Add the flour, bread crumbs, sugar, allspice, and salt. Toss again.

In another bowl, beat the eggs until frothy. Add the molasses, orange juice, lemon juice, and 1 cup brandy or rum. Mix well. Pour the eggs over the fruit mixture and, with a sturdy wooden spoon, beat until eggs are thoroughly incorporated. Cover loosely with plastic wrap, and refrigerate 4 to 8 hours.

Butter three 1-quart English pudding molds, or any similar bowls with lips. Divide the pudding mixture evenly among them; it should nearly reach the tops. Cover each bowl with a buttered piece of aluminum foil, pressing it down on top of the pudding and tucking it close to the sides of the bowl. On each bowl, center a kitchen towel on top of the foil; then secure it to the bowl by tying a length of kitchen cord underneath the lip. Bring the two opposite ends of the towel up and over the top of the pudding, and tie them together. Place the molds on racks in one or more large pots, and fill the pots with water reaching three-fourths of the way up the sides of the molds. Bring the water to a boil, reduce the heat, and steam the puddings, covered, for 6 hours. If the water evaporates, add more.

Lift the puddings out of the water by using the knotted towels as handles. Allow puddings to cool. Remove towels, but tie a new length of cord around the bowls to keep the foil in place. If making within 1 month of serving, refrigerate until ready to use. If making more than 1 month in advance, freeze. (Allow 24 hours to come to room temperature if frozen.)

TIME ALLOWANCE FOR FINAL PREPARATION: 2 HOURS.

For each plum pudding, place mold in large pot of boiling water, as for the initial steaming. Bring to a boil, reduce heat to low, and steam, covered, for 2 hours. Remove from water; discard foil, and run a sharp knife around the mold's edges. Place a serving plate on top, upside down. Turn both the mold and the plate over and give a vigorous shake. The pudding should slip out easily; if it does not, repeat.

Heat the remaining ½ cup of brandy or dark rum per pudding in a small saucepan. When it is quite warm, ignite it with a match. Pour the flaming liquid over the pudding and serve immediately, with or without hard sauce.

Each pudding will serve at least 8, as it is very rich.

MAY BE PREPARED UP TO 4 DAYS IN ADVANCE.

HARD SAUCE
½ cup unsalted butter, softened
1 cup confectioners' sugar
2 teaspoons brandy or rum (or substitute 1 teaspoon vanilla)

With an electric mixer or by hand, cream the butter in a small bowl until very soft. Gradually add the sugar, beating until smooth. Flavor with brandy, rum, or vanilla. Cover tightly with plastic wrap, and refrigerate until 2 hours before serving. Makes enough for 1 plum pudding.

YULE LOG

♦

MAY BE PREPARED UP TO 6 WEEKS IN ADVANCE AND FROZEN.

CAKE
Butter and flour for pan
5 eggs
1 cup sugar
1 teaspoon vanilla
1 cup flour
6 tablespoons unsalted butter, melted and cooled to room temperature
Confectioners' sugar for dusting

To make the cake: Preheat oven to 350 degrees.

Butter a jelly roll pan, 11 by 16 inches. Line with wax paper cut the same width as the pan but at least 4 inches longer, leaving 2 inches at each end. Butter the wax paper generously; then dust it with a little flour, shaking out any excess.

Place the eggs in a large mixing bowl. Start beating with an electric mixer or by hand. Gradually add the sugar, then the vanilla. Beat until the eggs have tripled in volume and are creamy in color. With a rubber spatula, gently fold in the flour, ⅓ cup at a time, taking care not to decrease the volume of the eggs. Fold in the melted butter, 2 tablespoons at a time.

Pour the batter into the prepared jelly roll pan, using the rubber spatula to spread it evenly. Place the pan in the oven and bake 12 to 14 minutes, until the surface of the cake is pale gold and firm, but not crisp, to the touch.

Set the pan on a cake rack. Cover with a damp kitchen towel, and allow it to cool until the towel stops steaming. Sift a layer of confectioners' sugar over another length of wax paper, also longer than the pan. Turn the cake onto the sugared wax paper, peeling off the paper used in the baking. Gently roll up the cake and the fresh wax paper jelly roll fashion. (The fresh wax paper will help support the cake as you roll.) Then wrap both in a fresh, damp kitchen towel. Set aside while you make the frosting.

CHOCOLATE BUTTER CREAM FROSTING
5 egg yolks
2 cups confectioners' sugar
1 cup milk
3 ounces unsweetened chocolate
¼ teaspoon salt
1 cup (2 sticks) cold unsalted butter, cut into ½-inch pieces
¼ teaspoon cinnamon
1 teaspoon vanilla
3 tablespoons unsweetened cocoa

To make the frosting: Combine the egg yolks and sugar in a medium-size saucepan, off the heat. Beat them with a wooden spoon until they form a paste. Meanwhile, combine the milk and unsweetened chocolate in a small saucepan, and heat them over medium to low heat until the chocolate has melted and the milk is scalded. Gradually pour the milk mixture into the eggs and, stirring occasionally over medium heat, bring the mixture almost to a boil. (It will thicken somewhat.) Do not let it boil, or it will curdle. Transfer the chocolate mixture to a mixing bowl and, with an electric mixer or by hand, beat until it has thickened considerably and the bowl is cool. (This may take 10 minutes. Do not become discouraged.)

With the mixer still running, take each piece of butter one by one and soften it between your fingers; then drop it into the chocolate. Do not add the next piece until the previous one has been incorporated. Repeat until all the butter has been well beaten in. Add the salt, cinnamon, vanilla, and cocoa; mix thoroughly.

FINAL ASSEMBLY
½ cup finely chopped pistachio nuts (or 2 tablespoons green crystallized
sugar)

Remove the cake from the towel and gently unroll it, leaving the wax paper beneath it. Using an icing spatula, spread two-thirds of the frosting over the surface of the cake to within one inch of the edges. Roll up the cake again. Do not worry if the cake splits; merely mold it together with your hands. Any cracks will be concealed later by frosting.

Transfer the cake to a serving platter, seam side down. Cut off each end on the diagonal. Spread all but 2 tablespoons of the remaining frosting over the "log" in lengthwise strokes. Then, with the tines of a fork, make lengthwise hatch marks on the frosting to simulate bark. Along one side of the log, press the pistachio nuts or green sugar to make "moss." From the diagonal pieces you have cut off the ends, take small pieces of cake; roll them into two little cylinders, and spread with the remaining frosting. Attach them decoratively to the log to represent stubs of branches. (Stabilize them with toothpicks if necessary, but remember to remove toothpicks when serving.)

Place log in the freezer, serving platter and all, without wrapping. When it has frozen and there is no danger of disturbing the decorative frosting, wrap it tightly in a plastic bag. Thaw for 6 hours before serving.

SERVES 10 TO 12.

A PROVENÇAL TWIST TO FISH FOR SIX

Scrod Provençal

Saffron Rice and Peas

Raspberry Mousse

We who live in New England are fortunate to be able to enjoy numerous varieties of fish, many year round. I am thinking in particular of the cod family, which includes not only the Atlantic cod itself, but haddock, pollack, hake, and about fifty-five other species. To many people's surprise, "scrod" is not a separate species but an indicator of size: It is either a cod or a haddock weighing between 1½ and 2½ pounds. We sometimes take this firm, pristine white-fleshed fish too much for granted, limiting ourselves to broiling, baking, or frying it. But with just a little effort, a fish that is considered almost pedestrian can become quite tasty and unique.

Scrod Provençal is a case in point. Its tomato sauce not only couples nicely with the delicacy of the fish, but simultaneously serves as both cooking liquid and sauce. (You may use canned tomatoes if you absolutely must, but even the most peaked winter tomatoes work better.) With the fish, serve saffron rice and peas to absorb the sauce's lovely liquidity.

The dish is a nice visual foil for the white and red of the scrod Provençal, pleasing the eye as well as the palate.

To finish off a most satisfying meal, I offer one of the first desserts I ever learned to make. I was about twelve when I read this recipe in my school newspaper, and I determined to surprise my mother and prove to her that I could "cook." So deceptively easy is raspberry mousse to prepare, so pretty to behold, and so thoroughly satisfying that my mother promptly shelved her fundamental doubts about my culinary potential and confessed that maybe—just maybe—there was hope for me in the kitchen.

SCROD PROVENÇAL

SAUCE MAY BE PREPARED UP TO 48 HOURS IN ADVANCE;
FISH SHOULD BE PURCHASED FRESH THE DAY IT IS TO BE USED.

1 cup coarsely chopped onion
2 teaspoons minced garlic
¼ cup olive oil
¼ cup coarsely chopped mushrooms
¼ pound baked ham, finely chopped
5 medium-size tomatoes (about 2 pounds), peeled, seeded, and coarsely chopped
½ teaspoon rosemary, crushed
1 bay leaf
3 tablespoons pitted black olives, sliced (optional)
¼ teaspoon salt
Freshly ground black pepper
1 cup dry white wine
2½ to 3 pounds filleted and skinned cod or haddock

In a large skillet, over low heat, sauté the onion and garlic in the olive oil until wilted. Add the mushrooms and ham, and continue cooking until the mushrooms have exuded their juices. Add the tomatoes, rosemary, bay leaf, olive slices (if desired), salt, pepper, and wine, and bring to a boil over high heat. Reduce heat and simmer, uncovered, for 15 minutes. Cool. Remove the bay leaf and discard. If prepared more than 4 hours in advance, transfer to storage container and refrigerate until 1 hour before final preparation.

TIME ALLOWANCE FOR FINAL PREPARATION: 40 MINUTES.

Preheat the oven to 375 degrees.

Place half the sauce in the bottom of an 8-by-11-inch baking dish or its equivalent. Layer the fish fillets on top, overlapping if necessary. Spread the remaining sauce over the top. Bake 30 minutes or until the sauce is bubbling. Serve immediately.

SERVES 6.

SAFFRON RICE AND PEAS

MAY BE PARTIALLY PREPARED UP TO 36 HOURS IN ADVANCE.

2 tablespoons unsalted butter
½ cup finely chopped onion
1 cup rice
2 cups chicken stock, preferably homemade (page 286)
½ teaspoon salt
¼ teaspoon saffron
1 (10 ounce) package frozen baby peas, thawed; or 1½ cups fresh peas, parboiled until just tender

Preheat oven to 350 degrees.

In a flameproof casserole, melt the butter over low heat. Add the onion and sauté it until just wilted, about 5 minutes. Add the rice and stir to coat all the grains thoroughly with butter. Cook, stirring, 1 minute. Pour in the chicken stock. Add the salt and saffron and bring to a boil. Cover, immediately transfer to the oven, and bake 20 minutes.

Remove from the oven. (The rice will *not* be completely cooked.) Toss the rice, then add the peas. Cover and hold in a cool corner of the kitchen. (Refrigerate only if the dish is being held longer than 5 hours. Remove from the refrigerator and uncover 1 hour before final preparation.)

TIME ALLOWANCE FOR FINAL PREPARATION: 15 MINUTES.

Preheat the oven to 375 degrees.

Bake the rice and peas, covered, 10 minutes, tossing occasionally, or until they are steaming hot. Do not overcook or the peas will harden and lose their bright green color.

SERVES 6.

RASPBERRY MOUSSE

MAY BE PREPARED UP TO 48 HOURS IN ADVANCE.

¼ cup strained fresh lemon juice
1 package unflavored gelatin
2 (10-ounce) packages frozen raspberries, thawed
1 cup heavy cream, whipped

Pour the lemon juice into a small saucepan, and sprinkle the gelatin over it. When the gelatin has absorbed the liquid, place the pan over low heat and stir until the gelatin has dissolved.

Place one package of thawed raspberries (do not drain) in a medium-size mixing bowl. Add the gelatin, mixing well. Refrigerate until the berries and their juices have thickened, but do not permit them to become solid. The mixture should have the consistency of mayonnaise. If too solid, remove from the refrigerator and allow to warm, stirring until the desired consistency is achieved. Gently fold in the whipped cream, blending until no traces of white remain. Transfer to a 1-quart ring mold, cover with plastic wrap, and refrigerate until ready to serve. Hold the remaining package of raspberries in the refrigerator until ready to serve.

TIME ALLOWANCE FOR FINAL PREPARATION: 5 MINUTES.

Run a knife around the edges of the mold to loosen the mousse.

Set the mold in a bath of hot water for 1 to 2 minutes. Remove from the water and place a serving dish, upside down, on top of the mold. Turn the mold and dish over and give a firm shake; the mousse should slip out. (If not, repeat the procedure.) Fill the center of the mold with the remaining raspberries. To serve, cut the mousse in wedges and spoon the raspberries over the mousse.

SERVES 6.

A WARMING
VEAL STEW
FOR FOUR

Veal Stew with Port

Baby Red Potatoes with Parsley

*Green Bean and Beet Salad
with Creamy Basil Dressing*

Ice Cream

Super-Simple Fudgy Brownies

A few years ago, February found me briefly in England, where I had the luck to be visiting particularly hospitable friends in Kent. Their kitchen was a haven I still dream about and covet. Built on the foundations of an old mill, it has two walls of densely packed stone, and some of the mill's old timber beams are embedded in the ceiling. The hearth is mammoth, and in the chill of winter my hosts always keep a fire going. On the night of my visit they were serving a stew of venison that had been marinated and then cooked in a fine old port. The combination was truly inspired, the rich body of the port, with its fruity overtones, perfectly enhancing the flavor of the meat.

Although occasionally I am fortunate enough to come into possession of venison, I am afraid I do not have a constant supply. As a consequence, when I returned home, I determined to try the stew, substituting veal for venison. Judging from the smiles of pleasure on the faces of friends who have partaken of the dish with me, I think it is quite successful.

I like to serve small boiled potatoes, preferably the red-skinned variety, with the stew but cooked separately. And, since the stew is packed with sweet leeks, I think a vegetable salad such as green beans and beets with creamy basil dressing is quite satisfying.

For dessert, a good, creamy ice cream is perfect, especially if accompanied by chewy, moist brownies. The recipe I am giving here is my aunt's. She hated to cook but had two specialties: the best Toll House cookies I have ever eaten, and equally sensational brownies, which she managed to mix in one pot. (She didn't enjoy washing up, either.)

VEAL STEW WITH PORT

MAY BE PARTIALLY PREPARED UP TO 48 HOURS IN ADVANCE;
MUST BE PARTIALLY PREPARED AT LEAST 8 HOURS IN ADVANCE.

2 pounds boneless veal stew meat
1½ cups medium-dry port
6 large leeks, thoroughly cleaned, white parts only, roots trimmed
6 tablespoons unsalted butter
2 teaspoons minced garlic
1 tablespoon fresh thyme leaves (or 1 teaspoon dried)
3 tablespoons vegetable oil
½ cup flour
1 teaspoon salt
½ teaspoon freshly ground black pepper
1½ cups chicken stock, preferably homemade (page 286)
2 tablespoons minced fresh parsley

Remove and discard all fat and sinew from the veal. Cut the meat into ½-inch cubes. Place in medium-size mixing bowl and barely cover with port, using 1 to 1½ cups. Toss to coat all the veal thoroughly. Cover with plastic wrap and refrigerate undisturbed for 6 to 8 hours.

Place a sieve over another mixing bowl. Drain the veal into the sieve, catching and reserving the port in the bowl beneath. Place the veal on paper toweling and pat dry with more toweling.

Cut the leeks lengthwise in half, then again in quarters. Slice the quarters crosswise very thin. Melt 3 tablespoons of the butter in a large skillet, preferably one with high sides. Over moderately low heat, sauté the leeks and garlic in the butter until wilted, stirring occasionally, about 5 minutes. Sprinkle in the thyme, and toss to mix. Transfer to a 3-quart flameproof casserole.

Add the remaining 3 tablespoons butter and the oil to the skillet. Increase the heat to high. Meanwhile, in a medium-size paper bag, combine the flour, ½ teaspoon of the salt, and ¼ teaspoon of the pepper. Place a generous handful of the veal in the bag, close securely and shake vigorously. When the butter and oil are foaming, remove the flour-coated pieces of meat from the bag, shaking off any excess, and fry them until they are brown on all sides, tossing frequently. As they are done, transfer them with a slotted spoon to the casserole. Repeat until all the meat is floured and browned.

Discard any oil remaining in the skillet. Pour the reserved port into the pan and, over moderate heat, scrape up any particles left clinging to the bottom. Add the chicken stock and the remaining ½ teaspoon salt and ¼ teaspoon pepper. Bring to a boil. Pour the liquid over the leeks and veal. Mix thoroughly. Cool. Cover and hold, refrigerated, until 1 hour before final preparation. Bring to room temperature.

TIME ALLOWANCE FOR FINAL PREPARATION: 1¾ HOURS.

Preheat oven to 300 degrees.

Place the casserole on top of the stove and, over moderate heat, bring to a boil. Transfer to a rack in the middle of the oven and bake, covered, for 1½ hours. Sprinkle with parsley and serve immediately.

Reheating note: Stews benefit from holding; their flavors mellow particularly well if allowed to rest 24 to 48 hours before serving. Therefore, if you prefer to cook the stew completely ahead of time, it is fine to do so. Bake it the prescribed time, cool, and hold, refrigerated, until one hour before you plan to reheat it. Allow about 40 minutes in a 300-degree oven for it to become steaming hot.

SERVES 4.

BEAN AND BEET SALAD
WITH CREAMY BASIL DRESSING

SALAD MAY BE PARTIALLY PREPARED UP TO 4 HOURS IN ADVANCE;
DRESSING MAY BE PREPARED UP TO 48 HOURS IN ADVANCE.

SALAD

4 small beets, leaves trimmed and reserved for another use
1 pound green beans, ends trimmed
12 to 16 leaves Boston lettuce, washed and dried
½ yellow pepper, stem and seeds discarded
3 tablespoons minced red onion

Place the beets in salted water to cover in a small saucepan. Bring to a boil, lower the heat and gently cook until tender, about 30 minutes. (Test with the tip of a knife to make certain. Time depends on size and age of beets.) Drain and refresh under cold water. Trim root and stalk ends, and slip skins off. Cut into thin slices, and reserve in a small bowl, covered with plastic wrap, until time for final preparation.

Place the green beans in a steamer, and steam just until tender, about 5 to 8 minutes. Refresh under cold water, drain, and hold in a separate bowl, covered with plastic.

TIME ALLOWANCE FOR FINAL PREPARATION: 10 MINUTES.

On each of 4 salad plates, place 3 or 4 leaves of Boston lettuce. On each plate, over half the lettuce leaves, arrange the beans, side by side. Over the other half, spread out the sliced beets.

Cut the yellow pepper into julienne strips about ¼ inch by 1 inch. Sprinkle them evenly over the four salads. On top of the peppers, scatter the onion pieces. Give the dressing (below) a shake or two; then drizzle it over the vegetables.

SERVES 4.

CREAMY BASIL DRESSING

¼ cup packed fresh basil leaves
2 tablespoons white wine vinegar
¼ teaspoon sugar
½ teaspoon Dijon mustard
1 tablespoon mayonnaise
½ cup olive oil
Salt and freshly ground black pepper to taste

Place the basil leaves in the bowl of a food processor fitted with a steel blade. Whirl until finely minced. Add the vinegar, sugar, and mustard; whirl 2 seconds. Add the mayonnaise, and whirl until just blended. With the motor running, add the olive oil in a steady stream. Stop the motor, and taste and adjust the seasoning. Transfer to a jar equipped with a tight-fitting lid, and store in a cool section of the kitchen. Shake briefly before using.

SUPER-SIMPLE FUDGY BROWNIES

MAY BE PREPARED UP TO 24 HOURS BEFORE SERVING.

½ cup unsalted butter
2 ounces unsweetened chocolate
½ cup sugar
¾ cup firmly packed dark brown sugar
2 eggs
¼ teaspoon salt
½ cup flour
½ teaspoon baking soda
1 teaspoon vanilla
½ cup chopped walnuts or pecans

Preheat oven to 350 degrees. Generously grease an 8-inch-square baking pan.

Over very low heat, melt the butter and chocolate in a 1- to 2-quart saucepan. Stir occasionally, and guard against scorching. Add the white and brown sugars, and stir until dissolved. Remove the pan from the heat, and allow the mixture to cool. When the bottom of the saucepan is comfortable to the touch—it should not have been very hot at any time—beat in the eggs, one at a time, until they are thoroughly incorporated and the chocolate is shiny. Stir in the salt. Add the flour and baking soda, and stir until smooth. Add the vanilla and nuts, and mix thoroughly. With a rubber spatula, scrape the batter into the greased pan. Place in the center of the oven, and bake 30 minutes, or until a knife inserted in the center comes out clean. Be careful not to overbake, or the brownies will be dry.

Cool on a rack. While the brownies are still warm, cut them into squares, but leave them in the pan until thoroughly cooled. Serve with scoops of vanilla ice cream.

YIELD: SIXTEEN 2-INCH-SQUARE BROWNIES.

STUFFED PORK CHOPS FOR TWO

Cranberry-Stuffed Pork Chops

Italian Green Beans with Almonds

Baked Potatoes with Sour Cream

Spiced Oranges

My mother, a marvelous self-taught cook, always lectured me on the importance of bones in intensifying the flavor of meat. "Never bone a roast," she used to say, "unless it's for ease in carving. Don't filet a fish, either. You'll lose half its goodness."

She was right, of course; bones impart added flavor to meats, just as they do to soups. The point is illustrated by chops, those succulent nuggets of meat almost entirely surrounded by bone. Veal and lamb are the king and queen of chops, in terms of both taste and price, but pork chops are princely items, particularly when cut extra thick to allow for a "pocket" filled with stuffing. They make a good, hearty winter dish.

To accompany the chops, I suggest pretty, green green beans. Buy the larger Italian beans or pole beans; avoid the rather pitiful winter string beans. Whatever beans you buy, please don't gray them by overcooking.

For dessert, orange slices spiked with a spicy wine syrup add color and nutrition to the meal, rounding it off happily in a not-too-caloric fashion.

CRANBERRY-STUFFED PORK CHOPS

MAY BE PREPARED UP TO 8 HOURS IN ADVANCE.

2 large loin pork chops, 1 inch thick
⅓ cup fresh or frozen cranberries, coarsely chopped, plus 1 tablespoon sugar
   (if unavailable, substitute ¼ cup whole cranberry sauce)
¼ teaspoon crushed thyme
¼ teaspoon ground sage
½ teaspoon grated orange rind
1 tablespoon minced fresh parsley
2 tablespoons toasted bread crumbs
1 teaspoon thinly sliced scallions
¼ teaspoon salt
Freshly ground black pepper
½ teaspoon crushed rosemary

Have your butcher make a "pocket" along the loin side of each pork chop. (Or do this yourself by laying the pork chop flat and making a 4-inch incision halfway between the top and bottom of the chop along the side, piercing deep into the meat until the tip of the knife meets the bone.)

In a mixing bowl, combine the chopped cranberries and sugar (or cranberry sauce) with the thyme, sage, orange rind, parsley, bread crumbs, scallions, and salt. Toss until well combined. Spoon into the "pockets," and close the openings with skewers or thread. Wrap the chops in plastic or aluminum foil, and refrigerate until 1 hour before final preparation.

TIME ALLOWANCE FOR FINAL PREPARATION: 1 HOUR.

Preheat oven to 375 degrees. Preheat broiling unit if separate from the oven.

Rub both sides of the pork chops with pepper and crushed rosemary. Place in baking pan and bake 40 minutes without disturbing. The meat should be tender when pierced with the tip of a knife; if not, roast 5 minutes more. Brown in broiler for 5 minutes on each side. Remove thread or skewers, and serve immediately.

SERVES 2.

ITALIAN GREEN BEANS WITH ALMONDS

MAY BE PARTIALLY PREPARED UP TO 6 HOURS IN ADVANCE.

½ pound Italian green beans or Kentucky Wonder pole beans
½ teaspoon sugar
1 tablespoon unsalted butter
2 tablespoons slivered almonds
Salt and freshly ground black pepper to taste

Trim the ends of the green beans; then cut them crosswise in ½-inch pieces. Half fill a 1-quart stainless steel saucepan with water. Add the sugar, stir to dissolve, and then add the green beans. When the water returns to a boil, lower the heat to medium, and cook approximately 8 minutes, until the beans are just tender but still bright green. Drain immediately, and refresh under cold water to stop cooking. Reserve in a strainer placed over a bowl in a cool corner of the kitchen.

TIME ALLOWANCE FOR FINAL PREPARATION: 10 MINUTES.

In a 10-inch skillet, preferably with a nonstick surface, melt the butter over moderate heat. When it foams, drop in the almonds and sauté them, stirring occasionally, until they are tan and toasted. Add the cooked beans and toss to mix. Increasing the heat, cook, stirring frequently, for 3 to 5 minutes or until heated through. Taste and adjust seasonings.

SERVES 2.

SPICED ORANGES

MAY BE PREPARED 24 HOURS IN ADVANCE;
MUST BE PREPARED AT LEAST 4 HOURS BEFORE SERVING.

¾ cup sugar
¾ cup water
¾ cup dry white wine
2 cloves
1-inch section of cinnamon stick
2 slices lemon
½ teaspoon vanilla
3 large navel oranges, peeled and white pith removed, sliced thin

In a medium saucepan, combine the sugar and water over medium heat, and stir until the sugar has dissolved. Add the wine, cloves, cinnamon, and lemon slices. Boil over moderate heat for 10 to 15 minutes, until the syrup has been reduced by half. Remove from heat, and add vanilla.

Place the oranges in a heatproof serving bowl, and strain the syrup over them. Toss once or twice to make certain the syrup permeates the fruit. Cover loosely with plastic wrap, and refrigerate at least 4 hours. Serve chilled.

SERVES 2.

A CREAMY JULIENNE FOR FOUR

Creamed Julienne of Turkey and Ham

Thin Buttered Noodles

Sautéed Cucumbers

Cranberry Kisel

Myriads of new products appearing in the markets offer culinary opportunities not imagined before. One such product is the so-called "turkey cutlets"—actually presliced sections of breast meat—which afford the cook the use of turkey meat at a reasonable price without forcing a commitment to a whole bird or a large section. Like chicken breasts, turkey cutlets are extremely versatile and can often be substituted for far more costly veal. This menu combines turkey cutlets with baked ham. (Don't bake a whole ham yourself, though—go to the deli.) The meats are cut into thick julienned strips and combined in a flourless cream sauce. Together they provide an extremely pleasant and somewhat novel taste sensation in their coupling of delicate and smoky flavors.

With the turkey and ham, I suggest noodles to absorb the sauce, and sautéed cucumbers as a "different" vegetable. If your guests have never tried them before, this menu is the right moment, for they are the perfect crisp and toothsome foil to a moderately rich entree.

Cranberry kisel, a New England adaptation of a Russian pudding, presents a slightly tart finish to an unquestionably different meal.

CREAMED JULIENNE OF TURKEY AND HAM

MAY BE PREPARED UP TO 8 HOURS IN ADVANCE.

4 tablespoons unsalted butter
1½ pounds turkey cutlets, cut into ¼-inch strips
½ pound baked ham, cut into thick ¼-inch strips
½ pound mushrooms, stems trimmed, thinly sliced
1 tablespoon minced shallots
1 tablespoon Dijon-style mustard
1½ cups heavy cream

In a 12-inch skillet, melt 3 tablespoons of the butter over medium to high heat, taking care not to let it brown. Add the turkey strips and sauté them, stirring frequently, until all traces of pink have disappeared, about 5 minutes. Add the ham strips, distributing them evenly among the turkey, and sauté them a minute longer. With a slotted spoon, transfer the meat to a plate and reserve. When cool, cover with plastic wrap and refrigerate until 1 hour before final preparation.

To the juices remaining in the pan, add the final tablespoon of butter. Lower the heat and sauté the mushrooms and shallots until the mushrooms have exuded their juices. Mix in the mustard, blending well. Turn off the heat and reserve in the skillet, covering loosely with plastic or foil when cool. It is not necessary to refrigerate the mushrooms.

TIME ALLOWANCE FOR FINAL PREPARATION: 10 MINUTES.

Remove the wrap or foil from the skillet, and place the pan over high heat. Add the cream and allow it to cook for about 5 minutes, stirring frequently until it has thickened somewhat and been reduced by about one-third. Add the turkey and ham, toss well to coat in the cream, and continue cooking, stirring constantly, for 3 to 4 minutes, until the meat is heated thoroughly.

SERVES 4.

SAUTÉED CUCUMBERS

MAY BE PARTIALLY PREPARED UP TO 4 HOURS IN ADVANCE;
MUST BE PARTIALLY PREPARED AT LEAST ¾ HOUR IN ADVANCE.

3 to 4 cucumbers, about 2 pounds
1 tablespoon salt
2 tablespoons unsalted butter
Freshly ground black pepper
2 tablespoons minced fresh chives

Trim ends off cucumbers and peel. Cut lengthwise in half and, with a teaspoon, scrape out all the seeds. Cut cucumbers crosswise into 1½-inch lengths. Place in a colander, sprinkle with 1 tablespoon salt, toss well, and allow to drain at least ½ hour or until final preparation.

TIME ALLOWANCE FOR FINAL PREPARATION: 10 MINUTES.

Place cucumbers on paper toweling and pat completely dry with more toweling.
Melt butter in a large skillet over medium to high heat, taking care not to let it burn. Add the cucumber pieces. Cook, tossing frequently, for 3 to 5 minutes, or until they feel tender but not soft when pierced with the tip of a sharp knife. Their texture should be crisp. Season to taste with salt and pepper. Sprinkle with chives, toss again, and serve immediately.

SERVES 4.

CRANBERRY KISEL

MAY BE PREPARED UP TO 48 HOURS IN ADVANCE;
MUST BE PREPARED AT LEAST 2½ HOURS IN ADVANCE.

2 cups cranberries, picked over, bruised or rotten ones discarded
1½ cups plus 2 teaspoons water
½ cup sugar
1 tablespoon grated orange rind
2 teaspoons cornstarch
1 cup heavy cream, whipped (optional)

Place the cranberries and 1½ cups water in a stainless steel or enamel saucepan and bring to a boil. Lower heat and simmer until the berries are very soft, about 15 minutes.

Transfer contents of pan to a blender or a food processor fitted with a steel blade. Add the sugar and orange rind. Whirl until pureed. Strain through a sieve and return to the saucepan.

In a cup or small bowl, make a paste of the cornstarch and the remaining 2 teaspoons water, and add to the cranberry puree. Bring to a boil, lower heat, and simmer 2 to 3 minutes, stirring constantly, until the puree has thickened slightly. Pour into 4 dessert bowls and refrigerate, covered with plastic wrap, for at least 2 hours before serving. Serve plain or with dollops of whipped cream.

SERVES 4.

A CHEESE
LUNCHEON
FOR SIX

Welsh Rabbit on Horseback

Millionaire's Salad

*Pecan Ice Cream Balls with
Butterscotch Sauce**

"Welsh rabbit"—sometimes spelled "rarebit"—was a favorite of my mother's for many years. She loved parties and people, and one of my most vivid childhood memories was of mother's midnight returns from evenings out, with groups of friends she had enticed home for an impromptu supper. Nine times out of ten, she would reach into the "icebox" and come out with a generous hunk of good, aged cheddar cheese. In no time at all she managed to assuage her friends' hunger with a delectable rendition of Welsh rabbit.

This smooth blend of cheese, beer, and eggs is eaten by the English today most often as a "savory"—a small, appetite-stimulating course just before dessert. It originated, so the story goes, centuries ago when a poor Welsh hunter returned home rabbitless, and his wife improvised with a supper of melted cheese. The name was changed from "rabbit" to "rarebit" because some unnamed snob decided "rarebit" sounded more refined.

However you want to spell and/or pronounce it, I have adapted Welsh rabbit into a more substantial luncheon dish, served in all its tangy glory over crisp English muffins and briefly sautéed tomatoes. With it, I suggest a salad named, in fun, "millionaire's salad." It actually isn't very costly, because it requires only small amounts of costly ingredients, but their prices (particularly the radicchio, a bittersweet crimson-and-white lettuce that bears an uncanny resemblance—in appearance only—to red cabbage) seem staggering at first glance.

Dessert is a sweet tooth's dream: balls of ice cream coated with toasted pecans and bathed in a creamy butterscotch sauce. I suggest vanilla ice cream, but feel free to substitute any compatible flavor. No matter what you choose, it will be pure, calorie-filled bliss.

RABBIT ON HORSEBACK

MAY BE PARTIALLY PREPARED UP TO 6 HOURS IN ADVANCE.

6 tablespoons plus 6 teaspoons unsalted butter
½ teaspoon salt
½ teaspoon paprika
½ teaspoon dry English mustard
3 or 4 drops Tabasco
1 teaspoon Worcestershire sauce
¾ pound cheddar cheese, coarsely grated
¾ cup beer
1 egg, lightly beaten
1 teaspoon arrowroot or cornstarch
6 English muffins, split
12 tomato slices, ½ inch thick (3 or 4 large tomatoes)
2 tablespoons minced fresh parsley

Make the cheese rabbit by melting 2 tablespoons of the butter in the top of a double boiler, over moderate heat, and combining it with the salt, paprika, mustard, Tabasco, and Worcestershire. Stir until well blended; then add the cheese and stir occasionally until it is soft. Slowly add ½ cup of the beer, blending well after each addition. Add the beaten egg and the arrowroot to the remaining ¼ cup beer, and stir until smooth. Gradually beat the mixture into the cheese. Stir constantly until the rabbit has thickened and is smooth. Do not let it come close to a boil, or it may separate. If preparing well in advance, cover and remove from heat. Spread each English muffin with ½ teaspoon butter. Place on a cookie sheet and cover with plastic wrap.

TIME ALLOWANCE FOR FINAL PREPARATION: 10 MINUTES.

Preheat broiler, and arrange a rack 3 inches from the heat.

Place the double boiler with the rabbit in the top section over low heat and, stirring occasionally, reheat the cheese.

In a large (12-inch) skillet, preferably nonstick, melt the remaining 4 tablespoons butter. Add as many tomato slices as you can without overcrowding and, over moderate heat, fry 1 minute on each side. Repeat until all are done.

While the tomatoes are being fried, toast the English muffins in the broiler until just golden. Transfer 2 halves to each plate. Top each with a fried tomato slice. When the rabbit is hot, ladle 2 or 3 generous spoonfuls over each muffin half. Sprinkle with parsley and serve immediately.

SERVES 6.

MILLIONAIRE'S SALAD

MAY BE PARTIALLY PREPARED UP TO 3 HOURS IN ADVANCE.

SALAD
1 small head radicchio
6 small heads endive
1 bunch watercress, tough stems removed
½ green pepper, seeds removed, cut in julienne strips
⅓ English cucumber, unpeeled, sliced thin
2 hard-boiled eggs, mashed (page 46)
3 tablespoons minced scallions
4 ounces black lumpfish caviar

To make the salad: Separate the radicchio leaves, wash, and dry. Remove the outer leaves from the endive, and quarter each endive lengthwise. Line a salad bowl with paper toweling and group the radicchio, endive, watercress, and green pepper in it, unmixed. Refrigerate until ready to assemble. Also refrigerate, in separate containers, the sliced cucumber, eggs, scallions, and caviar, well covered.

DRESSING
1 teaspoon Dijon-style mustard
¼ teaspoon salt
Freshly ground black pepper
½ teaspoon basil
¼ cup red wine vinegar
½ cup olive oil

To make the dressing: In a small jar, combine the mustard, salt, pepper, basil, and red wine vinegar, and stir until the mustard and salt are dissolved. Add the oil, cover the jar tightly, and shake well. Set aside until final preparation.

TIME ALLOWANCE FOR FINAL PREPARATION: 10 MINUTES.

On 6 individual salad plates, arrange the radicchio, endive, watercress, and green pepper attractively. Place the cucumber slices on top. Spoon 1 heaping teaspoon caviar over each salad, sprinkling it around as evenly as possible. Sprinkle the mashed egg and scallions over the caviar. Shake the dressing well so that the oil and vinegar will combine, and drizzle 2 dessertspoonsful over each salad.

SERVES 6.

PECAN ICE CREAM BALLS
WITH BUTTERSCOTCH SAUCE

MAY BE PARTIALLY PREPARED UP TO 24 HOURS IN ADVANCE.

2 2½-ounce packages pecan pieces
1 quart vanilla ice cream
1 cup light cream
2 tablespoons unsalted butter
¾ cup firmly packed dark brown sugar
1 tablespoon light corn syrup
Pinch of salt

Preheat oven to 350 degrees.

Finely chop the pecan pieces. Toast them 4 to 5 minutes in the oven, stirring once or twice, until they are just a little darker. Cool.

While the nuts are toasting and cooling, remove the ice cream from the freezer, and allow it to soften slightly. When the nuts have returned to room temperature, spread them out on a pie plate or shallow dish. With an ice cream scoop, scoop a ball of ice cream. Drop it into the nuts, and roll it around quickly to coat it on all sides. Transfer the ball to a cookie sheet, preferably nonstick. Repeat until you feel you have enough ice cream balls for 6 people—or until you have finished the ice cream. (If your scoop is small, allow 2 scoops per person.) Work quickly so that the ice cream does not become too soft. Freeze the balls on the cookie sheet until hard. Transfer them to a plastic bag, and hold in the freezer until serving time.

Make the butterscotch sauce by combining, in a small saucepan, the cream, butter, brown sugar, and corn syrup. Place over low heat, and stir until sugar has dissolved and the butter melted. Continue to cook, stirring occasionally, until the sauce thickens and turns somewhat darker, about 20 minutes. Reserve the sauce in a jar, or in the same saucepan, until time for final preparation.

TIME ALLOWANCE FOR FINAL PREPARATION: 5 TO 10 MINUTES.

The butterscotch sauce may be served warm or at room temperature. If it is to be served warm, simply heat it up over low heat, stirring occasionally. Place the ice cream balls in a large serving bowl or in individual dessert dishes, and serve with the butterscotch sauce.

SERVES 6.

FLAKY FISH PIE
FOR SIX

Mandy Vine's Fish Pie

*Boiled Potatoes with
Parsley and Butter*

Zucchini and Avocado Salad

Praline Mocha Chiffon Pie

One spring I enjoyed a vacation in the Bahamas with my two sun- and water-oriented children. While there, I met a delightful young Englishwoman named Mandy Vine, and one sultry afternoon we started talking about food. As we bandied recipes back and forth, Mandy opted very generously to share with me one of her own favorite do-aheads, her fish pie. She didn't give me specifics, but what she told me was enough to keep the concept bubbling in my mind and fire me up to try to duplicate what she had described just as soon as I got home.

I have no idea whether Mandy Vine, now back at her home in Henley-on-Thames in England, would recognize my creation as her particular fish pie, although it includes all her components, but I must tell you that the six guests to whom I served it were delightfully enthusiastic. Contained in a free-form package of puff paste, the pie filling is a marvelous mix of smoked haddock (finnan haddie) and fresh haddock, mushrooms, onions, and red pepper, all bound together in a heady fish velouté. Coming to the table puffed and gloriously golden, it is every bit as impressive to behold as it is to consume. (For the nervous pastry novice, let me assure you it is not at all difficult to construct.)

With it I suggest serving a slightly different salad, a tempting combination of raw zucchini and avocado, dressed in a simple sauce of dill, sour cream, and yogurt, whose flavors actually improve with doing ahead. The dessert, praline mocha chiffon pie, is a superlative combination of fluff and crunch—but not so rich that your conscience will force you to refuse a second helping.

MANDY VINE'S FISH PIE

MAY BE PARTIALLY PREPARED UP TO 48 HOURS IN ADVANCE.

1½ pounds finnan haddie (smoked haddock)
1 pound skinned haddock fillets
1 small onion, peeled and cut in half
2 cups plus 1 tablespoon water
2 cups dry white wine
4 tablespoons unsalted butter
¾ cup thinly sliced onion (about 1 medium)
½ pound mushrooms, thinly sliced
1 small red pepper, cored and seeded, cut in ¼-inch dice
3 tablespoons flour
½ teaspoon salt
¼ teaspoon freshly ground white pepper
¼ cup minced fresh parsley
1 (17¼-ounce) package frozen puff pastry, thawed
2 eggs
¼ cup heavy cream
3 tablespoons minced fresh dill weed

Place the finnan haddie and haddock in a medium-size saucepan with the halved onion. Cover with 2 cups water and the dry white wine. Bring to a boil, lower heat, and simmer, partially covered, for about 10 minutes, until the fish is opaque and cooked through. Drain the fish, reserving the liquid. Shred the fish into bite-size pieces, discarding any bones, and transfer to a medium-size mixing bowl.

Melt 2 tablespoons of the butter in a 10- to 12-inch skillet. Over moderately low heat, sauté the sliced onion, mushrooms, and red pepper until just soft, about 5 minutes. Add to the flaked fish, and toss gently until mixed.

Bring 2½ cups of the reserved fish stock to a boil in a small saucepan. Meanwhile, melt the remaining 2 tablespoons butter in another saucepan. Add the flour and cook, stirring, over moderate heat for about a minute until a thick paste has formed. Gradually add 2 cups of the heated stock, stirring constantly until thickened. Season with salt and pepper. Pour 1 cup of the sauce over the fish mixture, add the minced parsley, and toss gently to bind the ingredients. (Add up to ¼ cup more sauce, if necessary.) If not proceeding immediately, cover with plastic wrap and refrigerate until 1 hour before final preparation.

To the sauce remaining in the saucepan, add ½ cup more heated fish stock and stir until blended. If not proceeding immediately, transfer to a bowl or jar, cover tightly and refrigerate until final preparation. (Any leftover stock may be discarded or saved for another use.)

TIME ALLOWANCE FOR FINAL PREPARATION: 1 HOUR.

Preheat oven to 400 degrees.

On a lightly floured surface, roll out the two sheets of puff pastry until they measure approximately 10 by 13 inches. (Roll one about 1 inch longer and wider than the other.) Reserve the pastry scraps. Transfer the smaller rectangle to a baking sheet or jelly roll pan. Mound the fish mixture on top of it, coming to within 1 inch of its edges. Moisten the edges with water; then lay the larger piece of pastry over the filling. Pinch the edges of both pieces together, sealing them tightly. Cut a round hole in the center of the top. Out of aluminum foil, fashion a chimney to fit and insert it in the hole. Cut one or two free-form fish out of the reserved pastry scraps. Moisten one side, and adhere them to the "pie" in a decorative manner.

In a small saucer, beat 1 egg with 1 tablespoon water until well blended. Brush the water over the surface of the pie. Transfer the pie, still on its baking sheet, to a rack positioned in the center of the oven. Bake 40 to 45 minutes, or until beautifully puffed and golden brown.

While the pie is baking, finish the sauce by reheating it in a saucepan over moderate heat. Add the remaining egg and beat well to break it up; then add the cream. Bring almost, but not quite, to a boil, stirring constantly. Add the dill weed, taste, and adjust the seasonings, and keep warm until ready to serve.

When the pie is done, carefully slip it off the baking sheet onto a preheated platter. Transfer the sauce to a serving bowl. The pie should be cut in thick slices and the sauce ladled over each slice.

SERVES 6.

ZUCCHINI AND AVOCADO SALAD

MAY BE PREPARED UP TO 24 HOURS IN ADVANCE;
MUST BE PREPARED AT LEAST 1 HOUR IN ADVANCE.

4 to 5 small zucchini, ends trimmed (2 to 2½ pounds)
1 tablespoon salt
⅓ cup thinly sliced red onion rings
½ cup plain yogurt
½ cup sour cream

2 tablespoons minced fresh dill weed
Salt and freshly ground black pepper to taste
1 large ripe avocado, peeled, stoned, and sliced

With a mandoline or by hand, cut the zucchini into paper-thin slices. As you finish cutting one, transfer the slices to a colander, and sprinkle with some of the salt. Repeat until all the zucchini are sliced and salted. Place the colander in the sink to drain, with a heavy weight on top. Allow to drain at least 30 minutes.

Transfer the zucchini to lengths of paper toweling, and cover with more to absorb any remaining moisture. Place in a salad bowl, add the onion rings, and toss gently to mix.

Make the dressing by combining the yogurt, sour cream, and dill weed. Stir to blend thoroughly. Spoon just enough over the zucchini to coat it. (Do not be too generous; the zucchini will continue to exude more moisture, and there will be more than enough dressing—somewhat thinner—to cover all the salad. Save any remaining dressing for another salad. It will hold, refrigerated, for at least 1 week.) Add the avocado slices and toss gently. Taste for and adjust seasoning. Cover with plastic wrap and refrigerate until serving time. Toss once or twice just before serving.

SERVES 6.

PRALINE MOCHA CHIFFON PIE

MAY BE PARTIALLY PREPARED UP TO 6 HOURS IN ADVANCE.

1 unbaked 9-inch pie shell
⅓ cup unsalted butter
½ cup firmly packed brown sugar
½ cup finely chopped pecans
1 package unflavored gelatin
¼ cup water
4 eggs, separated
⅓ cup unsweetened cocoa
1¼ cups sugar
¼ teaspoon salt
1 cup hot, strong coffee
½ cup cream
¼ cup shaved semisweet chocolate (optional)

Preheat oven to 425 degrees.

Prick the pie shell all over with the tines of a fork. Line the pie shell with aluminum foil, and weight it down with dried beans or uncooked rice. Bake 10 minutes.

Meanwhile, melt the butter and the brown sugar in a small saucepan, stirring until they are well blended, and cook until the mixture bubbles vigorously. Remove from heat, and stir in the pecans. Remove the weighted foil from the pie shell; spread the praline mixture evenly over the bottom of the lightly baked shell. Return the pie to the oven, and bake 5 minutes longer. Cool thoroughly.

Sprinkle the gelatin over the water to soften. Beat the egg yolks well. Combine the cocoa, ½ cup of the white sugar, and the salt in a small bowl, and add the hot coffee. Stir until the cocoa and sugar are dissolved. Pour into the beaten yolks, and mix well. Transfer the mixture to a 1-quart saucepan and, over moderate to low heat, cook the custard, stirring constantly, until it coats the back of a spoon. Remove from the heat, add the softened gelatin, stir to blend, then cool. Refrigerate, watching carefully, until the mixture thickens to the consistency of mayonnaise.

Meanwhile, beat the egg whites until foamy; then beat in ½ cup of the white sugar, 1 tablespoon at a time. Beat until stiff. Fold the thickened custard into the whites, blending only until all traces of white disappear. Pour the filling into the praline-lined pie shell, which should be cool; mound the filling into the center. Refrigerate until just before serving.

TIME ALLOWANCE FOR FINAL PREPARATION: 5 MINUTES.

Whip the cream until stiff, sweetening to taste with the remaining sugar. Swirl it attractively over the top of the mocha chiffon. Garnish with shaved chocolate if desired.

YIELD: ONE 9-INCH PIE.

DINNER FOR SIX: ONE POT SERVES ALL

Lentil-Sausage Stew

Royal Spinach Salad

French Bread

Sherry Cherry Jubilee*

Sometimes a busy cook needs a dish or two that are super do-aheads, to be made whenever there's free time—perhaps on the weekend—and reheated when needed. If the dish is something whose flavors intensify with holding, as in stew, so much the better.

This lentil-sausage stew will serve six generously. It might even satisfy eight healthy appetites, but I erred on the conservative side so that you could have some left over to serve another time. Or you might just want to divide the stew in half after it is done and freeze the remaining portion. Then again, you might want to double it and freeze several meals. Whatever, it is the kind of a stew in which the addition or deletion of a few ingredients doesn't make much difference. Take the basic recipe, and give rein to your imagination.

Like the stew, the rest of the menu is planned for six. The salad is a nice one, rather like a Caesar salad but with spinach. After the stew, the refreshing sherry cherry jubilee, light and fruity, seems just right. Both the stew and the dessert can be made well in advance, and both dishes should keep everybody happy.

LENTIL-SAUSAGE STEW

◆

MAY BE PREPARED UP TO 48 HOURS IN ADVANCE.

2 tablespoons unsalted butter
2 teaspoons cumin seed
1 cup coarsely chopped onions
1 cup coarsely chopped carrots
1 cup coarsely chopped celery
1 pound lentils, rinsed thoroughly
4 cups beef stock
28-ounce can whole, peeled tomatoes with their juices
1 teaspoon salt
¼ teaspoon freshly ground black pepper
2 tablespoons cider vinegar
1 pound cooked garlicky sausage, such as kielbasa or linguica, cut crosswise
  in ½-inch slices
1 12-ounce bag of baby carrots, peeled (or ¾ pound carrots, peeled and cut
  in half lengthwise and then crosswise into 1-inch pieces)
¼ cup minced scallions, including 2 inches of green leaves
¼ cup minced fresh parsley

In a 4-quart casserole or stainless steel pan with a tight-fitting lid, melt the butter over low to moderate heat. Add the cumin seeds and sauté briefly. Add the onions, carrots, and celery. Sauté, stirring occasionally, until the onions and celery have wilted, about 10 minutes. Toss in the lentils, beef stock, tomatoes, salt, pepper, and vinegar. Stir until well mixed, breaking up the tomatoes in the process.

Increase the heat. When the liquid is boiling, cover the pot, lower the heat, and simmer gently for 45 minutes, stirring once or twice. Add the sausage and the baby carrots (and up to 1 cup water if you think the stew is too dry). Bring the liquid to a boil again, lower the heat, cover and simmer 30 minutes, or until the carrots are tender.

The stew may be served at this point, garnished with the scallions and parsley, but its flavors develop if it is allowed to rest—the longer, the tastier, up to 48 hours—in the refrigerator, tightly covered. Bring it to room temperature 1 hour before final preparation.

TIME ALLOWANCE FOR FINAL PREPARATION: 30 MINUTES.

Stir the stew a few times. If it seems too dry, add a bit of stock or water, but remember that you do not want it runny, like a soup. It will become slightly more liquid as it is heated.

Heat it, covered, over low heat, stirring ocassionally, until it is just below the boiling point. Serve direct from the casserole or from a large heated bowl, sprinkling its surface with the scallions and parsley.

SERVES 6.

ROYAL SPINACH SALAD

DRESSING MAY BE PREPARED UP TO 24 HOURS IN ADVANCE;
SALAD SHOULD BE PREPARED 1 TO 2 HOURS IN ADVANCE.

DRESSING
1 egg
¼ cup olive oil
¼ cup vegetable oil
2 tablespoons strained fresh lemon juice
1 teaspoon Worcestershire sauce
½ teaspoon salt
Freshly ground black pepper
1 teaspoon minced garlic
2 tablespoons thinly sliced scallions, white parts only

To make the dressing: Drop the egg into a small mixing bowl. With a whisk, beat it well. Slowly whisk in the oils and lemon juice. The mixture will thicken somewhat. Add the Worcestershire sauce, salt, and pepper, and blend. Finally add the garlic and scallions. Transfer the dressing to a jar with a tight-fitting lid. Close and shake vigorously for a few seconds. Refrigerate until ready to use.

SALAD
10 ounces fresh spinach, unwashed
½ pound mushrooms, sliced
1 cup unseasoned croutons, preferably homemade
¼ cup freshly grated Parmesan cheese
1 ripe advocado, peeled, pitted, and sliced

To make the salad: Line a salad bowl with paper toweling. Tear off the tough stems from the spinach, and tear any very large leaves into smaller pieces. Sprinkle the mushrooms and croutons on top. Cover loosely with a kitchen towel, and refrigerate to crisp until just before final preparation.

TIME ALLOWANCE FOR FINAL PREPARATION: 5 MINUTES.

Remove the paper toweling and kitchen towel from the salad bowl. Give the dressing a few vigorous shakes. Pour over the salad, and toss to coat the leaves. Add the Parmesan cheese; toss again. Add half the avocado slices, and gently mix into the rest of the salad. Garnish the surface of the salad with the remaining avocado.

SERVES 6.

SHERRY CHERRY JUBILEE

◆

MAY BE PREPARED UP TO 48 HOURS IN ADVANCE;
MUST BE PREPARED AT LEAST 6 HOURS IN ADVANCE.

17-ounce can pitted dark sweet cherries
2 cups strained fresh orange juice
1 tablespoon grated orange rind
1 cup sugar
2 packages unflavored gelatin
1 cup plus 1 tablespoon dry sherry
1 cup heavy cream, whipped

Drain the juice from the can of cherries into a 2-quart saucepan. Reserve the cherries. Add the orange juice, rind, and sugar to the cherry juice. Over moderate heat, bring the mixture to a boil, stirring until the sugar is dissolved. Remove from heat.

Meanwhile, sprinkle the gelatin over 1 cup sherry to soften; then add it to the hot syrup. Stir until the gelatin has completely dissolved. Set the mixture aside to cool; then pour it into a 6-cup mold or dessert bowl and refrigerate. When the syrup begins to set but is not yet firm, fold in the reserved cherries, distributing them evenly under the surface of the jell. Refrigerate until firm. If preparing far in advance, cover tightly with plastic wrap.

TIME ALLOWANCE FOR FINAL PREPARATION: 10 MINUTES.

If you have molded the jubilee, run a knife around the edges of the mold to loosen it.

Set the mold in a bath of hot water for 1 to 2 minutes. Remove from the water and place a serving dish, upside down, on top of the mold. Turn the mold and dish over and give a firm shake, and the jubilee should slip out. (If it doesn't, repeat the procedure.)

Serve the jubilee either unmolded or direct from the dessert bowl accompanied by generous dollops of whipped cream.

SERVES 6.

AN ADULT BIRTHDAY PARTY FOR TEN

Oysters on the Half Shell with Ginger Shavings

Roast Filet Mignon with Béarnaise Sauce

Sautéed Potato Balls

Boiled Broccoli Flowerets with Brown Butter

Chocolate Raspberry Roll

Every once in a while comes a time when we are required to give a really smashing birthday party for someone important in our lives. It is something of a challenge to present a sumptuous meal and still be a part of the festivities.

A few years ago, my family gave a gala dinner to celebrate my mother-in-law's eightieth birthday. We gathered together as many of her family as could come to Boston, and I spent several nervous weeks pondering—and discarding—menus that did not obey Malabar's Law: "The hostess shall be with the party and not in the kitchen." I finally settled on the menu I am presenting here, having decided to go for broke and hang the expense. (Actually, it turned out not to be too costly; filet mignon goes farther than many other meats.) After all, it was a very special occasion, and I wanted the food to match the moment.

For entertaining, this menu is superbly simple. A roast is a roast is a roast, and, provided one doesn't forget and overcook it, it can't be destroyed. Potato balls are equally effortless, as is the broccoli. Serve the oysters, garnished with shreds of fresh gingerroot, while the filet is in the oven. And when the chocolate raspberry roll comes in, stick a candle in it (if you like), sit back, grin like a Cheshire cat, and wait for the raves.

Our evening was a tremendous success—except for one horrendous gaffe. I had been so concerned about the proper seating for my mother-in-law's family around the table that I totally forgot to set a place for her!

OYSTERS ON THE HALF SHELL WITH GINGER SHAVINGS

MUST BE ASSEMBLED JUST BEFORE SERVING.

1-inch section of thick gingerroot, peeled
5 dozen fresh oysters, unopened
Juice of 1 or 2 limes

Slice the peeled gingerroot as thinly as possible; then cut into matchstick-shaped pieces, again as thin as possible. It should yield 2 to 3 teaspoons. The gingerroot may be sliced in advance and refrigerated until time to assemble.

Just before serving, open the oysters and arrange them, on the half shell, on serving plates, allowing 6 oysters per person. Spoon a little of the ginger atop each oyster. Since fresh gingerroot is so pungent, ¼ teaspoon will be enough for 6 oysters. Sprinkle with lime juice and serve.

SERVES 10.

ROAST FILET MIGNON WITH BÉARNAISE SAUCE

SAUCE MAY BE PREPARED 2 TO 3 HOURS IN ADVANCE;
ROAST MAY BE PARTIALLY PREPARED UP TO 4 HOURS IN ADVANCE.

6- to 7-pound filet of beef, trimmed (roasting weight: 5 pounds)
Salt and freshly ground black pepper
4 or 5 large mushrooms
Watercress

For 10 people you will need a large filet, one that weighs at least 6 or 7 pounds before trimming. Have your butcher trim it well, cover the top with a thin layer of suet, and tie it down at 2-inch intervals. Sprinkle it lightly with salt and pepper. Remove the stems from the mushrooms and skewer them decoratively at even intervals on the top of the filet. Cover loosely with plastic wrap, and refrigerate until 1 hour before final preparation.

TIME ALLOWANCE FOR FINAL PREPARATION: 40 MINUTES.

Preheat oven to 450 degrees.

Remove the plastic wrap from the filet, and transfer the meat to a roasting pan. Roast it on a rack in the middle of the oven for 25 minutes. Place it on a heated platter, and let it stand for 10 minutes before carving. Garnish the platter with small bunches of watercress. This will produce a rare filet of beef. Cook it 5 minutes longer for medium.

BÉARNAISE SAUCE
2 tablespoons minced shallots
1 teaspoon dried tarragon leaves
⅓ cup tarragon vinegar
3 egg yolks
1 cup unsalted butter, melted and cooled
Salt and freshly ground black pepper to taste

Place the shallots, tarragon, and tarragon vinegar in a 1-quart saucepan. Over moderate heat, cook the mixture until the shallots and tarragon are soft and the liquid has almost completely evaporated. (The herbs should look wet, not dry.) Add the egg yolks, reduce the heat to very low, and whisk vigorously until the yolks start to thicken. Start adding the melted butter, drop by drop, checking the heat of the pan constantly. If the bottom of the pan is too hot to touch, remove it from the heat until it cools, but continue whisking and adding the butter as you do so. When you can touch the bottom of the pan with your hand, return it to the lowest possible heat. Keep whisking in the butter, drop by drop, until all is incorporated and the sauce has thickened to the consistency of mayonnaise. If the sauce should separate because it has become too hot, remove the pan from the heat, add an ice cube, and beat until the sauce has come together again—although it will be slightly thinner. Taste and adjust for seasoning.

Some people prefer béarnaise smooth and free of herbs. If you like it this way, simply strain it after the sauce has thickened, pressing down to extract all the herbal juices.

Leave the sauce in the pan in a warm section of the kitchen, partly covered. (Even better, hold it in a Thermos.) Just before serving, stir the sauce a few times. Do not reheat it. Transfer to a sauceboat, and serve with the filet.

SERVES 10.

SAUTÉED POTATO BALLS

MAY BE PARTIALLY PREPARED UP TO 12 HOURS IN ADVANCE.

10 large potatoes (4 to 5 pounds), peeled
½ cup unsalted butter
Salt and freshly ground black pepper to taste
2 tablespoons minced fresh parsley

With a melon baller, cut rounds out of the potatoes. They don't have to be perfect spheres, but try to shape them as neatly as possible. There will be quite a bit of potato trimmings left over; save them for mashed potatoes.

Drop the balls into a large saucepan of salted water, bring to a boil, and boil 5 minutes. Immediately drain and refresh the potatoes by filling the saucepan with cold water. Reserve them in cold water until time for final preparation.

Clarify the butter by melting it in a small saucepan over low heat. When it is completely melted, spoon off the white foam that has risen to its surface. Carefully pour all the remaining butter—except the milky residue in the bottom of the pan, which should be discarded—into a 12-inch skillet. Reserve until time for final preparation.

TIME ALLOWANCE FOR FINAL PREPARATION: 20 MINUTES.

Drain the potato balls, and pat them dry with paper toweling. Heat the clarified butter. Add the potatoes and sauté over high heat, shaking the pan every few minutes, until they are golden brown on all sides. Sprinkle with a little salt and pepper and the minced parsley.

SERVES 10.

CHOCOLATE RASPBERRY ROLL

MUST BE PREPARED 3 TO 4 HOURS IN ADVANCE.

8 ounces semisweet chocolate morsels
¼ plus 2 tablespoons raspberry-flavored liqueur, such as Framboise
7 eggs, separated, at room temperature
¾ cup plus 2 tablespoons sugar
Pinch of salt
½ cup unsweetened cocoa

½ cup seedless raspberry preserves or jelly, melted
1½ cups heavy cream
3 tablespoons coarsely grated semisweet chocolate

Preheat oven to 350 degrees.

Prepare a 10-by-15-inch jelly roll pan by greasing its bottom and sides liberally with softened butter. Cut a piece of wax paper a few inches longer than the pan and narrow enough to fit compactly on its bottom. Place it in the pan, letting a couple of inches stick out either end to act as handles. Butter it well, and set aside.

Place the chocolate morsels in the top of a double boiler with ¼ cup raspberry-flavored liqueur. Over low heat, melt the chocolate. Meanwhile, beat the egg yolks until creamy. Gradually add ¾ cup sugar, and continue beating until the mixture is thick and lemon-colored. Scrape the melted chocolate into the egg mixture, and stir until blended. In another bowl, beat the egg whites with a pinch of salt until stiff but not dry. Add one-third of them to the chocolate mixture to lighten it; then fold it into the whites carefully until no white remains visible. Turn the batter into the jelly roll pan, spreading it out evenly to all the corners. Bake 15 minutes, or until there is slight resistance when the surface is gently prodded with a finger. Turn off the oven, and let the cake remain inside 5 minutes. Remove it from the oven, set it on a rack to cool, and cover it with a damp kitchen towel. When steam is no longer rising from the towel, it has cooled to room temperture, and you may proceed.

Sift a thin layer of cocoa over a piece of wax paper slightly larger than the jelly roll pan. Turn the cake, still in its pan, over on the wax paper. Lift off the pan, and carefully peel off the wax paper with the "handles." With a brush, coat the surface of the cake with the melted seedless raspberry preserves or jelly.

Whip the cream with the remaining 2 tablespoons sugar until it is of spreading consistency. Beat in the remaining 2 tablespoons raspberry-flavored liqueur. Spread all but one-third of the cream over the roll, smoothing it out to within an inch of its edges. Using the wax paper underneath as a guide, roll the cake lengthwise like a jelly roll and slide it, seam side down, onto a board or platter to fit. Spread the remaining cream over its surface, swirling it decoratively. (This will disguise any cracks or crevices.) Do not be afraid to mold the roll with your hands into a more attractive shape if it has slumped somewhat. Sprinkle the surface with the grated chocolate. Refrigerate at least 3 hours before serving.

SERVES 10.

SATISFYING SEAFOOD GUMBO FOR SIX

New Orleans Seafood Gumbo

Hearty Oatmeal Bread

Watercress and Grapefruit Salad with Poppy Seed Dressing

Baked Chocolate Pudding

New Orleans seafood gumbo is technically a soup, I suppose, but it comes very close to being a stew. It is a filling, hearty blend of crunchy vegetables, bright red tomatoes, pods of okra, rice, crabmeat, and shrimp in a bath of chicken stock, which acts more as a moisturizing agent than as a soup base. For a light supper, or as noontime protection from winter's freezing blasts, this particular soup/stew can't be beat.

Since the gumbo is so satisfyingly filling, all that needs to be served with it is a dense hearty oatmeal bread. I prefer to offer it toasted, slathered in butter, but you might like to serve it just slightly warm, reheated briefly in the oven. A light, fruited salad bathed in a vinaigrette with a hint of sugar rounds things off nicely.

For dessert, I suggest a baked chocolate pudding that, although it doesn't puff, bears a textural resemblance to a soufflé. With a food processor or blender, it's simple to make. Serve it warm just out of the oven if you can time things right, but don't despair if you can't—it's just as good at room temperature. Offer it with mounds of whipped cream, and I doubt you'll have any left over to snack on the next day.

TIME ALLOWANCE FOR FINAL PREPARATION: 25 MINUTES.

To reheat the bread: Preheat oven to 325 degrees.

Remove wrap from bread and warm in the oven for 15 minutes (20 if the bread has been refrigerated).

The bread may also be served sliced and toasted. Serve accompanied by unsalted whipped butter.

YIELD: 2 LOAVES 7 INCHES IN DIAMETER.

BAKED CHOCOLATE PUDDING

◆

MAY BE PREPARED UP TO 12 HOURS IN ADVANCE.

8 ounces semisweet chocolate morsels
2 cups light cream, scalded
¼ cup sugar
4 eggs
Pinch of salt
1 teaspoon vanilla
¼ cup chocolate syrup (optional)
1 cup heavy cream, whipped or plain

Preheat the oven to 325 degrees.

Place the chocolate morsels in a blender or in the bowl of a food processor fitted with a steel blade. Pour in the scalded cream, and whirl until smooth, scraping down the sides if necessary. With the machine still going, add the sugar through the feed tube, and then the eggs one at a time. Whirl until the sugar has dissolved and the mixture is smooth and shiny. Add the salt and vanilla. Whirl to mix.

Pour the mixture into a 1-quart soufflé or baking dish. For a decorative design, pour a thin stream of chocolate syrup onto the surface of the pudding, starting at the center and spiraling outward toward the dish's rim. (Although it contributes little to the flavor of the pudding, it makes an attractive presentation.) Bake 60 to 70 minutes, or until the top of the pudding is firm and springy to the touch. Serve hot or at room temperature, accompanied by a pitcher of heavy cream or a bowl of whipped cream.

SERVES 6.

LABOR-SAVING DINNER FOR TWELVE

All-in-One Chicken

Kneadless Rye Bread

Mixed Green Salad with Vinaigrette Dressing*

Walnut-Apricot Roll

Here is a chicken dish, marvelously economical and easy to prepare, that can be served year round, although it is particularly satisfying, with its pungent built-in gravy, on a winter's night.

Placed in a very hot oven an hour before dinner, all-in-one chicken requires only small intervals away from guests for basting and turning. Considering the number of self-contained vegetables the dish contains, it really does not even require a salad, although simple mixed greens, tossed with a vinaigrette dressing, make a delightful palate-cleanser between entree and dessert. Homemade, well-warmed rye bread is a gratifying tool for soaking up the chicken's juices, but, if you're pressed for time, crisp, hot French bread is a fine substitute. (A bonus: if any chicken is left over, strip the meat from the bones, discard the bones and skin, and cut the carrots and potatoes into smaller pieces. Voilà: You have a wonderful, hearty soup, to be reheated for another meal.)

The walnut-apricot roll is as wickedly rich as the chicken dish is simple and pure. Both harmonize beautifully—and neither requires any last-minute labor. Despite the number of guests, the meal can be relaxing for everyone.

TIME ALLOWANCE FOR FINAL PREPARATION: 25 MINUTES.

Preheat oven to 325 degrees.

Remove wrap from bread and warm in the oven for 15 minutes, or 20 if the bread has been refrigerated. Bring to the table on a bread board, steaming hot, accompanied by lots of sweet butter.

YIELD: 1 LOAF ABOUT 8 INCHES IN DIAMETER.

WALNUT APRICOT ROLL

MAY BE PARTIALLY PREPARED UP TO 10 HOURS IN ADVANCE;
MAY BE COMPLETED UP TO 4 HOURS IN ADVANCE.

¾ cup dried apricots
½ cup apricot preserves
½ cup sugar
6 eggs, separated
1 cup firmly packed dark brown sugar
8 ounces walnut pieces (about 1¾ cups), ground fine
1 teaspoon baking powder
Confectioners' sugar
1½ cups heavy cream, whipped

Preheat oven to 350 degrees.

In a small saucepan, simmer the apricots in water to cover for 20 minutes or until tender. Drain, reserving juices. Place apricots in a blender or a food processor fitted with a steel blade. Add apricot preserves and white sugar. Whirl 2 to 3 minutes, adding apricot juice if mixture seems too thick, until puree is smooth and sugar has dissolved. Set aside.

In a medium-size mixing bowl, beat the egg yolks with the brown sugar until double in volume and light in color. Beat in 1½ cups of the ground walnuts, reserving the rest for garnish, and the baking powder. In another bowl, beat the egg whites until stiff. Spoon one-third of the whites into the nut batter, and blend to lighten. Gently fold in the remaining whites. Pour the batter into a 10-by-15-inch jelly roll pan that has been buttered, lined with wax paper cut to fit, and buttered again. Bake 20 minutes.

Remove the cake from the oven, cover it with a dampened dish towel, and set it on a rack to cool for 15 minutes. Remove the towel.

Cut off a piece of wax paper 20 inches long. Sift a light dusting of confectioners' sugar evenly over the wax paper. Turn the cake out of the pan upside down onto the sugared paper. Carefully roll the cake up lengthwise sandwiched between the two wax papers. Cover completely with a dampened towel. Set aside until ready to complete the roll. It is not necessary to refrigerate it.

TIME ALLOWANCE FOR FINAL PREPARATION: 10 MINUTES.

Remove the towel from the cake and gently unroll it. Carefully peel off the top piece of wax paper. Spread the surface of the cake with the pureed apricots, then top with two-thirds of the whipped cream, spreading it only to within one inch of the cake's edges. Using the bottom piece of wax paper as a guide, gently reroll the cake lengthwise, jelly roll fashion. Transfer it to a serving dish, seam side down. Do not be concerned if the cake cracks; mold it together with your hands, pressing it into shape. Spread the remaining whipped cream over the top and sides, and sprinkle with the reserved ground walnuts. Refrigerate until ready to serve.

The roll will hold, refrigerated, for 4 hours. It is not advisable to complete it any earlier before serving time.

SERVES 12.

TIME TO TRY
VEAL KIDNEYS
AT DINNER
FOR TWO

Veal Kidneys in Wine Sauce

Brown Rice Pilaf

*Snow Pea Salad with
Mustard Dressing*

Bananas Foster

There's no doubt that kidneys are an acquired taste, along with—for most people—liver, tripe, sweetbreads, or brains. But once you like kidneys, you'll find them hard to resist.

Now, there are kidneys and kidneys. The best are from calves, or veal, as calf is known in food vernacular. (Why do we say "veal kidneys" and "calves' liver"? It's a whim of the English language I've never understood.) In addition to veal kidneys, there are beef, lamb, and pork kidneys, but they are all stronger in flavor because of the increased age of the animals, and not half so delectable. Like all organ meats, kidneys should be eaten as soon as possible after slaughter and ideally should not be frozen. Of course, there are only two kidneys per animal, so more often than not what we receive at the market or eat in a restaurant has been frozen. Moreover, I must confess that, when I notice a supermarket having a veal sale, I rush in and scoop up all the veal kidneys I can find and freeze them immediately, breaking my fundamental rule, simply because they are scarce and my family adores them. We use them up pretty fast, and today's recipe is our favorite.

Rice is a natural with kidneys. It absorbs the wonderful sauce like a sponge. I particularly like brown rice for its flavor and texture, to say nothing of its superior nutritional value. It does take longer to cook than white rice, and sometimes one variety takes longer than another. Give yourself some latitude, and don't decide the rice is done simply because the prescribed cooking time is up. Taste a kernel or two, and use your own judgment.

Bless our greengrocers for putting snow peas on their shelves year round these days. With proper cooking—not more than blanched—they always taste crunchy and look so pretty. Today's salad is a different and colorful one, and, in the depths of winter, reminds us of bright things budding ahead.

Bananas Foster, an old New Orleans treat, is a dramatic finale to an intimate dinner, especially if prepared flaming at the table. A seemingly simple combination of vanilla ice cream and bananas mellowed in rum and brown sugar, it's a dessert that's hard to beat.

VEAL KIDNEYS IN WINE SAUCE

MUST BE PARTIALLY PREPARED 1½ HOURS IN ADVANCE.

1 pound veal kidneys
2 teaspoons strained fresh lemon juice
3 tablespoons unsalted butter
3 tablespoons minced shallots
½ pound mushrooms, trimmed, left whole if small (or halved or quartered,
*   depending on size)*
2 teaspoons Dijon-style mustard
¼ cup dry red wine
2 tablespoons minced fresh parsley

To be at their best, veal kidneys must be as fresh as possible. Moreover, they can be ruined by overcooking. When prepared properly, they should be a delicate gray-brown on the outside and nicely pink inside.

Slice the kidneys crosswise into 1-inch pieces. With a sharp knife, cut quarter-size chunks of the kidney meat away from the white core, discarding the core as you progress. Drop the kidney pieces into a bowl of water acidulated with the lemon juice, and allow to soak for 1 hour. Drain in a sieve at least 10 minutes; then spread the kidneys out on paper toweling to eliminate any hint of moisture.

TIME ALLOWANCE FOR FINAL PREPARATION: 20 MINUTES.

In a 12-inch skillet, melt the butter over low heat. Add the shallots and cook them, stirring occasionally, until slightly wilted. Increase the heat to moderate and toss in the mushrooms. Shaking the pan, sauté them until they just start to soften, about 5 minutes. Add the kidneys and, stirring constantly, sauté just until all traces of pink disappear, about 3 minutes. Add the mustard, stir to blend, and cook 1 minute longer. Increase the heat to high, pour in the wine, and stir until assimilated.

Holding the skillet by its handle, tip the pan to about a 30-degree angle. Push the

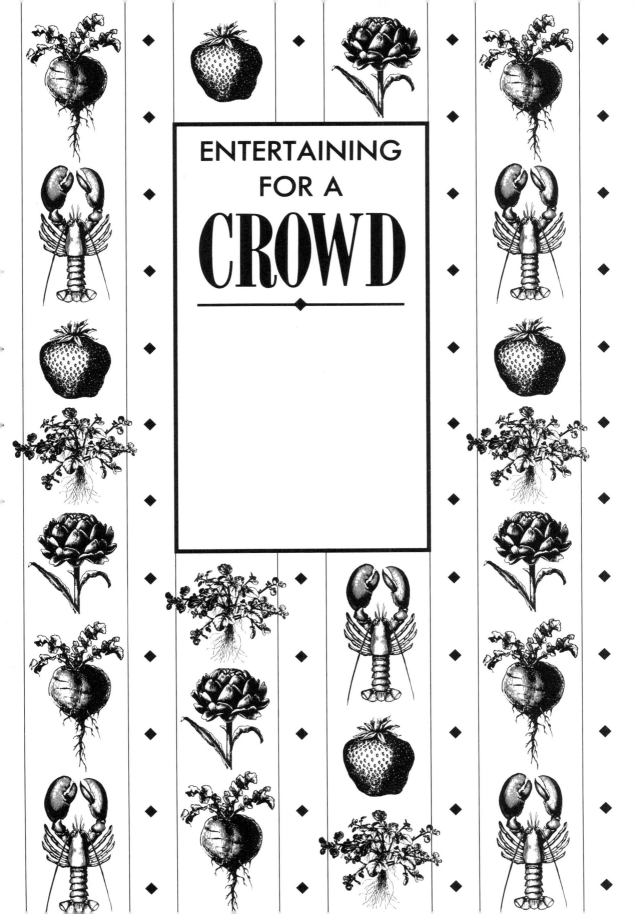

ENTERTAINING
FOR A
CROWD

Entertaining a large group presents a whole new set of logistics problems, whether that entertainment takes the form of a buffet dinner, a cocktail party, or an all-day "at home."

The most important thing to consider is size. You must evaluate the area where you plan to do the entertaining in terms of the number of people you would like to include. Do not decide to pay back all your social obligations of the last ten years in a studio apartment that measures twenty by fifteen feet. Your guests would feel like sardines. Your party is a reflection of yourself and your family and your life style. You want the event to be remembered in glowing terms.

If you are socially in debt to many people and your quarters are minimal, plan several smaller parties. My mother, for example, was a splendid hostess living in a small apartment in New York. When she entertained, being a very practical person, she would give three consecutive parties, all within a week. (Usually it was one every other night, the evenings in between being used to catch her breath.) That way, she explained, the silver had to be polished only once, the "good" china needed to be retrieved from the highest shelves in her kitchen only once, and the mass of flowers with which she decorated the living and dining rooms generally stayed pretty fresh, with only a few additions and deletions. The savings in effort and money were considerable.

Freedom of circulation is very important at a party. People packed too densely simply can't move either to get more food and drink, or to sashay over to an amiable-looking stranger or join an old friend. And too many people in a given area makes for too much noise. There is nothing worse than being forced to scream at your partner in order to make yourself heard.

So plan your space. Eliminate furniture where you can, or move it to improve traffic flow. Decide which rooms you will use and how many people would be able to fit comfortably in them at the height of the party. Locate your bar (or bars, if it's really a large party) where your guests will easily be able to get to them—and, more important, away from them. Position your food at one central spot, with a few food "satellites" scattered in other locations. Distribute bowls of nibbles, such as nuts or olives, around the rooms on small tables.

Carefully plan where you'll send people to leave their coats or umbrellas. (It can rain or snow, and the host must be prepared for all contingencies.) If necessary, rent a coat rack and, if possible, place it in a vestibule or lobby where the guests can dispose of their gear before entering your party. (This is not always feasible, to be sure, but it certainly helps.) A clean, presentable garbage can can be a handy receptacle for wet umbrellas and their puddles.

Make certain you have a good supply of paper napkins, cocktail or others. I once gave a large cocktail party and totally forgot them. One hundred pairs of crumb- and butter-laden hands and fingers, to say nothing of profusely sweating glasses—what a disaster.

Similarly, there are certain basic rules to follow when you are giving a large buffet dinner, if the size of your home or the scope of your furnishings precludes seating the guests at tables. It doesn't matter whether you're feeding ten or a hundred: If your guests are going to have to balance their plates on their laps or on small tables, or even trickier, eat while standing, then remember that *all food must be fork-manageable*. Do not even offer knives. Offer rolls or bread already buttered. If the entree is going to be meat in one form or another, make sure it is presented in bite-size pieces, as in a stew or a stroganoff—or that it is soft enough to cut easily with the side of a fork, like fish (no bones, please), hamburger, or lasagne. Forget spaghetti; eating it neatly even at a table is something of an art. Similarly, vegetables should be fork-easy—no asparagus or the like. If you are serving a salad, don't get carried away by large, artistically arranged leaves. Make certain they are cut up into bite-size pieces, not left whole.

Hire help if need be. Generally, at large events you can do with several extra hands. After all, if you are entertaining a goodly number, your costs are going to be high anyway. Spend a little more, and you and your guests will have better service and more fun.

As for plates and glasses, try to use your own or rent some. Think of plastic as a last resort. If I am serving good food and drink, I believe the implements should complement them. A lovely platter, a nice glass—they all contribute to the party's ambiance.

Keep flowers to a minimum at large events. Only the first guests really notice them. Then the rooms become too full of people for anybody to observe that nice spray of dogwood or quince blossoms in the corner. A low bouquet on the buffet table might be appropriate, but only if it does not usurp too much space. Similarly, forget about the romantic light of candles. Large parties need good lighting, and candles just don't fit the bill. Furthermore, they tend to smoke, and in a crowd they are something of a fire hazard. Too many people and a candle knocked over, and it just might be your last party.

The final key to success in giving a large party is paying strict attention to your guest list. If you assemble a group of twenty, make certain that each guest knows at least two others; thirty, three others; forty, four others. That way you'll have a good party. Each guest, seeing a familiar face or two or three across the room, immediately feels more at ease and confident. Recognizable faces are like security blankets—they comfort. Entertaining for a crowd is a lot of work, there's no doubt. There's a lot of food to be prepared, countless details to attend to. But, with proper organization and care, a large party can be a really gala occasion. Who knows? You may gain a reputation as the hostess with the mostest. It's worth a try.

BUFFET DINNER FOR TWENTY-FOUR

Soused Shrimp

Crudités with Dip

Assorted Nuts

Roast Tenderloin of Beef, Thinly Sliced

Buttered Pumpernickel Bread

Horseradish and English Mustard

"Chinese" Chicken Salad

Strawberries and Crème Fraiche*

Ultimate Pecan Pie

When I am giving a party for a large number of people, I don't like to experiment with exotic foods. There are too many folks with aversions or allergies to particular foods that might interfere with their enjoyment of the evening—and my satisfaction as a hostess. After all, who wants to prepare enough food to feed an army of twenty-four and find two-thirds of the sweetbreads (which I happen to adore in any of their many guises), or some other somewhat esoteric foodstuff, left over?

So this menu for a large crowd strikes me as just perfect. There is at least one dish on the table—if not several—to satisfy everyone. How many people do you know who don't adore shrimp (except those with seafood allergies, and they'll have plenty of alternatives) or a nice, rosy-pink sliver of beef tenderloin? Similarly, chicken salad, while prosaic, is always popular, and I offer in the recipe a rather novel manner of cooking the chicken, since the host has to deal with three birds, not one. Instead of simmering them on top of the stove—which might necessitate three good-size pots—or cooking them one at a time, slow-roast them together in the oven. They'll turn out wonderfully moist this way and, at the same time, render their fat, which contributes so much to the quality of the salad's dressing. My mother gave me this idea; she would make homemade mayonnaise specifically for chicken salad by substituting rendered chicken fat for the normal vegetable oil. It makes a much more chickeny salad.

For dessert, give your guests a choice: They can nibble on plain strawberries or dunked in thick, tart crème fraiche, or they can have a sweet tooth's dream, rich, chocolate-studded pecan pie, the truly ultimate pecan pie. Of course, if they have room, there's no reason they can't have both.

Whatever, I'm sure you'll not be burdened with a single leftover—but just to make sure, here are certain quantity guidelines for those recipe-less items suggested in the menu:

- tenderloin of beef: one large one, about 5 to 6 pounds (trimmed), should be enough
- two loaves of cocktail-size pumpernickel bread, generously spread with unsalted butter
- 3 quarts of strawberries, washed and hulled
- 4 cups crème fraiche (page 301).

SOUSED SHRIMP

MUST BE PREPARED 1 TO 3 DAYS IN ADVANCE.

2 teaspoons salt
½ teaspoon freshly ground black pepper
1 teaspoon sugar
2 teaspoons paprika
¾ cup white wine vinegar
3 tablespoons Dijon-style mustard
1 cup olive oil
1 tablespoon white prepared horseradish
1 teaspoon minced garlic
½ cup finely chopped celery
½ cup finely sliced scallions, including 1 inch green leaves
½ cup minced fresh parsley
3 pounds shelled, deveined, cooked large shrimp (about 5 pounds unshelled)
Lettuce leaves

To make the marinade: Place the salt, pepper, sugar, paprika, and vinegar in a quart jar with a tight-fitting lid, and shake vigorously until the sugar and salt have dissolved. Add the mustard and shake again. Add the oil and horseradish, and shake until all the ingredients are well combined. Finally, toss in the garlic, celery, scallions, and parsley and shake a few more times.

Place the shrimp in a mixing bowl. Pour the marinade over them, and, with a salad fork and spoon, toss to coat well. Cover with plastic wrap. Refrigerate 1 to 3 days, turning occasionally to redistribute marinade. Remove from the refrigerator 1 hour before final preparation.

TIME ALLOWANCE FOR FINAL PREPARATION: 5 MINUTES.

Toss shrimp one final time. Line a decorative serving bowl with lettuce leaves. Mound the shrimp in the center. Serve with toothpicks on the side.

SERVES 24 AS AN HORS D'OEUVRE.

"CHINESE" CHICKEN SALAD

MAY BE PREPARED UP TO 48 HOURS IN ADVANCE.

CHICKEN SALAD
3 roasting chickens, 6 to 7 pounds each
3 medium onions, peeled and quartered
1 lemon, sliced thin
4 8-ounce cans water chestnuts, sliced thin
4 red peppers, cored, seeded, and coarsely chopped (or substitute green or
*   yellow)*
1 pound snow peas, ends trimmed, strings pulled off, cut into ½-inch seg-
*   ments*

Preheat oven to 275 degrees.

Rinse the three chickens, then pat dry inside and out. Insert one quartered onion in each cavity. Place the chickens, breast side down, on racks in roasting pans. Top each with one-third of the lemon slices. Bake undisturbed for 3 hours, or until the juices run clear when the thighs are pierced with a fork. If the juices are still pinkish after 3 hours, bake 20 minutes longer. Repeat until the juices run clear.

Remove the chickens from the oven. As soon as they have cooled enough to handle, tear off and discard the skin. (It is much easier to remove when the birds are still very warm.) Discard lemon slices. Allow the birds to cool to room temperature. Cut all the meat off the bones into ½-inch cubes, and transfer them to a large mixing bowl. Strain the rendered chicken fat left in the roasting pans into another bowl, reserving ¾ cup for the dressing. Add the water chestnuts, peppers, and snow peas to the chicken pieces. Mix well.

DRESSING

¾ cup rendered chicken fat (see procedure above)
3 cups unsweetened mayonnaise
¼ cup strained fresh lemon juice
½ cup soy sauce
2 tablespoons ground ginger
1 cup sour cream
Lettuce leaves
Watercress, tough stems removed
Cherry tomatoes, halved

To make the dressing: In a large mixing bowl, slowly beat the ¾ cup rendered chicken fat into the mayonnaise, teaspoon by teaspoon. (If by any chance you do not have ¾ cup, make up the difference with vegetable oil.) When it has been completely absorbed, add the lemon juice, soy sauce, ginger, and sour cream. Blend thoroughly.

Pour the dressing over the chicken and toss until all the pieces are coated. Cover the bowl with plastic wrap and refrigerate 1 hour before final preparation.

TIME ALLOWANCE FOR FINAL PREPARATION: *5 MINUTES.*

Line a very large salad bowl with lettuce leaves. Toss the chicken salad several times to redistribute the dressing, then spoon it over the lettuce, mounding it attractively. Garnish the bowl with sprigs of watercress and halved cherry tomatoes.

SERVES 24.

ULTIMATE PECAN PIE

◆

PASTRY AND FILLING MAY BE MADE UP TO 24 HOURS IN ADVANCE;
PIE SHOULD NOT BE ASSEMBLED, HOWEVER, MORE THAN 6 HOURS IN ADVANCE.

Pastry sufficient for three 9-inch tart or pie shells
6 eggs
1½ cups sugar
1½ cups dark corn syrup
½ cup unsalted butter, melted
1 teaspoon salt
2 teaspoons vanilla
½ cup dark rum
2 cups coarsely chopped pecans
¼ cup flour
1 12-ounce package semisweet chocolate morsels ("little bits" size,
* preferably)*
2 cups heavy cream, whipped
¼ cup dark rum

Divide the pastry into three parts. Roll out and line three 9-inch tart pans with 1-inch sides. (If you do not have three 9-inch tart pans, you may substitute regular pie plates. Since the filling is so rich, I prefer to use tart pans with their thinner layer of filling.) Trim edges. Cover well with foil or plastic wrap, and refrigerate until ready to assemble.

In a large mixing bowl, beat the eggs until they are slightly thickened. Slowly add the sugar, and continue beating until the batter is very thick and light yellow. Add the corn syrup, butter, salt, vanilla, and rum, mixing well. Place the pecan pieces in a sieve. Sprinkle with water. Add the flour, then shake vigorously to coat the nuts lightly. Add the nuts and chocolate bits to the batter. Stir gently to distribute. Cover with plastic wrap, and refrigerate until 1 hour before assembling the pies.

TIME ALLOWANCE FOR FINAL PREPARATION: 40 MINUTES.

Preheat oven to 350 degrees.

Stir filling. Divide evenly among the three tart shells. Place pies on rack in the middle of the oven and bake 30 minutes or until filling is set. Cool.

Serve at room temperature accompanied by whipped cream flavored with rum, if desired.

YIELD: THREE 9-INCH PIES.

SPRING COCKTAIL PARTY FOR FIFTY

Cheese Phyllo Triangles

Creamy Salmon Mousse

Guacamole with Crudités

Steak Tartare*

Buttered Cocktail Rye Bread

Olives

Assorted Nuts

In the event that you are lucky enough to be throwing a major cocktail party, here are suggestions for hors d'oeuvres for fifty. Because it can often be so hard to find help, I suggest a variety of tasty nibbles that require little last-minute attention and can be presented on a table rather than passed, encouraging your guests to help themselves.

All of them can be prepared well in advance, with the exception of baking the cheese phyllo triangles, unmolding the salmon mousse, and assembling the guacamole. You can bake the triangles an hour ahead and put them on a hot tray, or you can lure a friendly teenager into the kitchen to bake them in batches at intervals throughout the party. Unmolding the mousse takes only minutes. And, although I've allowed fifteen minutes for mashing and mixing the guacamole, you may well be able to do it in five or ten. (Do plan buying the advocados five or six days in advance, because you may find only hard ones at the grocery store. Rocklike avocados never made a guacamole. They have to be soft but not squishy.)

I hope you can locate a bartender, or even two. Without help in this department, the host or hostess really needs four hands. Allowing your guests to help themselves tends to create lots of spills and general disorganization—which, in the end, do not contribute to the conviviality of the party.

As for beverages, the usual hard stuff is being bypassed by many these days in favor of wine, although gin and tonics and rum with tonic or soda are still very popular. Don't forget soft drinks; they're a must. It is a good idea to have a bottle of cranberry juice or orange juice on hand as well.

So, sit back—or rather, stand up—and enjoy your guests. This do-ahead is planned so that you especially will enjoy your own party.

CHEESE PHYLLO TRIANGLES

MAY BE PREPARED UP TO 1 WEEK IN ADVANCE AND REFRIGERATED,
OR MAY BE FROZEN, WELL SEALED, FOR 1 MONTH.

CHEESE FILLING
½ cup minced scallions, including 1 inch of green leaves
½ cup minced fresh parsley
½ cup minced fresh dill weed
1 pound Swiss cheese, grated
1 pound Monterey Jack cheese, grated
7 eggs
1 tablespoon Dijon mustard
1 tablespoon Worcestershire sauce
2 teaspoons baking powder
½ teaspoon freshly ground black pepper

1 pound frozen phyllo pastry sheets, thawed overnight in the refrigerator,
 brought to room temperature for 2 hours
1 pound unsalted butter, melted
1 cup toasted homemade bread crumbs

To make the filling (which should be done first): In a large bowl of an electric mixer, combine the scallions, parsley, and Swiss and Monterey Jack cheeses. Beat briefly to combine. Mix in the eggs, one at a time, beating well after each addition. Add the mustard, Worcestershire sauce, baking powder, and pepper, and beat vigorously for 1 minute. Set aside while preparing baking sheets and phyllo dough.

Butter four baking sheets generously. Place 6 sheets of the thawed phyllo on a flat surface, one on top of another. Place the remaining dough between sheets of wax paper, and cover with a dampened dish towel. (Do not allow the reserved phyllo dough to dry out. Keep it refrigerated until needed.) Cut the 6 sheets crosswise into 3-inch-wide strips. Remove 6 strips. Stack the remaining phyllo dough between sheets of wax paper, and cover with a dampened dish towel. Separate the strips on a flat surface alongside of one another. Brush gently but rapidly with melted butter. Sprinkle the top half of each strip with toasted bread crumbs. Fold each strip in half on top of itself. Spoon about 1 teaspoon of the cheese filling ½ inch from the end of the pastry strip closest to you. Fold the pastry strip back over the filling so that the bottom edge meets the left edge, forming a right triangle. Continue folding back and forth, making triangles each time, tucking in any remaining dough at the end. Transfer the triangles to the baking sheets as they are made. (You may need more than 4 baking sheets, or you may have to reuse them. Buying throw-away aluminum ones can facilitate matters.)

Repeat process until all the filling is used up. Remove only 6 sheets of dough from the supply in the refrigerator at a time, and always place the surplus strips between wax paper and under a damp dish towel while you work.

Brush the triangles with melted butter. If you are planning to bake them within a week, refrigerate them, well sealed with plastic wrap, until 30 minutes before baking. If you are planning to freeze them, place the baking trays, uncovered, on the shelves of your freezer. When the triangles are solidly frozen, transfer them carefully to freezer bags and seal well. Thaw them for 1 hour before baking on well-buttered baking sheets.

TIME ALLOWANCE FOR FINAL PREPARATION: 45 MINUTES.

Preheat oven to 350 degrees.

Bake the triangles for 30 to 40 minutes, until nicely crisp and golden brown. Serve hot.

YIELD: ABOUT 100 TRIANGLES.

CREAMY SALMON MOUSSE

MAY BE PREPARED UP TO 24 HOURS IN ADVANCE.

2 cups dry white wine
2 cups water
1 bay leaf
1 carrot, peeled, cut in four pieces
1 small onion, peeled and halved
4 sprigs parsley
2 to 2½ pounds salmon steaks
1 cup homemade mayonnaise
¾ cup heavy cream
1 package unflavored gelatin
1 teaspoon salt
Freshly ground black pepper
¼ cup minced fresh parsley
2 tablespoons finely chopped scallions, including 1 inch green leaves
2 tablespoons chopped fresh chives
2 tablespoons finely chopped fresh dill weed
2 tablespoons strained fresh lemon juice
2 teaspoons Dijon-style mustard
4 ounces red salmon roe (optional)
Watercress sprigs (garnish)
Simple crackers such as Bremner Wafers

Make a court bouillon by combining the wine, water, bay leaf, carrot, onion, and parsley sprigs in a high-sided skillet or a wide saucepan large enough to contain the salmon steaks in one layer. Bring the liquid to a boil, lower the heat, and simmer, partially covered, for 10 minutes. Add the salmon steaks, return to a boil, then simmer, partially covered, for 15 minutes or until the fish seems tender when pierced with a knife. (Cooking time depends on the thickness of the steaks.) Transfer the salmon to a rack or plate to cool. Strain the broth and reserve ½ cup. When the fish is cool enough to handle, skin, bone, and flake it.

In an electric blender or a food processor fitted with a steel blade, place one-third of the salmon, one-third of the mayonnaise, and one-third of the cream. Whirl until smooth, scraping the mixture down when necessary. (It will be thick and will need some stirring to achieve a smooth consistency.) Transfer the first batch to a large mixing bowl and repeat twice more with the remaining salmon, mayonnaise, and cream.

Soak the gelatin in the reserved ½ cup fish broth. When it has softened, dissolve it in a small saucepan over low heat, stirring frequently. Blend the dissolved gelatin into the salmon mixture. Add the salt, pepper, parsley, scallions, chives, dill, lemon juice, and mustard, and mix until all the ingredients are thoroughly blended. Taste and adjust seasonings. You may want to add a bit more salt or lemon juice, depending on the flavor of the salmon.

Rinse a 5–6 cup mold or two smaller ones with cold water, and drain. For best results, use a simple mold. A plain mixing bowl makes a fine mold, even though it is not highly decorative. Fill with the salmon mousse. If you are using two molds, divide the mixture equally between them. Place the mousse in the refrigerator, covered with plastic wrap.

If you are planning to add the salmon roe, wait 30 minutes, or until the mousse is just beginning to firm up but is not yet solid. Spoon the roe over the surface of the mousse to distribute it evenly. Slowly and gently fold it into the mousse, taking care not to break any of the eggs. Refrigerate the mousse, well covered, until just before you are ready to unmold it.

TIME ALLOWANCE FOR FINAL PREPARATION: 5 MINUTES.

Remove and discard the plastic covering. Run a knife around the edge of the mold to loosen the mousse. Set the mold in a bath of hot water for about a minute. Remove it from the water, and place a serving dish upside down on top of the mold. Turn the mold and dish over, and give a firm shake. The mousse should slip out easily. If not, repeat the procedure. If, by any chance, you leave the mold in the hot water too long and the mousse liquefies too much at the edges, simply return it, still in its mold, to the refrigerator to firm up again.

Garnish the mold with sprigs of watercress. Serve the mousse with simple biscuits or crackers that will not conflict with its delicate flavor.

YIELD: ABOUT 5 CUPS MOUSSE.

GUACAMOLE WITH CRUDITÉS

♦ VEGETABLES MAY BE PREPARED UP TO 6 HOURS IN ADVANCE;
THE AVOCADO DIP SHOULD NOT BE PREPARED MORE THAN 1 HOUR IN ADVANCE.

SUGGESTED CRUDITÉS OR RAW VEGETABLES

1 pound carrots, peeled
1 bunch celery, stalks washed, leaves trimmed and discarded
1 small head of cauliflower, cored
3 or 4 small zucchini, ends trimmed
1 bunch broccoli, tough stalks cut off and discarded

GUACAMOLE DIP

3 large ripe tomatoes, peeled and finely chopped (about 1½ cups)
½ cup minced onion
¼ cup strained fresh lemon juice
4 medium avocados, fully ripened
¼ teaspoon salt
Freshly ground black pepper
4 to 10 dashes Tabasco, depending on desired "fire"

Prepare the raw vegetables. Cut the carrots and celery in 2- to 3-inch pieces, quartering the carrots at the thick end. Break the cauliflower into small, easy-to-manage flowerets. Quarter the zucchini, and cut into 2- to 3-inch lengths. Cut the broccoli into flowerets. Rinse them well. Shake them dry. Place in plastic bags, and refrigerate until ready to assemble the dish.

Place the tomatoes in a small bowl, cover with plastic wrap, and refrigerate. Place the onion in another bowl, cover with plastic, and refrigerate. Put the lemon juice in a small glass, cover with plastic, and refrigerate. Do not do anything with the avocados.

TIME ALLOWANCE FOR FINAL PREPARATION: 15 MINUTES

Cut the avocados in half and peel them. Discard the pits. Place the halves in a large, flat dish such as a pie plate. With a fork, mash the avocados against the bottom of the dish until they are broken up and fairly smooth. Do not attempt to mash out all the lumps; guacamole is not meant to be a puree. Add the tomatoes, minced onion, and lemon juice. Continue to mix and mash until they are well blended and the tomatoes have broken down somewhat. Add the salt, pepper, and Tabasco, starting with only a few drops and tasting as you add. Some like guacamole hot, others only mildly spicy.

With a rubber spatula, scrape the guacamole into 3 or 4 small bowls. Place each bowl in the center of a large serving platter, and surround it attractively with the raw vegetables. Cover the guacamole loosely with plastic wrap until ready to serve. Guacamole does tend to discolor if prepared too far in advance; hence it is really advisable to prepare it last.

Tortilla chips, the traditional accompaniment to guacamole, may be substituted for the raw vegetables. Allow 2 (12-ounce) packages in place of the crudités.

SERVES 50 AS AN HORS D'OEUVRE.

AFTERNOON TEA FOR TWENTY

Assorted Tea Sandwiches

Delicate Tea Cake

Assorted Tea Cookies, Including Almond Lace Curls

Tea and Coffee

Sherry and Dubonnet

Teas are not the easiest form of entertaining. They require a lot of preparation and a lot of hopping about during the event. The kettle has to be kept full of boiling water, which in turn has to be transferred to the teapot as needed. Someone has to keep pouring. Sandwich and cookie trays have to be kept full. And empty cups have to be removed, washed, and returned to the table.

If you want to enjoy your own party—and, as hostess, you should be mingling, not pouring—hire some help or, even better, lasso a few willing teenagers who can perform some of the chores. (They're often more adept than adults.) Choose some close friends to do the pouring, but give them, too, enough time to circulate. Most important, do ahead all that you can—as early as you can.

There's no question that tea sandwiches are an art, and they require some dexterity. Don't be discouraged if a few of the first "rolls" or "sleeves" crack and look as if a two-year-old had made them. You'll get the hang of it very fast.

The tea cake offered here, a cross between a pound cake and a sponge cake, is truly delicate. Its flavor and texture come through best in thin slices. Do not serve it in normal cake-slice pieces.

As for the cookies, you probably have a score of delicious ones up your sleeve, and I leave the assortment to you. But do try the almond lace curls—they're heavenly. One word of caution, though: The batter spreads out wildly during the baking. You don't want giant cookies for your party, because the curls are extremely fragile and break easily. Cookie crumbs you do *not* need. Try for less than a teaspoon of batter as you spoon it on the cookie sheet. The result will be far prettier and infinitely more manageable from your guests' point of view. The curls are so special they'll disappear fast. If you have the time, it might be wise to double the recipe. Should you be lucky enough to have some left over, you'll earn many points with your family.

ASSORTED TEA SANDWICHES

SANDWICHES MAY BE PREPARED UP TO 6 HOURS IN ADVANCE
IF PROPERLY WRAPPED;
SPREADS MAY BE PREPARED UP TO 48 HOURS IN ADVANCE.

Asparagus and Hollandaise rolls*
Watercress and Boursin sleeves*
Curried egg wheels*
Cucumber on coriander rounds*
Smoked salmon on pumpernickel squares
Black caviar with scallion cream cheese on white rounds
Minced tongue with pickles on brown bread triangles
(* recipe follows)

Allow approximately 6 tea sandwiches per person, with an extra couple of dozen thrown in for good measure. Several ideas are listed above, or invent your own combinations, even using leftovers from the refrigerator. Just bear in mind the following rules:

The one thing to avoid in tea sandwiches is mayonnaise; it makes for messy, soggy creations. Use butter, flavored with herbs or plain; cream cheese lightened with drops of heavy cream; or cheese spreads, such as Boursin. Do not used whipped butter or whipped cream cheese. Sauces such as hollandaise and béarnaise, which solidify when chilled, also work very well. Have all spreads in softened condition when ready to prepare sandwiches.

As you complete the sandwiches, lay them on a jelly roll pan or cookie sheet on lightly dampened dish towels and cover them with wax paper. (You may make several layers, just keep repeating dampened towels and wax paper.) Refrigerate, covered with more dampened towels, when finished. Remove from refrigerator 1 hour before serving, but keep toweling on until the last minute.

If using a commercial bread, buy the "very thin" sliced bread.

Use the freshest bread possible, especially when making "rolls"; bread that is even slightly stale will crack as you roll it. For ease in rolling, after trimming the crusts, run a heavy rolling pin across both sides of the bread; it becomes more malleable that way.

Be generous with greens. Dip edges of sandwiches in minced parsley; green enhances their appearance, and an important part of tea sandwiches' success lies in their visual presentation.

ASPARAGUS AND HOLLANDAISE ROLLS

3 tablespoons strained fresh lemon juice
2 egg yolks
½ cup unsalted butter, melted and cooled
¼ teaspoon salt
Freshly ground black pepper
Dash cayenne pepper
1 12-ounce jar asparagus spears (about 20), drained, rinsed, and patted dry
10 slices very thin white bread, crusts trimmed, both sides rolled with rolling pin

To make the hollandaise "spread": Pour the lemon juice in a small saucepan and, over moderate heat, reduce it by half. Lower the heat and add the egg yolks. Whisk them until they have thickened somewhat, always watching the heat and lifting the pan off the heat if the bottom becomes too hot to touch. Beat in the melted butter, drop by drop, until it is all incorporated, removing the saucepan briefly from the heat if necessary. Add the salt, pepper, and cayenne. The sauce should thicken to the consistency of mayonnaise. If it separates from too much heat, remove the pan from the heat and add an ice cube. Beat vigorously. The sauce will be slightly thinner but will come together again. Refrigerate the hollandaise for 2 hours (or longer) so that it solidifies somewhat. Allow it to soften slightly before attempting to make the rolls. You want it to be easily spreadable.

Place the asparagus spears on paper toweling close at hand. Cut the crustless, rolled bread slices in half a few at a time. Cut each asparagus spear in half. Spread the bread generously with the hollandaise. Place an asparagus on one end of each piece of bread, crosswise, and roll the bread and asparagus up. Trim off any excess bread and asparagus (not the pretty little tip, though) with a sharp knife. Pinch the end of the bread together to seal the roll, using more hollandaise if necessary as a sealer. Place the roll, seam side down, on dampened tea towel. Repeat until all the asparagus are used up. Obviously, the ones with the tips peeking out will be prettier, but the non-tip pieces make for nearly as nice sandwiches. Cover with wax paper and refrigerate as described.

YIELD: 20 ASPARAGUS ROLLS.

WATERCRESS AND BOURSIN SLEEVES
10 slices very thin brown bread, crusts trimmed, both sides rolled with roll-
ing pin
1 5-ounce container Boursin cheese, softened
1 bunch watercress, tough stems removed, washed and dried

Cut the bread in half diagonally. Spread each half with a generous quantity of Boursin cheese. Select a few sprigs of watercress and lay them on the bread, their leaves at the apex of the bread triangle, their stems at the cut side. Starting at one of the smaller angles, roll towards the opposite small angle. The "sleeve" should have a little head of watercress peeking out between arms of bread. Pinch gently together to seal the ends. Place the sleeves on dampened cloth towels and repeat until all the bread is finished. (You will probably have a little cheese and a few sprigs of watercress left over. Use them up with more bread, if you prefer. These are very colorful, gay sandwiches.) Cover with wax paper and refrigerate, following the procedure given above.

YIELD: 20 WATERCRESS SLEEVES.

CURRIED EGG WHEELS
2 hard-boiled eggs, shelled (see page 46)
3 tablespoons unsalted butter, softened
2 teaspoons curry powder
¼ teaspoon salt
Freshly ground black pepper
10 slices very thin brown bread, crusts trimmed, sides rolled with rolling pin
½ cup minced fresh parsley

Place the eggs in a shallow bowl and mash them well with a fork. Add the butter and mix to blend. Sprinkle the curry powder, salt, and pepper over the eggs and beat until thoroughly blended.

Spread each trimmed slice of brown bread with the curried egg mixture. Roll up each slice, pinching the ends to seal well. With a sharp knife, cut each roll into 4 pieces. Dip one cut side into the minced parsley to coat it with green. Set each "wheel" non-parsley side down on dampened kitchen towels. Repeat until all the bread is used up. Cover with wax paper and refrigerate, following the procedure given above.

YIELD: 40 WHEELS.

CUCUMBERS ON CORIANDER ROUNDS

5 tablespoons unsalted butter, softened
3 tablespoons minced coriander leaves
10 slices very thin white bread, crusts trimmed
40 thin slices English cucumber (about 1)
Salt
Coriander (or cilantro) leaves

Combine the softened butter and minced coriander and mix well.

With a 1½-inch cutter, cut 4 rounds from each slice of bread. Spread the rounds generously with the coriander butter. Place a slice of cucumber on top of each round. Sprinkle sparingly with salt. Garnish each round with a tiny coriander leaf. Place on dampened kitchen towels, and cover with wax paper and refrigerate, following the procedure given above.

YIELD: 40 ROUNDS.

To serve: Arrange a combination of tea sandwiches in pretty groupings on doily- or napkin-covered trays.

DELICATE TEA CAKE

MAY BE PREPARED UP TO 48 HOURS IN ADVANCE.

15 to 20 whole blanched almonds
4 eggs
4 egg yolks
1½ cups sugar
2 teaspoons vanilla
2 teaspoons grated lemon rind
1 cup unsalted butter, melted and cooled
1½ cups cake flour
2 tablespoons cornstarch
¼ teaspoon mace

Preheat the oven to 350 degrees.

Grease and lightly flour a 9-inch tube or bundt pan. Arrange the almonds decoratively around the bottom of the pan. Combine the eggs, egg yolks, and sugar in a large mixing bowl and set it in a pan of hot water. Place the pan over very low heat and, stirring the mixture occasionally so that the eggs do not solidify, heat until the eggs are slightly warm to the touch—about 10 minutes. Do not let the water boil.

While the eggs are warming, add the vanilla and lemon rind to the melted butter. Stir to mix. Combine the flour, cornstarch, and mace. Sift twice.

When the eggs are warm, remove them from the water and beat them until they are cool, thick, and tripled in volume. Alternately, in three parts, sprinkle them first with one-third of the flour mixture, gently folding it in, and then with one-third of the melted butter, gently folding it in. The lighter your touch, the lighter the cake. End with the butter and continue to fold until no trace remains.

Pour the batter into the prepared pan, taking care not to disturb the arrangement of almonds. Bake 40 to 50 minutes, or until the cake is golden and a toothpick inserted in the center comes out clean. Cool the cake on a rack for 10 minutes, then remove it from the pan and cool it completely.

Serve the cake in thin, quarter-inch slices.

Freezing note: Properly sealed, this cake freezes beautifully and may be held in the freezer for 6 weeks. (If frozen longer than 6 weeks it loses its delicate flavor.)

YIELD: ONE 9-INCH TUBE CAKE.

ALMOND LACE CURLS

MAY BE PREPARED UP TO 24 HOURS IN ADVANCE.

1 cup unsalted butter
1 cup sugar
2 tablespoons flour
¼ cup light cream
1 cup blanched almonds, finely ground
1 teaspoon vanilla

Preheat the oven to 350 degrees.

Place the butter in a medium-size saucepan and, over low heat, melt it. Add the sugar and stir until it is dissolved. Add the flour, cream, and ground almonds and mix well. Finally stir in the vanilla.

Grease and flour two large baking sheets. Spoon 5 or 6 scant teaspoons of the batter—well separated—onto one sheet. Place in the oven and bake for approximately 8 minutes, or until the cookies are golden brown. Do not prepare and bake the other cookie sheet simultaneously. Wait until the first batch is half done, then prepare the second.

When the first batch of cookies is done, remove the sheet from the oven and let the cookies stand 1 minute to cool and firm. Then, working rapidly, scoop a cookie up with a spatula and roll it around the handle of a wooden spoon, curling it around itself into a little tube. Set on paper toweling to cool further and drain off any excess butter. (The cookies will be quite buttery at first.) If the cookies start to harden before you finish rolling them, return them briefly to the oven to soften. Repeat until all the batter is used.

Please note: These cookies are very crisp and delicate. Do not store them in a covered container or they will soften. Place them on plates, loosely covered with plastic wrap.

YIELD: APPROXIMATELY 5 DOZEN CURLS.

AN ITALIAN DINNER FOR TWENTY

Assorted Antipasti

Layered Lasagne

Mixed Green Salad with Vinaigrette Dressing*

Hot Buttered Garlic Italian Bread

Apricot Macaroon Trifle

Dinner parties with a particular theme often contribute to the festivity of the occasion. You can ask your guests to come in certain clothing or certain colors. (I once went to a splendid red-and-white affair where the hostess wore tomato red, from her spiked heels up to a wig of the same hue. Most of the guests were more moderate in dress, but the vibrancy of the colors contributed greatly to the spirit of the evening.) Or you can create a meal around a specific theme, such as a particular kind of ethnic food or even a style of presentation. How about a forkless meal, for example? Many Indian or Mexican dishes would fall into this category very nicely.

This buffet dinner for twenty has a certain Italian ambiance—if you permit me a liberal interpretation for the dessert. The meal begins with mixed antipasti, passed on trays with drinks and napkins. Antipasti (meaning, literally, "before the pasta") are an excellent form of finger food and offer your guests a variety of choices. Happily they can be assembled according to your own taste and the size of your budget. Given a little imagination and artistic flair, they make a very pretty presentation. Since the layered lasagne (my version of an Italian favorite) is probably one of the least expensive entrees you've served in many a day, splurge a little on the antipasti, using good-quality imported prosciutto and maybe even a beautiful batch of vinaigrette-bathed boiled shrimp.

Though inexpensive, the layered lasagne with its aromatic sausage and tomato sauce tastes like a million. While the number and variety of its ingredients sound like a supermarket inventory sheet, the dish is surprisingly simple to prepare. So much can be done ahead of time that it's a hostess's dream come true.

Speaking of dreams, the meal climaxes with the apricot macaroon trifle. It's almost sacrilegious to call it a "trifle." This novel interpretation is a far cry from the traditional British sponge-cake version. It's anything but trifling with its layers of Italian—you see, I remain true to my theme—almond macaroons, sparked with sherry and intensified with apricot puree and whipped cream.

ASSORTED ANTIPASTI

MAY BE PARTIALLY PREPARED UP TO 6 HOURS IN ADVANCE.

The following are simply suggestions for a large assortment of hors d'oeuvres. Use as many or as few of them as you like, in any proportion that you like. Fill 2 or 3 large trays with a mixture of all, arranged as decoratively and appetizingly as possible. Quantities are approximate, for guidance merely.

> *prosciutto and melon**
> *stuffed Spanish olives (1 10-ounce jar)*
> *marinated artichoke hearts (1 12-ounce jar)*

marinated mushrooms*
seeded breadsticks (1 or 2 4-ounce packages)
stuffed grape leaves (1 12-ounce jar)
stuffed celery*
salami cornucopias (½ pound sliced thin, skin removed)
deviled eggs (2 dozen, halved)
pepperoni slices (12 ounces, skin removed)
provolone slices (12 ounces)
(* recipe follows)

PROSCIUTTO AND MELON

1 large cantaloupe or honeydew melon
8 ounces imported prosciutto ham

Cut the melon into 8 wedges. Seed and skin each wedge. Cut each wedge crosswise into ½-inch-thick pieces. Cut the prosciutto into small lengths large enough to wrap around the melon piece. Wrap each melon piece with prosciutto, securing with toothpicks. Refrigerate, well wrapped, until time for serving.

MARINATED MUSHROOMS
MUSHROOMS SHOULD MARINATE
FOR AT LEAST 4 HOURS BEFORE SERVING.

4 tablespoons strained fresh lemon juice
½ teaspoon Dijon-style mustard
¼ teaspoon salt
Freshly ground black pepper
½ teaspoon oregano
¾ cup olive oil
1 clove garlic, peeled and halved lengthwise
12 ounces perfect white small mushrooms, ends trimmed

In large bottle equipped with a tight-fitting lid, such as a 1½-quart mayonnaise jar, combine the lemon juice, mustard, salt, and pepper. Stir until the mustard is blended with the juice and the salt has dissolved. Add the oregano, olive oil, and garlic. Cover the bottle tightly and shake well. Add the mushrooms, cover, and shake again.

Marinate for at least 4 hours or as long as 6, shaking occasionally. Just before serving, drain completely. Discard the garlic and serve the mushrooms in small bowls with toothpicks.

STUFFED CELERY

1 (8-ounce) container whipped cream cheese, softened
1 8-ounce wedge Saga blue cheese, softened, skin removed
¼ teaspoon garlic salt
1 bunch celery, leaves trimmed, cleaned, stalks cut in 3-inch lengths (discard
 tough outer stalks)
Paprika

In a mixing bowl, combine the cream and Saga cheeses and the garlic salt and beat until thoroughly blended. Mound attractively on the celery pieces. Wrap well and re-frigerate until time to serve. Just before serving, sprinkle with paprika.

LAYERED LASAGNE

THE MEAT SAUCE MAY BE PREPARED UP TO 4 DAYS IN ADVANCE,
OR THE ENTIRE DISH MAY BE PREPARED, BUT NOT BAKED, 24 HOURS IN ADVANCE.
LAYERED LASAGNE FREEZES VERY WELL, BUT IT IS PREFERABLE
TO FREEZE IT BEFORE THE FINAL BAKING.

MEAT SAUCE

1 pound Italian hot sausage, skinned
1 pound Italian sweet sausage, skinned
1 tablespoon fennel seed
1½ cups chopped onion
1 tablespoon minced garlic
1 cup chopped green pepper
1 cup chopped carrots
1 cup chopped celery
½ pound thinly sliced mushrooms
2 teaspoons basil
1 tablespoon oregano
2 bay leaves
¼ to ½ teaspoon crushed red pepper, depending on taste
1 tablespoon salt
½ teaspoon freshly ground black pepper
2 (6-ounce) cans tomato paste
3 (35-ounce) cans Italian plum tomatoes

1 pound lasagne
1½ pounds mozzarella cheese, sliced
3 pounds whole-milk ricotta cheese, softened
Freshly grated Parmesan cheese (about 1½ to 2 pounds)

In a 14-inch skillet with 5-inch sides, or a 4-quart casserole, break up the sausage into large chunks. Turn on the heat to moderately low, and sauté it slowly, stirring occasionally, until it begins to exude its oil. Add the fennel, and continue to break up and sauté the meat until all traces of pink disappear. Add the onions, garlic, green pepper, carrots, celery, mushrooms, basil, oregano, bay leaves, red pepper, salt, and pepper and cook until the vegetables are soft, about 10 minutes. Add the tomato paste and tomatoes and stir until well blended. Bring the sauce to a boil, lower the heat, and simmer, uncovered, for 2 hours, stirring occasionally. If preparing just the meat sauce, remove from heat, cool, cover, and refrigerate until 1 hour before assembling the entire dish.

To assemble, remove the sauce from the heat (or have it at room temperature, as indicated above) while you cook the lasagne in a 6-quart (or greater) kettle of salted boiling water for 2 minutes less than the directions call for on the box's label. (This should be about 10 minutes.) Immediately drain and rinse under cold water.

Scoop off any excess oil that has risen to the top of the sauce. In a deep 6-quart ovenproof casserole (or two smaller ones) spoon one-third of the meat sauce over the bottom. Cover the sauce with two layers of lasagne, followed by half the mozzarella slices and half the ricotta. Repeat. Cover the last layer of cheese with the remaining meat sauce. Cover tightly with plastic wrap and the casserole's own lid and refrigerate until 1 hour before final preparation. To facilitate the lasagne's coming to room temperature, remove the lid and plastic wrap once it is out of the refrigerator.

TIME ALLOWANCE FOR FINAL PREPARATION: 1¾ HOURS.

Preheat the oven to 350 degrees.

Cover and bake the layered lasagne undisturbed for 1½ hours. Serve immediately, accompanied by bowls of freshly grated Parmesan cheese.

SERVES 20.

APRICOT MACAROON TRIFLE

MAY BE PARTIALLY PREPARED UP TO 12 HOURS IN ADVANCE.

2 pounds dried apricots
3 cups sugar
1 cup medium-dry sherry
1 1-pound box of Amaretti di Saronno almond macaroons (available at specialty stores and some supermarkets)
3 cups heavy cream
4 tablespoons finely chopped slivered almonds (optional)

In a large saucepan, soak the apricots in water to cover for 45 minutes. Place the saucepan over moderately low heat, add the sugar, and stir until it is dissolved. Cook the fruit until very tender, about 15 minutes. Puree the apricots and their juice, in two batches, in a food processor fitted with a steel blade until very smooth. Scrape the puree into a bowl and reserve.

Have at hand two 3-quart soufflé dishes, or glass bowls with high sides. Pour the sherry into a shallow soup bowl or pie plate. Remove and discard the paper covering the macaroons. Whip 2 cups of the cream until stiff. Then assemble the trifle as follows:

Dip 12 macaroons into the sherry. Arrange them in one layer in the bottom of one of the bowls. Spread one-sixth of the apricot puree on top, followed by a quarter of the whipped cream. Repeat with another layer of 12 sherried macaroons, apricot puree, and cream. Repeat with a third layer of 12 sherried macaroons and puree, but do not finish with the cream. Cover tightly with plastic wrap and refrigerate until ½ hour before final preparation. Repeat the process with second bowl.

TIME ALLOWANCE FOR FINAL PREPARATION: 10 MINUTES.

Whip the remaining 1 cup cream until stiff. Either pipe it decoratively on top of both trifles or spread it with a spatula in pleasant swirls. Garnish with finely chopped almonds if desired, or serve unembellished.

SERVES 20.

FALL
COCKTAIL PARTY
FOR THIRTY

*Layered Cheese Mold with
Pesto and Crackers*

*Toasted Ramekins with
Two Fillings*

*Sausage Crescents with Sweet
Mustard Sauce*

Cashews

Black and Green Olives

A cocktail party for thirty isn't a terrifying thing to contemplate in terms of preparation because you don't really have to wine and dine all that many people. Still, it's nice to offer something unusual to eat, particularly in party season, when appetites can become rather jaded. The hors d'oeuvres offered on today's menu are different, you may rest assured. The layered cheese mold, with the green of the pesto visually enhancing it, is both subtle and piquant. The sausage crescents are nicely nippy. But my favorite are the toasted ramekins, filled with a curried chicken or a mix of dilled crabmeat and mushrooms. (The idea of creating little toasted bread saucers instead of small pastry shells was the brainchild of John Clancy, head chef of the "Time-Life Foods of the World" test kitchen. They take less time to make than tiny tarts and are less rich.) Try creating some of your own original fillings. Just make sure the binding agent is thick, or the filling will soak through. I often make a large supply of ramekins ahead of time and freeze them. Then, when I have unexpected company, I am usually able to come up with something quite presentable.

Since the sausages and ramekins are meant to be offered hot from the oven, if you don't have someone to help you bake and serve them while the party's buzzing, bake them a bit ahead and set them out on a hot tray, where they'll remain warm and fresh.

LAYERED CHEESE MOLD WITH PESTO

MAY BE PREPARED UP TO 4 DAYS IN ADVANCE;
MUST BE PREPARED AT LEAST 12 HOURS IN ADVANCE.

½ cup pine nuts
2 cloves garlic, peeled and sliced
1 cup tightly packed fresh basil leaves, stems removed
1 cup tightly packed fresh parsley leaves, stems removed
½ teaspoon salt
⅓ cup olive oil
¾ cup freshly grated Parmesan cheese
2 tablespoons unsalted butter, softened, plus 1 pound unsalted butter, softened
2 (8-ounce) packages cream cheese, softened
Basil and parsley leaves for garnish (optional)

To make the pesto: Toast the pine nuts in a 10-inch skillet, preferably one with a nonstick surface. Cook them over moderate heat, tossing frequently, until they are light brown on all sides. Take care they do not burn.

While the machine is running, drop the garlic slices through the feed tube into the bowl of a food processor fitted with a steel blade and whirl until they are finely minced. Add the pine nuts, basil, parsley, and salt, and whirl until minced. With the motor still going, slowly pour the olive oil in through the feed tube. Add the cheese and the 2 tablespoons butter, and whirl until well blended. Scrape the mixture into a small bowl and reserve. Wash and dry the food processor.

Place the cream cheese and remaining 1 pound of butter into the processor fitted with a steel blade. Whirl until smooth and well blended.

Cut a 20-inch length of cheesecloth and moisten it with water. Line a 6-cup bowl or pudding mold with the cloth, allowing the excess to drape over the edges. With a rubber spatula, smooth one-fifth of the cheese mixture into a layer in the bottom of the mold. Spoon one-fourth of the pesto mixture over the cheese, running it as close to the edge of the bowl as possible. The layers will be soft, but try not to mix them, so that when the cheese mold is presented, chilled and firmed, it will have distinct white and green layers. Repeat with another fifth of the cheese and another fourth of the pesto until the ingredients are used up. Finish with a cheese layer. Fold the ends of the cheesecloth over the mold, and press the top lightly to compress it. Cover well with plastic wrap and refrigerate at least 10 hours or until ready to serve.

TIME ALLOWANCE FOR FINAL PREPARATION: 5 MINUTES.

Remove the cheesecloth from the cheese mold. Invert the cheese on a serving platter, and surround it with assorted crackers. Garnish it with additional basil and parsley leaves, if desired.

SERVES 30 AS AN HORS D'OEUVRE.

TOASTED RAMEKINS WITH TWO FILLINGS

RAMEKINS MAY BE PREBAKED AND STORED IN THE REFRIGERATOR FOR UP TO 72 HOURS, OR FROZEN FOR 2 MONTHS.
FILLINGS MAY BE PREPARED UP TO 24 HOURS IN ADVANCE.

TOASTED RAMEKINS
48 slices "Very Thin" white bread
1 cup unsalted butter, melted

Preheat oven to 425 degrees.

Roll a rolling pin across each piece of bread twice to render the slices more flexible. With a 3-inch cookie cutter, cut one round out of each slice. Using a pastry brush, brush one side of a round with the melted butter. Buttered side down, carefully press each round into a 2¾-inch muffin cup, molding it gently until it conforms to the shape of the cup. Be sure to center the bread in the cup, or it will come out lopsided. Repeat with all the bread. (Save and freeze the bread scraps for homemade bread crumbs.) Bake the ramekins for 10 to 12 minutes, or until lightly browned. Cool. Remove from muffin cups, and drain on paper toweling to absorb any excess butter. Store in a plastic bag in the refrigerator, or freeze until ready to fill.

CURRIED CHICKEN FILLING
½ pound boned skinless chicken breast
Pinch plus ½ teaspoon salt
¼ cup unsalted butter
¼ cup finely chopped onion
1 tablespoon curry powder
¼ cup flour
1½ cups light cream

Place the chicken breast in a small skillet and cover with water. Over moderate heat, bring to a boil; then lower the heat and simmer for 10 to 12 minutes or until the breast feels firm to the touch. Immediately drain and refresh under cold water. Cool.

With a sharp knife, cut the chicken into pieces as small as you can manage—¼- to ½-inch cubes. Sprinkle with a pinch of salt. Reserve.

Melt the butter in a small saucepan over low heat. Add the onion and sauté, stirring frequently, until the onion is wilted, about 5 minutes. Add the curry powder and blend well. Add the flour, increase the heat to moderate, and stir for 1 minute. (This will eliminate any raw taste in the curry and flour.) Gradually pour in the cream, stirring constantly so that no lumps form. Add the remaining ½ teaspoon salt. Bring to a boil, lower the heat, and let the sauce simmer for 5 minutes, stirring occasionally. Remove from the heat and add the reserved chicken, tossing to coat all the pieces well. Cool. Either fill the ramekins now or transfer the filling to a bowl and refrigerate, covered with plastic wrap, until 1 hour before final preparation. (Makes enough filling for 24 ramekins.)

DILLED CRAB AND MUSHROOMS FILLING

½ pound crabmeat, thawed if frozen
¼ cup unsalted butter
3 tablespoons finely chopped onion
¼ pound mushrooms, stems trimmed, coarsely chopped
¼ cup flour
1½ cups light cream
½ teaspoon salt
Freshly ground black pepper
2 egg yolks, lightly beaten
¼ cup minced fresh dill weed

Pick over the crabmeat and discard any cartilage. Place in a sieve and allow to drain.

Melt the butter in a small saucepan over low heat. Sauté in it the onion and mushrooms, stirring frequently, until both are soft and the mushrooms' juice has completely evaporated, about 10 minutes. Add the flour and stir briskly to blend. Increase the heat to moderate and, stirring constantly, cook the flour for about 1 minute to eliminate any raw taste.

Still stirring, add the cream in a slow stream. Do not allow any lumps to form. Bring to a boil, lower the heat, and simmer 5 minutes. Add the salt and pepper. Remove from the heat and beat in the egg yolks. Add the drained crabmeat and dill weed and mix well. Either fill the ramekins at once, or transfer the mixture to a bowl and refrigerate it, covered, until 1 hour before assembling and final preparation. (Makes enough filling for 24 ramekins.)

TIME ALLOWANCE FOR FINAL PREPARATION: 20 MINUTES.

Preheat the oven to 450 degrees.

Divide the fillings evenly among the 48 toasted ramekins, allowing about 1 tablespoon filling each.

Arrange the ramekins on ungreased cookie sheets and bake for 5 minutes or until hot. Serve immediately or hold on a hot tray.

YIELD: 48 FILLED RAMEKINS.

SAUSAGE CRESCENTS WITH SWEET MUSTARD SAUCE

CRESCENTS MAY BE PARTIALLY PREPARED AND FROZEN UP TO 1 MONTH IN ADVANCE, OR MAY BE PARTIALLY PREPARED AND REFRIGERATED UP TO 8 HOURS IN ADVANCE. SAUCE MAY BE PREPARED UP TO 24 HOURS IN ADVANCE.

3 (8-ounce) packages frozen sausage patties, thawed
1 (17¼-ounce) package frozen puff pastry, thawed
2 egg yolks
2 tablespoons light cream
2 tablespoons heavy cream
2 tablespoons Dijon mustard
2 tablespoons red currant jelly

Crumble the sausage meat into a large skillet, and cook it, slowly, stirring frequently, until all traces of pink have disappeared. Continue to break up the meat into the smallest possible pieces as it cooks. With a slotted spoon, transfer the sausage to paper toweling to drain.

Meanwhile, prepare the pastry. Hold one of the sheets in the refrigerator while you work on the first. On a floured surface, roll out the pastry into a large rectangle about 12 inches wide, 16 inches long, and ⅛ inch thin. It is important that the pastry be thin. If your measurements are larger or smaller than those given, don't worry as long as the pastry is ⅛ inch thin. Trim any uneven edges. Divide the rectangle into long strips about 3 inches wide. Cut each strip into 3-inch squares. Cut each square in half diagonally.

On each triangle, place about 1 teaspoon of the sausage meat, spreading it out along the widest side. Roll the triangle from the wide end toward the opposite point. Shape into a crescent. Place on an ungreased baking sheet and refrigerate while you repeat the process with the second sheet of puff pastry.

To freeze: Make a wash by combining the egg yolks with the light cream, and brush each crescent with the mixture. Place the crescents, on the baking sheets, in the freezer until they are hard. Slip them off the sheets into plastic bags, seal tightly, and hold in the freezer until 2 hours before final preparation. While they are still hard, arrange them in rows on ungreased baking sheets.

To hold unfrozen: Place the crescents, on the baking sheets, in the refrigerator, lightly covered with plastic wrap. Bring them to room temperature 1 hour before final preparation. Make a wash by combining the egg yolks with the light cream, and brush each crescent with the mixture.

Make the sweet mustard sauce by combining the heavy cream, mustard, and currant jelly in a small saucepan. Cook it over moderate heat, stirring constantly, until the jelly melts and is assimilated. Cool and transfer to a small dipping bowl.

TIME ALLOWANCE FOR FINAL PREPARATION: 45 MINUTES.

Preheat oven to 375 degrees.

Bake the crescents 20 to 25 minutes, or until golden brown. Place the sweet mustard sauce in the center of a serving platter and arrange the crescents decoratively around it.

YIELDS APPROXIMATELY 96 CRESCENTS.

BUFFET FOR SIXTEEN

Baked Country Ham

Baking Powder Biscuits, Split and Buttered

Potato Salad Senegalese

Baked Mixed Vegetables

Ice Cream–Filled Cream Puffs *

Chocolate and Caramel Sauces *

There is such a mystique to baked country hams that many people resist serving them. But when they are properly prepared, their distinctive rich, salty taste makes them a rare treat and a perfect item for a large buffet or cocktail party.

All "country" hams are dry-cured. That is, after being smoked, they are rubbed with salt or a mixture of salt, sugar, and even pepper; covered in muslin; and "aged" or hung for a period of years—the longer the better, in fact, although at the end of many years they may look repulsively moldy. (A good scrub is advised before soaking.)

This recipe for baked country ham comes from an old friend and native Virginian, James Deetz. So inspiring was what he correctly described as his foolproof method that I sent away to The Cheese Shop in Williamsburg, Virginia, for an Edwards country-style hickory-smoked ham. (Country hams may also be ordered from Smithfield Ham Co., P.O. Box 447, Smithfield, VA 23430 or from Callaway Gardens, Pine Mountain, Georgia 31822.)

Please remember that country hams, despite the long soak, are still pretty salty. They should be served warm or at room temperature, sliced very thin. Baking powder biscuits slathered in sweet butter are a good accompaniment, as is the mildly curried potato salad Senegalese. The baked mixed vegetables, a Romanian dish, are a party giver's delight. Aside from a lot of initial chopping, the dish requires no attention at all, and it is so flexible that any vegetable deletions, additions, or substitutions the cook would like to make—such as adding celery, eggplant, peas, or corn, to name just a few—present no problems.

BAKED COUNTRY HAM

◆

MUST BE PARTIALLY PREPARED AT LEAST 24 HOURS IN ADVANCE.

1 dry-cured country ham, 10 to 15 pounds
6 cups water
1 teaspoon dry English mustard
1 cup apricot preserves

Because country hams are dry-cured in a mixture of sugar, salt, and preservatives, it is necessary to soak them for a prolonged period to eliminate the excessively salty taste.

Scrub the ham briskly to get rid of any surface salt and mold that may have accumulated during its aging. Place it in a roasting pan large enough to contain it in its entirety, and cover it with water. Soak at least 12 hours or as long as 24, changing the water every 4 to 6 hours.

Preheat oven to 350 degrees.

Drain the ham, rinse the pan, and return the ham to it, fat side up. Pour 6 cups water in the bottom of the pan. Cover the pan (preferably with its own lid; if none is available, seal it securely with a double thickness of aluminum foil.) Place the ham in the oven and increase the oven temperature to 500. When the oven temperature has reached that point, time the baking for 15 minutes. After 15 minutes turn off the heat. Do not open the oven.

Leave the ham in the oven 3 hours. Turn the heat back on to 500, and when it has reached that point, bake the ham another 15 minutes. Turn the heat off again, and let the ham stay in the oven, undisturbed, for another 3 hours or as long as overnight, if you are cooking in the evening. Again, do not open the oven.

TIME ALLOWANCE FOR FINAL PREPARATION: 20 MINUTES.

With a sharp knife, cut off the skin of the ham and all but a thin layer of fat. Rub the fat with the dry mustard.

Spoon the apricot preserves into a small saucepan, and bring them to a boil, stirring frequently to prevent scorching. Boil 3 minutes; then press through a strainer. Discard fruit. Brush the glaze over the cool ham, repeating several times to build up a generous coating. (The glaze will not adhere if the ham is hot.) Serve the ham at room temperature.

SERVES 16.

POTATO SALAD SENEGALESE

MAY BE PREPARED UP TO 24 HOURS IN ADVANCE.

5 pounds "waxy" new potatoes
2 cups unsweetened mayonnaise, preferably homemade
1 cup sour cream
⅓ cup cider vinegar
2 teaspoons prepared white horseradish
2 teaspoons salt
½ teaspoon freshly ground black pepper
4 teaspoons curry powder
2 teaspoons sugar
1 cup finely chopped red onion
4 tart apples, peeled, cored, and thinly sliced
Paprika
20 cherry tomatoes, halved

Place the potatoes in a saucepan with water to cover, and bring to a boil. Lower the heat and cook, partially covered, 20 to 30 minutes, or until very tender when pierced with a small knife. Drain. Fill the saucepan with cold water. When the potatoes are cool enough to handle, peel them. Set aside.

Make the dressing by combining in a small mixing bowl the mayonnaise, sour cream, vinegar, horseradish, salt, pepper, curry powder, and sugar. Stir until completely blended.

Cut the potatoes into ¼-inch slices. Add the chopped onion and apple slices, and spoon the dressing over the salad. Toss gently but thoroughly until all ingredients are well coated. Cover with plastic wrap, and refrigerate until 1 hour before final preparation.

TIME ALLOWANCE FOR FINAL PREPARATION: 5 MINUTES.

Remove plastic wrap. Toss salad to redistribute dressing. Sprinkle with paprika, and garnish with cherry tomato halves.

SERVES 16.

BAKED MIXED VEGETABLES

MAY BE PARTIALLY PREPARED UP TO 12 HOURS IN ADVANCE.

2 cups thinly sliced carrots (about 1 pound)
½ pound green beans, ends trimmed, cut in ½-inch pieces
1½ pounds tomatoes, peeled and cut into small chunks
2 small summer squash, thinly sliced (about 1 pound)
2 small zucchini, thinly sliced (about 1 pound)
1 Spanish onion, peeled and thinly sliced (about ½ pound)
1 cauliflower (about 1¼ pounds) cut into flowerets, stalk discarded
1 green pepper, seeded and cut into ¼-inch strips (about ½ pound)
1 red pepper, seeded and cut into ¼-inch strips (about ½ pound)
1 cup shredded cabbage
¾ pound new potatoes, peeled and cut in ½-inch dice
1 cup chicken broth
½ cup olive oil
5 teaspoons minced garlic
2 teaspoons salt
1 bay leaf, crumbled
1 teaspoon summer savory
1 teaspoon tarragon

In a large shallow casserole or baking dish (preferably one with a tight-fitting lid), combine the carrots, beans, tomatoes, squash, zucchini, onion, cauliflower, green and red peppers, and cabbage. Toss to mix well. Cover tightly and set aside in a cool spot in the kitchen (or refrigerate if preparing well in advance) until final preparation.

TIME ALLOWANCE FOR FINAL PREPARATION: 1¼ HOURS.

Preheat oven to 350 degrees.

Add the potatoes to the vegetable mixture, and toss well. In a small saucepan, combine the broth, oil, garlic, salt, bay leaf, savory, and tarragon. Bring to a boil. Pour it over the vegetables, toss again, cover the casserole tightly with either a lid or a double thickness of aluminum foil, and bake until the vegetables are tender, about 1 hour.

SERVES 16.

CHRISTMAS BRUNCH FOR SIXTEEN

Hot Mulled Cider *

Chicken "Pie"

No-Knead Christmas Coffee Rings

Hot Fruit Compote

So much Christmas food planning centers on the main repast—whether it be turkey, goose, or roast beef—that little thought is given to the other meals of that very important and exciting day. In my family, for example, we have tea or coffee while we open our stockings, gulp down a late breakfast of eggs and bacon afterwards, and then rush back to the "big" presents. Our dinner generally is served in midafternoon, when everyone is weak with hunger and fatigue.

Some families are smarter. Take the Brewsters of Plymouth, Massachusetts. They have a Christmas brunch tradition that goes back as long as any of them can remember. Each branch of the family opens stockings at home with a small breakfast. Afterwards all the Brewsters—all seventy-five or eighty of this four-generation clan—converge at the home of one family, wish each other good Christmas cheer, deliver last-minute presents, and partake of a soul-satisfying brunch of chicken pie and coffee, served buffet style. Later the individual families return to their own abodes to open their "tree" presents and, still later, to sit down to their own Christmas dinners.

Inspired by the Brewsters, I offer three of my own recipes for a Christmas brunch. It is planned for sixteen, a number I arbitrarily selected as being more average than seventy-five. The food can be nicely done ahead, leaving the hosts free to mingle under the mistletoe with their family and friends.

Why chicken, you may ask, when so many Christmas dinners feature turkey or goose? I have no proper answer, except that chicken is what the Brewsters serve, and have been serving, and who am I to quarrel with a tradition, that, for all I know, may have come over with the *Mayflower?*

CHICKEN "PIE"

MAY BE PREPARED IN THREE STAGES, STARTING 48 HOURS IN ADVANCE.

2 roasting chickens, 6 to 7 pounds each
2 yellow onions, peeled
3 carrots, broken in thirds
2 stalks celery, broken in thirds
10 sprigs parsley
5 bay leaves
2 pounds small white onions, peeled
2 pounds medium-size mushrooms, ends trimmed
2 red peppers, cored, seeded, and cut in ½-inch dice
5 cups homemade chicken stock (from the liquid in which the birds were
*   cooked)*
7 tablespoons chicken fat
7 tablespoons flour
1 tablespoon salt
½ teaspoon freshly ground black pepper
2 cups light cream
10 drops Tabasco
1 tablespoon tarragon
½ pound snow peas, stems and strings removed, cut in thirds crosswise
1 (17¼-ounce) package frozen puff pastry, thawed

First stage of preparation (up to 48 hours in advance): Pull out any fat clinging to the cavities of the chickens, and save for another use. Wash birds. Place them side by side on their backs in a 4-inch-deep roasting pan equipped with a tight-fitting lid. (If you don't own one, you may use a deep kettle, but a kettle will require more water to cover the birds and will result in a less intense stock.) Pour water into the roasting pan halfway up the chicken. (In a kettle you will have to cover both birds because presumably one will be positioned on top of the other.) Drop in the yellow onions, carrots, celery, parsley, and bay leaves. Bring the water to a boil, cover the pan, lower the heat, and simmer the chickens for 45 minutes. Turn them over. (In a kettle, re-position them.) Simmer another 45 minutes. Pierce them in several spots with the tip of a knife. They should be very tender; if not, simmer 15 minutes longer. Carefully transfer the birds to a large platter. While they are cooling, raise the heat under the roasting pan or kettle, and reduce the stock by half.

As soon as the chickens are cool enough to handle, tear off their meat into gener-ous chunks, discarding the bone and skin. (If you do this before they are cold, it is much easier.) Reserve the meat in a very large bowl.

When the stock has reduced, add the white onions. Bring the liquid to a boil, then reduce the heat and simmer the onions, partially covered, for 25 to 30 minutes, or until just tender. Add the mushrooms and diced pepper, and simmer another 5 minutes. With a slotted spoon, remove the vegetables and place them in the bowl with the chicken. Strain the stock into a large bowl and when it is cool, refrigerate it, preferably overnight. Cover the chicken and vegetables with plastic wrap, and refrigerate them until 2 hours before the second stage of preparation.

Second stage of preparation (may be done up to 8 hours in advance): Carefully skim the solidified fat off the surface of the stock, and set it aside. Measure 5 cups of stock, place it in a saucepan, and slowly bring it to a boil. Save remaining stock for another use. In a large pot, or preferably the casserole in which you plan to serve the chicken "pie," heat 7 tablespoons of the chicken fat, reserving the remainder for another use. Add the flour and, with a whisk, beat it with the fat over moderately low heat until well blended. Add the salt and pepper. Cook 1 minute. Cup by cup, whisk in the hot stock, stirring each addition until it thickens before adding the next. Add the cream and bring the sauce to a slow boil. Mix in the Tabasco and tarragon, and cook 2 minutes, stirring constantly. Finally, add the chicken, onions, mushrooms, and peppers, and gently stir to mix. Taste and adjust the seasonings, if necessary. Remove from the heat and, when the chicken is cool, mix in the snow peas. Cover the casserole and refrigerate if preparing more than 3 hours in advance. Remove from the refrigerator 2 hours before final preparation.

Preheat oven to 350 degrees.

On a floured surface, roll out the two pieces of puff pastry to rectangles of about 11 by 18 inches. With cookie cutters shaped in appropriate Christmas forms—such as Christmas trees, stars, reindeer—cut out the pastry pieces and transfer them to ungreased cookie sheets. Bake 25 minutes; then cool and set them aside, loosely covered with wax paper, until serving time.

TIME ALLOWANCE FOR FINAL PREPARATION: 20 MINUTES.

Set the chicken-filled casserole over low heat, covered. Slowly reheat it, stirring every few minutes so that the bottom of the casserole does not scorch, until it is steaming hot. (This period is sufficient for the snow peas to cook.) Serve it, if possible, warmed on a hot tray, accompanied by the pastry pieces on a separate platter.

(If you prefer, the chicken may be reheated, covered, in a preheated 300-degree oven, without stirring. It will take 45 to 60 minutes until steaming hot, depending on the size and shape of the casserole. This is an easier method and requires no attention, but the colors of the peppers and snow peas will fade somewhat.

SERVES 16.

NO-KNEAD CHRISTMAS COFFEE RINGS

MAY BE PREPARED SEVERAL WEEKS IN ADVANCE AND FROZEN,
OR 1 TO 3 DAYS IN ADVANCE AND REFRIGERATED.

1 cup warm water

5 tablespoons (or 6 packets) active dry yeast

1 tablespoon plus ¾ cup sugar

½ cup unsalted butter, softened

2 teaspoons salt

4 eggs

1½ teaspoons vanilla

6 cups unbleached flour

1 tablespoon cinnamon

1½ cups finely chopped walnuts

½ cup candied fruit

2 cups golden seedless raisins

¼ cup unsalted butter, melted

ICING

3 tablespoons water

1 tablespoon light corn syrup

¼ teaspoon vanilla

2 cups confectioners' sugar

In a small bowl, combine the warm water, yeast, and 1 tablespoon of sugar. Let proof (bubble and ferment) for 5 minutes while proceeding with the recipe. (If, after 10 minutes, it has not bubbled, discard and repeat the process.)

In a large bowl of an electric mixer, beat the softened butter until fluffy. Add the remaining ¾ cup sugar and the salt, and beat well. Beat in the eggs one at a time. Add the yeast mixture and 1½ teaspoons of vanilla, and mix thoroughly. Slowly add the flour, cup by cup, beating well after each addition. Add the cinnamon, and beat 5 minutes continuously. Let the dough rest 30 minutes.

Mix in the nuts, candied fruits, and raisins. Make sure they are well distributed within the dough. Dusting the surface of the dough and your hands with a little flour, transfer the dough to a well-buttered large bowl. Turn it over several times to coat it with butter. Cover the bowl with a towel, and set it aside in a warm, draft-free place until the dough has doubled in bulk, about 1 hour.

With your fist, punch down the dough. Divide it into three equal parts. On a lightly floured surface, roll each third into a rectangle about 6 by 16 inches. Brush the dough with some of the melted butter, and roll it up, lengthwise, like a jelly roll. Repeat with the remaining two portions of dough.

Lightly butter three 9-inch cake pans and the outside of one small jelly glass. Position the jelly glass in the center of one of the cake pans, and coil one portion of the dough around it, seam side down, pinching the ends together. Remove the jelly glass, and repeat with the remaining rolls. Brush the tops of the rings with the remaining melted butter (there should be just enough), and make thin slits on each surface with the tip of a sharp knife or a razor blade. Cover the rings with a towel, and let rise in a warm, draft-free spot until they have increased in size by about one-half, about 30 to 40 minutes.

Meanwhile, preheat the oven to 375 degrees.

When they have risen about 50 percent, bake the rings for 40 minutes. Just before they are finished baking, prepare the icing: In a small bowl or cup, combine the water, corn syrup, and ¼ teaspoon vanilla. Stir until the corn syrup has dissolved. Add the confectioners' sugar, and beat until smooth. Spread the icing on the rings while they are still hot. Remove them from their pans and cool them on a rack. Put them in plastic bags, tightly sealed, and refrigerate or freeze them until ready to use. Warm them in a slow oven just before serving.

YIELD: THREE 9-INCH RINGS.

HOT FRUIT COMPOTE

MAY BE PARTIALLY PREPARED UP TO 24 HOURS IN ADVANCE;
MUST BE PARTIALLY PREPARED AT LEAST 6 HOURS IN ADVANCE.

½ pound pitted prunes
2 (15-ounce) jars applesauce
2 teaspoons cinnamon
1 teaspoon nutmeg
½ teaspoon allspice
1 cup firmly packed light brown sugar
½ cup fruit-flavored liqueur, such as apricot brandy
2 (20-ounce) cans chunk-style pineapple, drained
3 (1-pound) cans sliced peaches packed in heavy syrup, drained
3 (1-pound) cans pear halves packed in heavy syrup, drained

Place the prunes in a saucepan, and cover them with water. Bring to a boil, lower heat, and simmer until tender, about 20 minutes. Transfer them, with ½ cup of their juice, to the bowl of a food processor fitted with a steel blade, and whirl for several seconds until they are broken up. Add the applesauce, cinnamon, nutmeg, allspice, brown sugar, and liqueur. Whirl until the sugar is dissolved and the mixture smooth.

In a large, ovenproof casserole or baking dish with a tight-fitting lid, place the drained pineapple chunks and peaches. Slice the pears and add them. Scrape the applesauce mixture on top, and gently toss the fruit to mix well. Cover and let rest at room temperature at least 6 hours or overnight.

TIME ALLOWANCE FOR FINAL PREPARATION: 70 MINUTES.

Preheat the oven to 300 degrees.
Bake the fruit, covered, for 60 minutes, or until hot. Serve immediately.

SERVES 16.

OPEN HOUSE FOR TWENTY

Eggnog, Cranberry Punch, and Bloody Marys

Moussaka

Spiced Rice with Pine Nuts

Mixed Green Salad with Vinaigrette Dressing*

Hot French Bread

Leoler's Lemon Chiffon Pie

An open house is a fine way to entertain. Fairly substantial amounts of food are needed, of course, but the preparation can be done well ahead, and the day itself can be low-key and comfortable. Appetites vary, so it is a thoughtful host who has a hot tray on the buffet table holding the food warm for the guests to eat when the urge strikes.

Moussaka, that magical Greek creation of creamy-topped eggplant, tomato, and ground lamb, is the perfect dish for an open house: soothing yet spicy, rich but not overwhelming. Some people will want to eat it with rice; for others, crusty French bread will be sufficient. No vegetables are necessary, save a salad.

For dessert I offer a marvelously piquant, airy pie: Leoler's lemon chiffon pie. Leoler was my grandmother's cook, and she cooked, with grace and abundance, until the day she died at age ninety. She never wrote down any of her recipes, but I did manage to persuade her to tell me her lemon chiffon pie recipe, and for that I and many of my guests have been grateful. The quantity of the lemon rind in the recipe may seem excessive, but have faith: It's what makes the pie. If you want to prepare one giant pie, you may fashion it in a paella dish or wok; the quantities are right. But, considering the free-wheeling schedule of an open house, three pies, served one at a time, would offer a better and more attractive presentation.

MOUSSAKA

EGGPLANT AND MEAT MAY BE PREPARED UP TO 24 HOURS IN ADVANCE;
SAUCE MAY BE PREPARED UP TO 6 HOURS IN ADVANCE.

> *8 eggplant, about 1 pound each, peeled and cut crosswise in ½-inch-*
> *   thick slices*
> *Salt for eggplant plus 2 teaspoons*
> *2 to 3 cups flour*
> *3 to 4 cups olive oil*
> *3 cups finely chopped onion (about 3 large)*
> *1 tablespoon minced garlic*
> *6 pounds lean ground lamb*
> *2 (28-ounce) cans Italian peeled tomatoes, drained and chopped*
> *3 cups tomato puree*
> *1 tablespoon oregano*
> *2 teaspoons cinnamon*
> *¼ teaspoon freshly ground black pepper*
> *1 cup plus 2 tablespoons freshly grated Parmesan cheese*

To make a dish in this quantity, it is vitally important to plan your equipment before proceeding. A frying pan with a diameter of 14 inches and 4-inch sides is ideal for frying the eggplant (no spatters) and making the meat sauce. If you do not own one, a flameproof casserole with roughly the same dimensions would do. Similarly, you will need at least three 14-by-9-by-3-inch baking dishes. Roasting pans, while not pretty, are a good substitute if you do not own enough baking dishes. Large, shallow ovenproof casseroles are also good. You do not have to stick to the dimensions given for the baking dishes, but allow for about that much area.

To prepare the eggplant and the lamb: Spread out several sections of paper toweling. Cover them with eggplant slices. Sprinkle with salt. Spread out another batch of paper towels on top of the first, and proceed as above until all the eggplant has been sprinkled. Weigh them down with a heavy platter, and let drain for 30 minutes.

Put the flour in a shallow roasting pan, and place it next to your stove top. Heat ¾ cup oil in a large skillet, preferably one with high sides, over high heat until it is smoking. Dust 6 to 8 slices of eggplant with flour, shaking off any excess, and fry them a minute or two on each side, until they are nicely brown but not burned. Immediately transfer them to paper towels to drain. Brown the remaining eggplant, adding oil as necessary.

Pour off any oil left in the skillet. Lower the heat to low-moderate, pour in ½ cup more oil, and add the onions and garlic. Sauté them until they are soft and slightly colored, about 8 minutes. Stir in the ground lamb, breaking up any lumps. Cook until all pink has disappeared. Add the tomatoes, tomato puree, oregano, cinnamon, 2 teaspoons salt, and pepper. Toss to mix. Bring to a boil over high heat and continue cooking briskly, stirring frequently, until most all the liquid in the pan evaporates, about 1 hour. Remove from the heat.

Assemble the moussaka as follows: In each of the three baking dishes, lay one-sixth of the eggplant slices side by side. Sprinkle the slices evenly with 2 tablespoons cheese for each dish. Spoon one-third of the lamb and tomato mixture over eggplant in each dish. Arrange the rest of the eggplant on top, and sprinkle each dish with 2 tablespoons cheese. If you are preparing the moussaka well in advance, cover the baking dishes with foil or plastic wrap, and refrigerate them until you are ready to add the sauce.

SAUCE
6 cups milk
3 tablespoons unsalted butter
9 eggs
¾ cup flour
1 teaspoon salt

To make the sauce: In one saucepan, heat 4 cups of the milk with the butter until bubbles start to form around the edges of the pan. Meanwhile, place the eggs in a 3-quart saucepan and beat them briskly. Add the flour and beat until smooth. Beat in the remaining 2 cups cold milk and salt. Put the saucepan over moderate heat and, stirring constantly, add the heated milk and butter in a slow stream. Continue stirring and cooking until the mixture thickens and nearly comes to a boil. Divide it among the three eggplant-lamb dishes, spreading it over the eggplant with a spatula. Sprinkle 2 final tablespoons cheese over each dish. If not ready to bake the moussaka at this point, cover the dishes again with foil or plastic wrap and refrigerate until 1 hour before final preparation.

TIME ALLOWANCE FOR FINAL PREPARATION: 70 MINUTES.

Preheat the oven to 350 degrees.

Remove the covering from the baking dishes, and transfer them to racks in the oven. Bake, uncovered, for 60 minutes, or until the meat is bubbling and the tops are golden brown.

SERVES 20.

SPICED RICE WITH PINE NUTS

MAY BE PARTIALLY PREPARED UP TO 24 HOURS IN ADVANCE.

10 tablespoons unsalted butter
1 cup finely chopped onion
1 tablespoon turmeric
1 tablespoon salt
4 cups long-grain rice
8 cups chicken stock, preferably homemade (page 286)
2 (6-ounce) packages pine nuts (pignoli)

Preheat oven to 350 degrees.

In a large flameproof casserole equipped with a tight-fitting lid, melt 6 tablespoons of the butter over low heat. Add the onion and cook until wilted, about 5 minutes. Stir in the turmeric and cook 2 minutes. Add the salt and rice, and mix until all the rice grains are coated with the spiced butter. Add the chicken stock and bring to a boil. Cover and transfer to the oven. Bake 25 minutes. Cool.

While the rice cools, melt the remaining 4 tablespoons butter. Add the pine nuts and, over moderately low heat, sauté them, stirring frequently, until they turn golden brown all over, about 5 minutes. Add them to the rice, and mix. Refrigerate the rice, covered, if preparing well in advance, removing it from the refrigerator 1 hour before final preparation; or store in a cool corner of the kitchen.

TIME ALLOWANCE FOR FINAL PREPARATION: 25 MINUTES.

Preheat oven to 350 degrees.

Place covered casserole in oven and reheat until rice is steaming hot, about 20 minutes. Serve immediately.

SERVES 20.

RECIPE DIVIDENDS

You may have noticed in some of my do-ahead menus that suggestions are given for an additional vegetable, soup, salad, or dessert for which there is no recipe immediately following. My reasoning is that most cooks know how to execute the suggested dishes without my guidance, or that good recipes for them are readily available in other basic cookbooks.

To help the cook, however, this chapter features as "dividends" some of the menu items that were marked with an asterisk as well as a few fundamentals such as home-made chicken stock.

Because the recipes sometimes apply to several menus, thus serving different numbers of people, the cook may have to multiply or divide the quantities accordingly. (The recipes are generally straightforward, and doubling, tripling, or halving shouldn't present any real difficulties unless the reader's math is shaky.)

HOMEMADE CHICKEN STOCK

◆

1 6-pound fowl
1½ pounds chicken wings
2 medium onions
4 cloves
3 large carrots, cut in thirds
6 celery stalks, 3 inches long, cut from the top of the bunch, including green
*   leaves*
1 clove garlic, unpeeled
8 sprigs parsley
2 bay leaves
1 teaspoon thyme
16 cups water
1 tablespoon salt

Rinse the fowl well, inside and out. Pull off and discard any clumps of fat left clinging to the cavity. Remove the neck and giblets from the cavity, and reserve the liver for another use. Place the fowl, its neck and remaining giblets, and the chicken wings in a large kettle. Position the onions (stuck with 2 cloves each), carrots, celery, garlic, parsley, bay leaves, and thyme around the bird. Cover with the water and sprinkle with salt. Bring the water to a boil over high heat, and skim off any foam that accumulates. Lower the heat and simmer, partially covered, for 2½ hours.

Remove the fowl from the kettle and allow it to cool. Let the stock continue simmering. When the bird can be handled, remove all meat and skin. (Just take the bigger pieces of meat; the bird does not have to be free of all flesh.) Discard the skin and save the meat for another use. Break up the carcass and return it to the simmering water. Continue simmering the stock, uncovered, for 2 hours more.

Strain the stock through a sieve into a large bowl, discarding all solid materials. When it has cooled, store it in the refrigerator. A layer of fat will form on its surface and solidify. Before using the stock, scrape off and discard the fat.

The stock will hold in the refrigerator for 2 weeks *provided the layer of fat, which acts as a seal, remains undisturbed.* If you wish to remove the fat and hold the stock, unfrozen, in the refrigerator, the stock may be boiled every 3 days for 5 minutes to kill off any bacteria that may be forming. The stock may also be frozen for 6 months.

YIELD: APPROXIMATELY 9 CUPS STOCK.

CHILLED CREAM OF WATERCRESS SOUP

½ pound potatoes, peeled and cut in ⅓-inch slices
3 large leeks, roots and green leaves removed, cleaned and sliced
2 bunches of watercress, washed
5 cups chicken stock, preferably homemade (page 286)
1 teaspoon salt
Freshly ground black pepper
2 cups light cream
1 cup milk
2 tablespoons minced fresh chives

Place the potatoes and leeks in a large kettle. Cut the tough stems off both bunches of watercress and add the stems to the pot. Pour in the chicken stock and bring to a boil. Lower the heat and simmer, partially covered, for 15 minutes or until the potatoes are soft when pierced with the tip of a sharp knife. Add the remaining watercress leaves and simmer for 5 more minutes. Do not let the cress cook longer than that or it will lose its bright green color.

With a ladle, transfer the soup in batches to the jar of a blender, and whirl until it is smooth and the watercress becomes small specks of green. As you puree each batch, pour it into a large tureen or mixing bowl.

After all the soup has been pureed, taste for seasoning and add up to 1 teaspoon salt and a generous grinding of pepper. Mix in the light cream and milk. Cover with plastic wrap and refrigerate until thoroughly chilled, at least 4 hours.

To serve, ladle into individual soup bowls and garnish with a sprinkling of minced chives. (The soup will be quite thick if made with homemade stock because of its natural gelatin. If canned broth is used, it will be much thinner. Add another ½ pound of potatoes if you are using canned broth and want a thick soup.)

The soup may also be served warm. Reheat it slowly until it is just below the boiling point.

SERVES 10 TO 12.

JELLIED CHICKEN CONSOMMÉ

9 cups homemade chicken stock (page 286) (see note below)
4 scallions, cut in 1-inch pieces
4 eggshells, crushed
4 egg whites, lightly beaten
Salt and freshly ground black pepper to taste
1 cup sour cream
2 tablespoons minced fresh chives

Please note: Do not attempt to make jellied chicken consommé with store-bought chicken broth. The canned broth does not contain enough natural gelatin for the soup to jell.

In a large saucepan, combine the chicken stock, scallions, eggshells, and egg whites. Taste for seasoning and adjust. Slowly bring to a boil, stirring constantly. Lower heat and allow to simmer, undisturbed, for 20 minutes.

Line a sieve with a double thickness of cheesecloth that has been wrung out in cold water. Carefully ladle the stock through the sieve. If you want to achieve a crystal-clear liquid, do not press the solids into the sieve but allow the liquid to seep through undisturbed. Discard all solid material.

Refrigerate the clarified stock until it has jellied, about 3 hours.

To serve, break up the jelly with a spoon or fork, and transfer to small soup cups. Spoon a dollop of sour cream and chives on top of each cup.

SERVES 8.

CREAMY BASIL DRESSING

¼ cup packed fresh basil leaves
2 tablespoons white wine vinegar
¼ teaspoon sugar
½ teaspoon Dijon-style mustard
1 tablespoon mayonnaise
½ cup olive oil
Salt and freshly ground black pepper to taste

Place the basil leaves in the bowl of a food processor fitted with a steel blade. Whirl until finely minced. Add the vinegar, sugar, and mustard; whirl 2 seconds. Add the mayonnaise, and pulse on and off until just blended. With the motor running, add the olive oil in a slow, steady stream. Taste and adjust the seasoning. Transfer to a jar with a tight-fitting lid. Store in a cool corner of the kitchen if the dressing is to be used within 4 hours; otherwise, keep the dressing refrigerated, but bring it to room temperature 1 hour before serving.

YIELD: ¾ CUP DRESSING.

BASIC VINAIGRETTE DRESSING

½ teaspoon Dijon-style mustard
¼ teaspoon salt
Freshly ground black pepper
1 tablespoon tarragon vinegar
1 clove garlic, peeled, cut in half lengthwise
4 tablespoons olive oil

Place the mustard, salt, pepper, and vinegar in a small jar with a tight-fitting lid, and stir until mustard and salt are dissolved. Add the garlic pieces and the oil, cover tightly, and shake vigorously. Hold in a cool corner of the kitchen until ready to use.

Before dressing the salad, remove the garlic pieces. Don't forget that the longer the garlic remains in the dressing, the stronger its flavor. Remove it after 1 hour if you do not like it too strong.

YIELD: ½ CUP DRESSING.

RUSSIAN DRESSING

2 cups mayonnaise
⅓ cup chili sauce
2 tablespoons strained fresh lemon juice
2 tablespoons minced sweet pickles
1 tablespoon minced fresh parsley

In a small bowl, combine the mayonnaise, chili sauce, and lemon juice, and blend well. Mix in the pickles and parsley.

Cover with plastic wrap and hold in a cool corner of the kitchen if using within 4 hours, or else refrigerate until 1 hour before serving.

YIELD: 2¾ CUPS DRESSING.

OIL AND LEMON DRESSING

4 tablespoons strained fresh lemon juice
½ teaspoon Dijon-style mustard
¼ teaspoon salt
Freshly ground black pepper
½ teaspoon sugar
¾ cup olive oil
1 clove garlic, peeled and cut in half lengthwise

In a 2-cup bottle with a tight-fitting lid, combine the lemon juice, mustard, salt, pepper, and sugar. Stir until the mustard has blended with the juice and the salt and sugar are dissolved. Add the olive oil. Cover the bottle tightly and shake briskly. Add the garlic halves. Cover again and store in a cool place. Just before serving, remove the garlic, recap the jar, and shake well.

YIELD: APPROXIMATELY 1 CUP.

POPPY SEED DRESSING

1 tablespoon onion juice (see instructions below)
½ cup honey
2 teaspoons Dijon-style mustard
½ teaspoon salt
⅓ cup white wine vinegar
1 cup vegetable oil
2 tablespoons poppy seeds

To make onion juice: Peel a small onion and grate on smallest holes of a 4-sided grater.

In a mixing bowl, combine the honey, mustard, salt, and vinegar and stir until they are well blended. Beat in the onion juice. Add the oil, a spoonful at a time, beating with a whisk after each addition until the oil is incorporated. Beat in the poppy seeds. Transfer to a jar with a tight-fitting lid and hold in a cool corner of the kitchen.

YIELD: APPROXIMATELY 1½ CUPS.

SIMPLE SALAD VINAIGRETTE

This is perhaps one of the simplest and best ways to prepare a salad, one that is commonly practiced in France. Don't be alarmed by a recipe without precise measurements. Provided you coat all the leaves well with the oil, if you should use too much vinegar, it will just roll off. The most important requisite for this salad's success, however, is the quality of the olive oil and vinegar you use. They must both be top-grade.

Allow 1 cup salad greens and 1 teaspoon sliced scallion per person.

Rinsed, dried salad greens mixed according to preference, such as water-
*   cress, bibb and Boston lettuce, romaine, chicory, arugula, Chinese cabbage*
Thinly sliced scallion, roots trimmed, white section only
Olive oil
Garlic salt
Salt and freshly ground black pepper
Vinegar such as tarragon or red wine
Cherry tomatoes (optional)

Line a salad bowl with paper toweling and place your salad greens on it. Sprinkle the scallions over the greens. Refrigerate the salad, uncovered, until just before serving, but for at least 30 minutes or as long as 2 hours. This period will help the salad crisp.

When you are ready to dress the salad, remove and discard the paper toweling. Holding your thumb over the oil's opening so that too much does not come flowing out at once, dribble approximately 1 tablespoon oil per one cup greens over the surface of the greens. Set the oil down and, with a salad fork and spoon, toss the greens until all the leaves are completely coated with oil. If you have not used enough oil, dribble some more on and toss again. Repeat until the leaves are well coated. Sprinkle some garlic salt over lightly. Sprinkle with salt and pepper. Toss again.

Place your thumb over the mouth of the vinegar bottle (if it does not come with a perforated plastic lid). Sprinkle approximately 1 teaspoon vinegar to 1 cup of salad greens over the surface of the salad. Toss the leaves with a fork and spoon until the vinegar is well distributed. Taste a leaf and see if you have used enough. If not, sprinkle some more vinegar over the salad and toss again. Do not worry about using too much vinegar; excess vinegar slips off the leaves and collects in the bottom of the bowl. Garnish with cherry tomatoes, if desired. Do *not* use sliced or quartered tomatoes, as their liquid will render the dressing watery.

ASPARAGUS WITH BROWN BUTTER

1 pound asparagus (or see alternatives below)
½ teaspoon salt
4 teaspoons unsalted butter

Trim the tough ends off the asparagus stalks and discard. Peel the stalks if you like, but it is not necessary.

Fill a 12-inch stainless steel or enamel-covered skillet with water, and bring to a boil. Add the salt. Carefully place the asparagus spears in the skillet, laying them all in the same direction. Return the water to a boil, lower the heat, and simmer the asparagus uncovered until it is tender but still bright green. Pierce the root end of a large stalk to check for doneness. Do not overcook. The asparagus should take approximately 5 minutes to cook, but timing depends on size and freshness.

Holding the asparagus back with a spatula, drain the skillet. Drop the pieces of butter on top of the asparagus and return the skillet to low heat. Keep shaking the skillet back and forth over the heat so that any residue of water will evaporate and the butter will melt. Watch carefully as the butter melts, for it will slowly brown. When it is a nutty brown color, remove the pan from the heat—if allowed to continue cooking, the butter will blacken and burn—and transfer the asparagus to a heated serving platter, positioning each spear in the same direction. Pour any butter remaining in the skillet over the vegetable. Serve immediately.

SERVES 2 TO 3.

The following vegetables may be treated in much the same manner:

> *3 cups broccoli flowerets, tough stems cut off*
> *½ pound fiddlehead ferns, tough stems cut off and discarded*
> *1 pint brussels sprouts, ends trimmed and cut with an "X"*

Instead of cooking these vegetables in a skillet, simply cook them in a saucepan filled with salted water. The cooking time should be just about 5 minutes for all of them, but keep checking with the tip of a sharp knife for tenderness, and watch their color. Drain and brown the butter as described above.

PAN-FRIED POTATOES WITH PARSLEY

> *1 pound potatoes, scrubbed*
> *1 to 2 tablespoons unsalted butter*
> *1 to 2 tablespoons oil*
> *½ cup chopped onions (½ medium onion)*
> *½ teaspoon salt*
> *Freshly ground black pepper*
> *3 tablespoons minced fresh parsley*

Place the potatoes in a saucepan in water to cover, and parboil for 15 minutes. Drain and cool under cold water. When they are cool enough to handle, peel them and cut into ¼-inch slices.

In a large skillet, melt 1 tablespoon of the butter and 1 tablespoon of the oil over moderate to low heat. When it is foaming, add the sliced potatoes, spreading them out over the bottom of the skillet so that, if possible, they are only 1 or 2 slices deep. Sauté them 5 to 8 minutes, moving them occasionally so that all slices get equally cooked. When all the slices are golden on one side, turn them over, adding the chopped onion. (Add more butter and oil if necessary.) Sauté another 5 to 8 minutes, until all are golden on both sides.

Transfer to a heated serving bowl, and sprinkle with parsley.

SERVES 4.

BABY RED POTATOES IN DILL BUTTER

1 pound small red potatoes, scrubbed
2 tablespoons butter
Salt and pepper
3 tablespoons minced fresh dill weed

Place the potatoes in a medium-size saucepan and cover with salted water. Bring to a boil, reduce heat, and simmer, partially covered, for 30 to 40 minutes, or until the potatoes feel tender when pierced with a sharp knife. (Timing will depend on the potatoes' size.)

Drain the potatoes, leaving them in the pan. Return the pan to low heat and shake it briefly until all liquid has evaporated. Add the butter and continue to shake until the butter has melted and coated all the potatoes. Add salt and pepper to taste.

Just before serving, sprinkle with the dill weed and toss until well distributed.

SERVES 4.

CREAMED PEAS AND ONIONS

1 pound small white onions
½ cup heavy cream
1 10-ounce package frozen peas, thawed and drained (or substitute 1 pound fresh peas, shelled)
2 teaspoons minced fresh mint (optional)

Drop the onions into a saucepan full of boiling water and boil them for 2 minutes. Drain and refresh under cold water. Immediately cut the root ends with a sharp paring knife and slip the skins off.

Return the onions to the same saucepan, cover with water, and bring them to a boil. Lower the heat and simmer, partially covered, for approximately 10 minutes, or until they are tender when pierced with a knife. (Timing depends on the onions' size.)

Drain the onions, leaving them in the saucepan. Add the cream. If you are using fresh peas, add them to the pot at the same time. Over full heat, reduce the cream by half; this will take approximately 5 minutes. Stir occasionally. If you are using frozen peas, add them after 4 minutes and allow them to cook in the cream for 1 minute.

Just before serving, add the mint, if you desire, and toss to distribute. Serve immediately.

SERVES 4.

STEAMED BROWN RICE

2 teaspoons salt
1 cup brown rice
2 tablespoons unsalted butter

In a 6- or 7-quart kettle, bring about 5 quarts of water to a rolling boil. Add the salt and slowly pour in the rice so that the water does not stop boiling. Stir occasionally to make certain no rice is sticking to the bottom of the pan.

Lower the heat to moderate and boil the rice 30 minutes. Drain the rice in a colander, and rinse it under cold water. Put 2 quarts fresh water into the same kettle and bring to a boil. Position the colander over the kettle, cover it with a folded dish towel and the pan's lid, and steam the rice 15 minutes.

Transfer the rice to a heated serving bowl and add the butter. Toss until the butter is melted. Serve immediately.

SERVES 4 TO 6.

MASHED TURNIPS

1 (2-pound) turnip, peeled and cut into 1-inch cubes
3 tablespoons unsalted butter
½ cup heavy cream
1 teaspoon salt
Freshly ground black pepper
½ teaspoon freshly ground nutmeg

Place the turnip cubes in a large saucepan and cover with water. Bring to a boil, lower the heat, and simmer, partially covered, for 20 to 30 minutes, or until the turnip pieces are very soft when pierced with the tip of a knife.

Drain the turnips and return the pan to low heat. Shake it over the heat for a few minutes to evaporate any excess water.

With a masher, hand-held electric beater, or heavy wooden spoon, mash the turnips until they are free of lumps. Add the butter and the cream, and beat vigorously. Add the salt, pepper, and nutmeg, and mix well.

Transfer the mashed turnips to a heated platter and garnish with a few more gratings of nutmeg. Any leftover Mashed Turnip can be successfully reheated in a double boiler. Warm it for approximately 20 minutes over boiling water.

SERVES 8.

SAUTÉED ZUCCHINI

1 tablespoon unsalted butter
1 tablespoon olive oil
1 pound small, young zucchini, ends trimmed and cut in ¼-inch slices
¼ cup minced shallots
Salt and freshly ground black pepper to taste
1 tablespoon minced fresh parsley

In a large skillet, melt the butter and oil over moderate heat. When they are foaming, add the zucchini and shallots. Using the stir-fry method, sauté the vegetables, stirring constantly, until they are barely tender and flecked with a little brown, about 3 to 4 minutes. Do not overcook. Taste for seasoning, and add salt and pepper to taste. Toss to mix.

Transfer immediately to a heated serving bowl, and garnish with parsley.

SERVES 4.

STIR-FRIED SNOW PEAS WITH YELLOW PEPPERS

1 tablespoon butter
1 tablespoon oil
½ cup thinly sliced onion
½ yellow pepper, stems and seeds removed, cut in thin slices
½ pound snow peas, ends trimmed, strings removed, washed
3 to 4 dashes "lite" soy sauce

Melt the butter by placing it and the oil in a wok or 12-inch skillet over moderate heat. Add the onion and sauté it until wilted, about 5 minutes. Increase the heat to moderately high and add the pepper and snow peas. Toss to coat with the oil, cover, and steam for 2 minutes. Toss again briefly, cover, and steam 1 more minute. The peas should be crisp, tender, and bright green. Take care not to overcook. Add the soy sauce, mix well, and serve immediately.

SERVES 4.

COLE SLAW WITH LIGHT MAYONNAISE

½ small cabbage (about ¾ pound), core removed, coarsely shredded
3 tablespoons minced fresh coriander (cilantro), or substitute parsley
3 tablespoons thinly sliced scallions, including 2 inches green leaves from each
½ small red pepper, cored, seeded, and cut in ¼-inch dice
3 tablespoons homemade mayonnaise
3 tablespoons plain yogurt

In a medium-size salad bowl, combine the cabbage, cilantro, scallions, and red pepper and, with a salad fork and spoon, toss well to mix.

In a small bowl, mix together the mayonnaise and yogurt until the two are well blended.

Pour the mayonnaise mixture over the cabbage and toss until all the leaves are completely coated.

SERVES 4.

STEAK TARTARE

3 pounds sirloin or filet of beef
4 egg yolks
1 cup finely chopped onion
½ cup capers, rinsed and drained
1 tablespoon salt
Freshly ground black pepper
3 tablespoons Worcestershire sauce
½ cup minced fresh chives
½ cup minced fresh parsley
6 anchovy fillets
Buttered slices of cocktail rye and pumpernickel bread

Shortly before serving the steak tartare, grind the meat twice in your meat grinder. (You can have the butcher do this for you, but the steak will taste much better for being freshly ground.)

Transfer the meat to a large mixing bowl and add the egg yolks, onion, capers, salt, pepper, and Worcestershire. With your fingers or two forks, mix thoroughly.

(Try to handle the meat lightly, without compressing it.) Taste for seasoning and adjust.

On a large piece of wax paper, combine the chives and parsley and mix well. Spread the herbs out over the paper. Shape the meat into a sausagelike roll and coat it all over with the chive-parsley mixture. Place it on a wooden plank or platter. Garnish the top with the anchovy fillets. Surround the steak with the buttered bread slices.

SERVES 30 AS AN HORS D'OEUVRE.

HERBED FRENCH BREAD

1 French baguette, about 24 inches long
1 stick unsalted butter, softened
2 to 3 cloves garlic, peeled and sliced thin or 2 teaspoons oregano

Preheat the oven to 325 degrees.

Cut the baguette into 1-inch slices, *but do not cut all the way through.* Spread each slice generously with the softened butter. Place a thin piece of garlic *or* a good sprinkling of oregano in each cut in the bread.

Wrap the bread well in aluminum foil and heat in the oven for 10 minutes. Open the foil and bake 5 minutes more.

Remove the pieces of garlic, if you have used them, and serve the bread immediately while it is steaming hot. (If you have used oregano, simply leave it untouched.)

SERVES 6 TO 8.

HOT MULLED CIDER

1 half-gallon jug cider
6 3-inch sticks cinnamon (or the equivalent)
30 whole cloves
½ cup strained fresh lemon juice
Freshly grated nutmeg

Place the cider in a large stainless steel kettle.

Cut a 12-inch length of double-thick cheesecloth and put the cinnamon and cloves in the center. Bring the ends and sides of the cheesecloth together, tie them securely so that a sac is formed, and place it in the cider. Add the lemon juice. Bring the cider to a boil, lower the heat, and simmer, partially covered, for 30 minutes.

Remove and discard the sac of cinnamon and cloves.

Ladle the mulled cider into mugs, sprinkle with a grating of nutmeg, and serve steaming hot.

YIELD: APPROXIMATELY 10 6-OUNCE SERVINGS.

ICE CREAM–FILLED CREAM PUFFS

1 cup water
½ cup unsalted butter, cut into pieces
½ teaspoon salt
2 teaspoons sugar
1 cup flour
4 eggs
1 quart ice cream, slightly softened

Preheat oven to 400 degrees.

In a heavy saucepan, bring the water, butter, salt, and sugar to a boil, and boil until the butter has melted. Remove the pan from the heat, and add the flour all at once. Beat the mixture with a large wooden spoon until it adheres to itself and forms a ball. Add the eggs one at a time, beating until each one is thoroughly incorporated before adding the next.

Generously butter a cookie sheet. Transfer the dough to a pastry sleeve fitted with a ¾-inch round tip, and squeeze out approximately 8 mounds, about 3 inches in diameter; or form mounds with heaping servingspoonfuls of dough. Bake 30 minutes. Prick the bottom of the puffs to allow the air to escape. Return them to the oven for 15 minutes, with the heat turned off, to dry.

Cool completely before filling.

To fill, cut the puffs in half horizontally. Place a scoop of ice cream in the bottom of each half, and top with its "lid."

Hold in the freezer until ready to serve.

YIELD: APPROXIMATELY 8 CREAM PUFFS.

CHOCOLATE SAUCE

½ cup unsweetened cocoa
½ cup sugar
½ cup firmly packed dark brown sugar
1 cup light corn syrup
½ cup heavy cream
3 tablespoons unsalted butter
Pinch of salt
Pinch of cinnamon
1 teaspoon vanilla

In a medium-size saucepan, combine the cocoa, white and brown sugars, corn syrup, cream, butter, salt, and cinnamon. Over moderate heat, bring to a boil, stirring constantly until the ingredients are dissolved and well mixed. Boil for 5 minutes. Remove from the heat. Stir in the vanilla.

YIELD: APPROXIMATELY 2 CUPS.

CARAMEL SAUCE

½ cup firmly packed light brown sugar
½ cup firmly packed dark brown sugar
½ cup light corn syrup
4 tablespoons unsalted butter
2 teaspoons strained fresh lemon juice
Pinch of salt
1 cup crème fraiche (page 301)

In a small saucepan, combine the light and dark brown sugars, corn syrup, and butter. Stir over moderate heat until the sugars are dissolved. Bring to a boil, and boil 5 minutes. Remove from the heat and add the lemon juice, salt, and crème fraiche. Return to the heat and stir until smooth. Bring to a brisk boil. Serve hot.

YIELD: APPROXIMATELY 2 CUPS.

CRÈME FRAICHE

1 cup heavy cream
¼ cup sour cream
¼ cup buttermilk

In a small bowl, combine the cream, sour cream, and buttermilk. Whisk briskly until all are well combined. Allow to sit in a warm spot in the kitchen for 8 to 12 hours (or longer) until the cream has thickened to the consistency of slightly whipped cream. (Whisk it several times during this period.)

Cover the bowl with plastic wrap or transfer the crème fraiche to a jar with a tight-fitting lid, and refrigerate until ready to use.

Crème fraiche will hold in the refrigerator for at least 1 month. To make another batch before the old is quite used up, and without buying another bottle of buttermilk, simply repeat the process with another cup of heavy cream, but substitute 1 tablespoon of the current batch of crème fraiche for the buttermilk. (The culture in the buttermilk grows and thickens the cream. The cycle can be repeated indefinitely.)

YIELD: 1½ CUPS.

INDEX TO MENUS ACCORDING TO NUMBER SERVED

INDEX